Children Talking about Books

by
Sarah G. Borders
and
Alice Phoebe Naylor

ORYX PRESS
1993

The rare Arabian Oryx is believed to have inspired the myth of the unicorn. This desert antelope became virtually extinct in the early 1960s. At that time several groups of international conservationists arranged to have 9 animals sent to the Phoenix Zoo to be the nucleus of a captive breeding herd. Today the Oryx population is nearly 800, and over 400 have been returned to reserves in the Middle East.

Copyright © 1993 by The Oryx Press
4041 North Central at Indian School Road
Phoenix, Arizona 85012-3397

Published simultaneously in Canada

Printed and Bound in the United States of America

∞ The paper used in this publication meets the minimum requirements of American National Standard for Information Science—Permanence of Paper for Printed Library Materials, ANSI Z39.48, 1984

Library of Congress Cataloging-in-Publication Data

Borders, Sarah G.
   Children talking about books / by Sarah G. Borders and Alice Phoebe Naylor.
        p.   cm.
   Includes bibliographical references and index.
   ISBN 0-89774-737-2
   1. Literature—Study and teaching (Elementary) 2. Children—Books and reading. I. Naylor, Alice Phoebe. II. Title.
LB1575.B6   1993
372.64′044—dc20   92-40386
                                                                    CIP

This book is dedicated to all the children
who participated in these discussions.
They are our teachers.

Contents

Foreword *by Jacque Touchton*   vii
Preface *by Alice Phoebe Naylor*   ix
Acknowledgments   x
Introduction *by Sarah G. Borders*   xi
Chapter 1: How to Use This Book   1
   Reading the Book Entries   1
   Parts of the Book Entry   1
   Using the Three Discussion Prompts   4
   References   6
Chapter 2: Functions of the Adult Leader   7
   Choosing the Books   7
   Providing an Environment   11
   Practicing and Learning from Mistakes   11
   Guiding the Discussion   11
   Listening   13
   Participating   14
   Other Things We Want to Say   14
   References   15
Book Entries   16
   Molly Bang, *Delphine*   16
   Judy Blume, *The Pain and the Great One*   20
   John Burningham, *Mr. Gumpy's Outing*   25
   Eric Carle, *A House for Hermit Crab*   30
   Beverly Cleary, "The Hard Boiled Egg Fad" from *Ramona Quimby, Age 8*   37
   Lucille Clifton, *Everett Anderson's Nine Month Long*   44
   Barbara Cooney, *Miss Rumphius*   49
   Carolyn Craven, *What the Mailman Brought*   58

Eleanor Estes, *The Hundred Dresses*   62
Mem Fox, *Wilfrid Gordon McDonald Partridge*   68
Mordicai Gerstein, *The Mountains of Tibet*   73
Patricia Reilly Giff, *Today Was a Terrible Day*   78
Helen Griffith, *Grandaddy's Place*   85
Ezra Jack Keats, *Whistle for Willie*   91
Leah Komaiko, *Annie Bananie*   96
Leo Lionni, *Frederick*   101
Arnold Lobel, *Fables*   108
Evaline Ness, *Sam, Bangs and Moonshine*   114
Cynthia Rylant, *Miss Maggie*   120
Cynthia Rylant, *The Relatives Came*   126
Robert D. San Souci, *The Talking Eggs: A Folktale from the American South*   134
Maurice Sendak, *Where the Wild Things Are*   140
Susan Shreve, "Cheating" from *Family Secrets: Five Very Important Stories*   146
Shel Silverstein, *The Giving Tree*   153
Isaac Bashevis Singer, *The Power of Light: Eight Stories for Hanukkah*   159
David Small, *Imogene's Antlers*   165
William Steig, *Spinky Sulks*   169
William Steig, *Sylvester and the Magic Pebble*   176
John Steptoe, *Mufaro's Beautiful Daughters: An African Tale*   183
Chris Van Allsburg, *The Wretched Stone*   189
Susan Varley, *Badger's Parting Gifts*   195
Judith Viorst, *The Tenth Good Thing about Barney*   199
Vera Williams, *A Chair for My Mother*   204
Audrey Wood, *Elbert's Bad Word*   209

Appendix A: Story Connections in Our Family *by Jane Tarman*   215

Appendix B: Selected Bibliographies of Children's Books   217
Bibliography   219
Subject Index to Book Entries   223
General Index   235

Foreword

by Jacque Touchton

I believe the most rewarding experience in teaching reading is hearing the delight in children's voices as they describe a story and its connection to their inner worlds. These insights are so personal and so fragile that they are rarely offered in the classroom setting. But, as a teacher, these connections between literature and life are the very ones that I continually strive to elicit from my students.

In *Children Talking about Books* the authors have mastered this art. This book does not present a "technique" or the usual "how to" story stretcher formula. It, instead, is a model that can teach us how to listen to children as they experience a story. And it shows us how to invite the dialogue that is so crucial to the child's process of gaining insight.

Jacque Touchton is a teacher of special students in Statesville, North Carolina, who uses literature across the curriculum.

Preface

by Alice Phoebe Naylor

Teachers and librarians who discuss literature with children are seeking ways to enable children to respond with something more than "It was interesting" or "It was good." Administrators and school boards fret that children are not being taught how to think. School counselors and therapists are looking for experiences that help children de-center, understand feelings, see other points of view, and make thoughtful choices. Parents who read with their families hope through this experience to raise children who share their values, see worth and dignity in others, and care about the world.

Our purpose in this book is to demonstrate how quality literature can engage children in reflective thinking about stories, themselves, and the world. Sarah Borders and I discuss books with children every chance we get. For us it is an enormously educational and satisfying experience. We learn about children and about books. We find that even when the woes of the world are weighing heavily on children, the process of sharing stories and conversation helps them face their lives with joy, dignity, and feelings of power. This book suggests books worthy of discussion, shows how interactions work, and encourages adults to bond with children. We created this book for teachers, reading specialists, counselors, librarians, and parents.

The body of the text comprises 34 book dialogues taken from real life and commentary on the discussion process. Readers will notice from scanning an entry that the teacher/counselor consistently uses three prompts to encourage the dialogues. Yet, each conversation takes a different course because the teacher/counselor (generically named teacher in the dialogues) listens, reflects, gives information, encourages, and, when appropriate, nudges children to higher levels of thinking or moral reasoning. The pattern we follow is based on response theory and the bibliotherapeutic process.

We have intentionally chosen to present our readers with sample dialogues and commentary rather than with 10 questions per book or with a prescribed lesson plan. We believe that adult booktalk leaders can provide children with encouragement to think and to create meaning. Different teachers, different books, different groups of children, different situations will suggest their own way of doing things. To encourage adults to take the plunge into literature discussions, we provide examples of what some children have said and how some leaders have encouraged response.

Acknowledgments

We are indebted to many teachers, counselors, and parents who conducted some of the discussions reported here. Thank you to our friends, colleagues, and relatives: Elizabeth Hipp, Kathleen Emdad, Phalbe Hendrickson, Roban Clear, Cheri Pace, Mimi Cunningham, Michelle Pendley, Jacque Touchton, Rion Scanlan, Mickie Vacca, Carol Leach, Cindy Minor, Kris Berman, Barbara Crouch, Jane Tarman, Stephen Borders, Susan Baumgardner, Terry Miller, Amy Miller, Belinda MacKinstry, Mardy Brown, Jane Jennings, and Monica Carpenter.

We thank Angela Ehrenfried, Paula Dugger, Michelle Call, and Susan Golden for their expertise and caring assistance with authors and titles.

For their loving support we thank Pamela Paisley, Glenda Hubbard, and Laura Swanson.

We especially thank our students who put up with our tape recorders, ulterior motives, and diversions from routine.

We would like to thank our families for allowing us to put a whole list of responsibilities on hold in order to complete this project.

Introduction

by Sarah G. Borders

HOW THIS BOOK CAME ABOUT

As an elementary school counselor I am a believer that guidance is an essential component for healthy development in children. Through the years I developed, collected, and used myriad activities for classroom and small group guidance. While I always enjoyed such activities, I often felt something lacking in the processing. I had the distinct impression that children were often answering with words and pat phrases that they thought I wanted to hear. In a drug education lesson, fifth grade children could respond in a chorus that they certainly would "say no" to drugs. They could recite the definition of peer pressure. But I began to wonder: How many would drop out of that chorus by eighth or ninth grade? How many would succumb to unhealthy influences? Dismal drug use statistics in our community corroborate my intuition.

My disenchantment with the superficial nature of some activities prompted me to give up *directing* children how to communicate, make choices, "say no," and act assertively. Instead, I began to read aloud and discuss books from the library.

What a difference! I was no longer limited to single-purpose lessons with stated guidance objectives such as reasons for behavior, self-esteem, cooperation, or identification of feelings. The literary transaction met all those minimal guidance goals, plus more. The children were, in effect, adding their own guidance goals as they created meaning from the interaction of the text with their own lives.

The change was immediate. The children and I were energized by the experience. We laughed at Spinky's sulk and cheered when Sylvester the donkey became himself again. We filed away for future reference how ritual helped overcome grief when Barney the cat died. The children's responses were real and heartfelt. The discussions were no longer punctuated with expected responses or "right" answers. Expressions on their faces no longer registered "Don't call on me!" or "What do you want me to say?" or "Am I right?" Instead, children referred to previous discussions with insights that were fresh and new to them and to me. Children remembered characters and story themes from previous sessions with surprise and satisfaction. In casual encounters in school corridors or the grocery store, children spoke to me of Ramona, Mr. Gumpy, or Wanda Petronski as if they were friends of ours.

I sensed that my students were beginning to de-center through identification with story characters. It gradually followed that they became more conscious of their feelings and those of their classmates. They laughed together, making discoveries about each other. In quiet conversations they shared sadness, or reflected about suffering in the world. As they became more experienced, they began to earnestly grapple with issues of right and wrong, good and bad.

I knew that I was on to something, but I was limited by not knowing what the best books were. My enrollment in Alice Naylor's children's literature class and subsequent work with bibliotherapy corroborated my earlier intuition, and led me down new paths of discovery. I enrolled in a specialist degree program and conducted research on this topic. Dr. Naylor served on my academic advisory committee. This book is a result of that collaboration.

We bring together the results of my research, my practical experience as a counselor, and Alice Naylor's expertise as a librarian, critic, and teacher of children's literature.

OUR THEORETICAL BASE

We are convinced by literary and developmental theory that story is a way to make meaning of human experience. Our experience, intuition, and professional reading tell us that literature reverberates in our lives and can act as a stimulus for the development of intellect and character. Robert Coles (1989), a psychiatrist and author who has interviewed thousands of children, names this the "moral imagination."

Because we adhere to the whole language philosophy, we believe the purpose of learning should be to create critical thinkers. Peterson and Eeds (1990) described "grand conversations" which involve children and teachers in dialogue about literature for purposes of understanding the author's intent and individual readers' responses. Responses to literature, according to Rosenblatt (1978), are based on a literary transaction between text and reader. Readers create meaning from the varied perspectives emanating from their own varied experiences. These theories provided the structure with which we began. Other assumptions emerged from our experience with children.

OUR ASSUMPTIONS

We have faith in metaphor. Good art makes us see ourselves and the world differently, better, and more clearly. In literature, metaphor has the capacity to "time release" in our lives, producing a kaleidoscope of meanings from the same story. Alice Naylor's research finds that the more a story serves as metaphor, the greater the range of responses among readers.

My study with fifth graders compared literature-based discussions with the didactic moral dilemmas common to guidance curricula. Both the experimental and the control groups displayed developmental growth as measured by the David Hunt Paragraph Completion Test, which assesses concrete to abstract thinking, and other-directed to self-directed attitudinal growth. However, I found significantly greater conceptual gains in those students who had participated in conversations about literature than among those who had discussed the dilemmas that were deliberately contrived to promote discussion of moral values (Borders and Paisley, 1992).

Adults are essential in stimulating and modeling growth in children. Children continually watch and imitate adults in their lives. Developmental theorists agree that growth in moral and cognitive thinking only takes place through interaction. Kohlberg's "Plus One" proposition (Sprinthall and Collins, 1984) describes how children are attracted to moral thinking at one stage higher than their current level. Therefore, children need to hear adult opinion and to have their own opinions heard.

Vygotsky (1986) found that children recreate the world in their efforts to understand it, and that adults are essential in providing necessary nudges to move children through their zone of proximal development (the extent to which each child is capable of learning more). The adult's role, as articulated in our sample conversations, is not to expect right answers but to respond to children's comments with honesty, information, and a collaborative point of view.

Stories help adults and children explore common experiences and dilemmas. We do not demonstrate one-way conversations. Armed with good stories, adults in a collaborative role with children can find themselves continually renewed in their own developmental journeys. Literature can be a powerful and safe vehicle for exploring unsafe issues that are all too prevalent in the world today. The story in Lucille Clifton's *Everett Anderson's Nine Month Long* (see entry) enabled Kathleen Emdad and her second grade students to have an honest, heartfelt discussion of their feelings and views on racism. The teacher did not know ahead of time that this would be the moral issue of discussion. The comments arose out of the children's biographies, their interaction with the pictures in this book, and their relationship with each other.

Story is bonding. We are continually amazed by children's eagerness to "step into and move through" (Langer, 1990) a story, and we are touched by the wisdom and depth of feeling they are willing to share afterwards. We have found that children who participate in group story discussions are bound to us and each other by the experience. We share a common memory of Everett Anderson, Wilfrid Gordon McDonald Partridge, and Delphine. These literary characters are portrayed so well that we, along with the children, consider them to be friends.

Stories are a joy. Tonetta (grade 3) describes her experience of sharing stories and conversations in the classroom this way:

> To: Mrs. Borders From: Tonetta—It is fun very very fun with you. I Love you anytime. I enjoy you. Tonetta.

Our purpose in presenting these experiences is to open doors of possibility to other adults and children. We also hope it is "fun very very fun with you."

REFERENCES

Borders, Sarah & Pamela Paisley. (1992). "Children's Literature as a Resource for Classroom Guidance." *Elementary School Guidance & Counseling* 27: 131-39.

Coles, Robert. (1989). *The Call of Stories*. Houghton Mifflin.

Langer, Judith A. (1990, Dec). "Understanding Literature." *Language Arts* 67: 812-16.

Peterson, Ralph & Mary Eeds. (1990). *Grand Conversations: Literature Groups in Action*. Scholastic-Tab, Ltd.

Rosenblatt, Louise M. (1978). *The Reader, the Text, the Poem: The Transactional Theory of the Literary Work*. Southern Illinois University Press.

Sprinthall, Norman A. & W.A. Collins. (1984). *Adolescent Psychology: A Developmental View*. Addison Wesley.

Vygotsky, Lev. (1986). *Thought and Language*. Translated by A. Kozulin. Mitchell Press.

Chapter 1
How to Use This Book

READING THE BOOK ENTRIES

We have organized the books discussed alphabetically by author. Almost all of these books can be used across many ages. We have selected books that have been sure-fire successes for us, or that provide an opportunity to discuss unusual aspects of life. We have tried not to use obviously didactic or pedagogical books. We rely on metaphor in the story to enable children to find parallels in their own lives.

PARTS OF THE BOOK ENTRY

Publisher, Date, and Illustrator

First we give the publisher of the book and the year of its publication. Most of the books have been published since 1980, but a few were published earlier. The illustrator is then named for books that rely heavily on the illustrations to tell the story.

Audience

We love all these books, so we can safely say that they could appeal to adults as well as children. However, as a guide, we include with each entry the lowest level of intended audience for the book. The "Books for Follow-Up Literature Studies" section at the end of each entry mentions two or three other titles with similar themes that range in level from kindergarten through sixth grade. If one of these titles varies in level from the main entry title, we call attention to it in the annotation.

Main Theme

We highlight one idea in each entry, the primary theme of the book from a literary perspective.

Other Possible Themes

We have attempted to second guess what topics may arise from the literature itself. Because theme is often an individual matter, we rest our choices on many years of experience and agreement between us. In discussion children often identify unexpected themes derived from their perspective. We have listed those that emerged in our discussions.

Values to Target

Although Sarah Borders identified values to assist counselors, this section is also addressed to teachers and parents whose intention is to focus on the development of personal and social skills and moral thinking. We hope that these targeted values clue all adults into the way in which literature discussions can promote healthy development of children: personally, socially, and psychologically.

About the Author

Long-term experience with book discussion leads children to stop using the pronoun "they" for the author. By telling them something about the author, children can be helped to realize that a story is created out of one person's perception of the world. This section offers facts, comments, or circumstances of the author that might serve as a by-way or road sign to understanding of the story the author created. We have relied on resources such as *Something About the Author (SATA)*, *Something About the Author—Autobiography Series (SATAAS)*, *The Dictionary of Literary Biography (DLB)*, *The Children's Literature Review (CLR)*, and *Junior Authors* for this information. Teachers interested in author studies may consult the sources for more details.

About the Illustrator

When the illustrations help tell the story or are particularly wonderful we include information on the illustrator. Children are engulfed in visual images in our culture and focusing on high-quality book illustrations provides an opportunity to enhance their visual literacy. How illustrations are designed to convey meaning is an important component of literature study.

About the Story

    This summary is not intended as a substitute for your reading of the story. This section will give you a sense of the setting, plot, and characters, thus helping you decide if this book meets your needs. Our reflections about the story are partially the result of having discussed the book with children, so we credit them for some interpretations and opinions we offer in this section.

Dialogue

    This is the fun part. Here we provide some sample responses and conversations that resulted from adult-led book discussions. The adult prompts are followed by the children's responses. The children take the discussions in directions that win our unending admiration. We often find that the fewer prompts we use, the better the discussion. The more we make comments instead of questions, the more comments children make. The less we talk, the more the children will talk.

    If we only ask questions, children search for right answers instead of for meaning from within their personal transaction with the text. When the children feel comfortable asking questions themselves, other children answer.

    Not all entries are identical. If something wonderful happened with a different kind of group or in a different way, we felt free to vary the entry. The format of discussions does not always have to follow a pattern. However, we have found that starting out by following a pattern such as this one helps children know what to expect and what to watch for and helps the adult feel more secure.

Insights

    Our process demands critique. We read and re-read our transcripts so that we can evaluate what happened in the transaction between story, children, and leader. We provide some of these insights, which appear in boxes before the start of children's responses to a prompt, to highlight the making of meaning as it takes place. Shared enjoyment and a sense of community are usually obvious. Sometimes the teacher leads the children to another level of thinking; sometimes a child amazes us with a particular insight. Some of our comments serve as models for assessing the progress of children along the developmental journey. For example, in Chris Van Allsburg's *The Wretched Stone,* we can observe Alan's progression to higher level thought and feeling. He no longer needs to be "tested" to determine his stage of cognitive and affective development.

Teacher Focus and Counselor Focus

Whole language teachers and counselors, while concentrating on assisting children to learn how to learn, constantly keep in mind their prescribed school curriculum goals. These sections seek to call to mind curriculum connections that can emerge from literature discussions. Teachers and counselors will see other connections as they experience the process themselves.

Making Connections

If we have tried a connecting activity ourselves, or heard about wonderful events other groups have created following a book discussion, we include them. We believe that children, and teachers, learn better when they create activities for themselves. However, we pass these ideas on because we like them. Also, we find that teachers appreciate reading about an activity so that they can adapt it for their own purposes and settings.

Books for Follow-Up Literature Studies

When children enjoy a discussion on a topic or a book by a particular author, we try to be ready to suggest other books or stories they can read, or that we might discuss in the future. We have included in this section some titles that may be read aloud in one session, but we have also included some chapter books. Literature studies of longer books can extend over several days or even weeks. Some of the upper grade books listed in this section may have to be read by the children before the discussions begin; or read in class over a longer period of time. Longer discussions will inevitably follow as children become more experienced with the process and comfortable with the group.

USING THE THREE DISCUSSION PROMPTS

The structure of each discussion is based on response theory, particularly the reduction of theories into the three categories of response we use in each entry. Patricia Kelly (1990) used the following prompts during a full year in her multi-ethnic class of 28 third graders to elicit first oral and later written responses to literature:

1. What did you notice about the story?
2. How did the story make you feel?
3. What does the story remind you of in your own life?

She concluded that not only were the students actively involved in learning, they were enthusiastic about literature. She found a noticeable difference in fluency and increased reflection of emotional involvement as students became accustomed to the process.

These prompts are effective catalysts to the bibliotherapeutic model described by Bodart (1980) and Schrank (1982). The process of interaction between readers and text as described by bibliotherapists consists of three steps.

1. *Identification*—The reader "enters" the story and is able to associate him or herself with a character or situation in the story.
2. *Catharsis*—The reader feels with the character such emotions as sadness, fear, or pride.
3. *Insight*—The reader begins to develop understanding or gains new perceptions regarding his or her life.

We adapted Kelly's question prompts to statements and found that discussions soon flowed right through the bibliotherapeutic model. The more we used these prompts, the more we noticed their effectiveness.

Prompt 1: *Talk about what you notice in the story.*

What children notice can and will include all aspects of the book—text, format, characters, illustrations, and more. You will be amazed at what the children notice that you never noticed at all.

There is no one right way to ask, "What did you notice?" Cheri Pace (see *Spinky Sulks* by William Steig) began by saying, "I noticed that you were very interested in the story." She then re-worded the question, asking, "What else did you notice?" Sometimes the leader simply states what she or he notices.

When children become familiar with this question, they eagerly seek the opportunity to tell what they notice. Kaaren Hayes, a teacher of preschool children, reports great excitement among three-year-olds who soon discern that they are absolutely wonderful at "noticing."

Prompt 2: *Talk about how the story makes you feel.*

Thoughts and feelings are not necessarily separate, so this also is "What do you think about...?" Children in the discussion of Judith Viorst's *The Tenth Good Thing about Barney* described "a feeling of crying." Mixed in the conversations about feelings were all kinds of related thoughts. Arnold Lobel's *Fables* inspires more thinking than feeling because of the nature of the genre.

The word "notice" in the first prompt elicits responses that establish a common knowledge shared by the group. This feelings prompt then works well as the second prompt because the group can draw on this shared knowledge to articulate feelings. With this easy question, concrete thinkers have their chance along with the more conceptual thinkers in the group. In the family reading of Barbara Cooney's *Miss Rumphius*, the three-year-old had plenty to contribute because he noticed the flowers over and over.

Once children share thoughts and feelings, the group is bonded and becomes a safer place to explore issues that may emerge with the third prompt.

Prompt 3: *Talk about what the story reminds you of in your life.*

This is where Judith Langer's (1990) "stepping out and objectifying" takes place. One's life is now the metaphor for the book. Our own experience helps us understand the book, and the book helps us understand our own experience.

The more children experience conversations, the more quickly they will move into understanding metaphorical meaning. However, good discussion can take place on many levels. In the discussion of Lucille Clifton's *Everett Anderson's Nine Month Long,* the children hardly talk about the book at all. The discussion was primarily concrete, but certainly profound.

REFERENCES

Bodart, Joni (1980). "Bibliotherapy: The Right Book for the Right Person at the Right Time and More" in *Top of the News* 36: 183-88.

Children's Literature Review. (1976 to date). Gale Research.

Commire, Ann, ed. (1971 to date). *Something About the Author.* Gale Research.

de Montreville, D. and Hill, E. D., eds. (1978 to date). *Junior Authors.* H. W. Wilson.

Estes, Glenn E., ed. (1985). *Dictionary of Literary Biography: American Writers for Children Since 1960.* Gale Research.

Kelly, Patricia. (1990). "Guiding Young Students' Response to Literature" in *Reading Teacher's Journal* 43(7): pp. 464-70.

Langer, Judith A. (1990). "Understanding Literature" in *Language Arts* 67: 812-16.

Schrank, F. A., (1982). "Bibliotherapy as an Elementary Guidance Tool" in *Elementary School Guidance and Counseling* 16(3): 218-27.

Something About the Author Autobiography Series. (1986 to date). Gale Research.

Chapter 2
Functions of the Adult Leader

We have learned that the adult leader of children's book discussions fulfills at least six functions.

1. Choosing the books
2. Providing an environment
3. Practicing and learning from mistakes
4. Guiding the discussion
5. Listening
6. Participating

CHOOSING THE BOOKS

We select titles on the basis of their quality first and their theme second. We find that multiple themes inevitably emerge from well-written stories. We do not ask, "What is this book good for?" We do ask ourselves, "Is this book good?"

How do we know when a story is good? Well, it's good when the children's eyes get big. Mem Fox (1990) noted that when children are so enraptured they forget to breathe, she knows her story is good.

Joan Aiken (1976) says that good literature has "quadruple, quintuple richness so that it can take extra wear and tear. A book ought to have something new to offer at every reading—a sort of graded series of concepts, graspable at each stage of development." Some guidelines for the selection process, based on elements of story, are described below.

Language

Words should be appropriate to the selection. Maurice Sendak's *Where the Wild Things Are* is a masterful blend of language, plot, and illustration. "Please don't go; we'll eat you up, we love you so," beg the monsters. The pictures and the language pick up the irony of *loveable* monsters. Audrey and Don Wood's pictures in *Elbert's Bad Word* draw readers into the elegant garden party with rich, rolling phrases like "Sir Hilary spilled his spritzer on Madam Friatta's feathered boa."

Words should give pleasure when read aloud. Often writing succeeds through the use of rhyme, rhythm, or repetition. Mem Fox is so good at choosing names for her characters that there is pleasure in the name itself. Wilfrid Gordon McDonald Partridge was the real name of her father. The name of the boy who "was not very old" resounds through the story. Leah Komaiko's *Annie Bananie* echoes with pathos, humor, and rhyming couplets that beg to be read aloud. "Annie Bananie, do not cry. Even best friends say good-bye."

The following descriptive passage is from *Maniac Magee* by Jerry Spinelli:

> To anyone else, it was a ratty old scrap of leather, barely recognizable as a baseball glove, fit for the garbage can. But Maniac knew at once this was Grayson's, the one he had played with all those years in the Minors. It was limp, flat, the pocket long since gone. Slowly, timidly, as though entering a shrine, the boy's fingers crept into it, flexed, curled the cracked leather, brought it back to shape, to life.

The wonderful choice of words propels the slow motion, yet retains the action of a poignant moment.

Setting

The details selected by the author should provoke images in the mind of the reader. In *The Relatives Came*, Cynthia Rylant writes:

> It was in the summer of the year when the relatives came. They came up from Virginia. They left when their grapes were nearly purple enough to pick, but not quite. They had an old station wagon that smelled like a real car, and in it they put an ice chest full of soda pop and some boxes of crackers and some bologna sandwiches, and up they came—from Virginia.

Without those details, which are repeated throughout the story, we cannot know enough about where we are to enter into the story. Children are prone to repeat aloud, "They're from Virginia." (See Rylant.)

Plot

The story line should engage readers, making them gasp in anticipation of what happens next. Stories have shape, starting in a certain place, building upward toward a climax, and then usually settling down to something similar to "happily ever after." Suspense is created through language. William Steig begins *Spinky Sulks* with "Spinky came charging out of the house and flung himself on the grass. He couldn't even see the dandelions he was staring at, he was so upset." Listeners immediately want to know why Spinky is upset. Even if action begins slowly and the shape of the plot is larger, the seeds of suspense are sown and sprout in the same way.

Illustrations

Miss Rumphius by Barbara Cooney is a lovely blend of picture and story. The illustrations are essential to the themes of beauty and generativity. Even the shape of the book was chosen with great care since the expanse of the wide double page captures the effect of the wind-borne lupines and the house by the sea.

In picture books, illustrations tell some of the story. In Rylant's *The Relatives Came,* the profusion of outrageous goings-on reflect the memory of feelings about "those relatives." The illustrations are not meant to be realistic. The nostalgic tone permits the disarray and bumbling behavior. Warmth and gaiety are revealed as much through the illustrations as the words.

Character

Characters should come alive for the reader, have dimension and individuality. Characterization is much more than a character simply having a name and playing a role in the plot. Ann Coleridge exhibits well-written characterization in *The Friends of Emily Culpepper*:

> Emily Culpepper is an old lady who enjoys cooking and travelling, but most of all she enjoys talking to her friends. One of her friends was the milkman, so she made him small and put him in a jam jar, so that she could talk to him any time she wanted to. (This is also a trifle suspenseful!)

Characters should behave consistently and in a believable fashion. Emily consistently puts friends in jars of one sort or another, but she is particularly attentive to the words of the policeman when he suggests that their families need them at home. We may be shocked by what she does, but it is in character.

Ramona, in the series of books by Beverly Cleary, consistently acts on her certainty that the only way to escape punishment is to be "extra good."

Theme

To find meaning, or theme, Kay Vandergrift (1980) suggests we ask ourselves the question, "Is there a pervasive morality woven into the fabric of the story rather than a contrived moral message?" In *The Mountains of Tibet* by Mordicai Gerstein, the word *choose* is used many times. The woodcutter is choosing. Gerstein says his intent was to explore the possibilities of choice in our lives. The reader recreates that theme, or meaning, during and after experiencing the book.

> There are thousands of kinds of people in this world...each with different dances and delicious dishes, and you may join any kind you like!
> The woodcutter looked and saw all the peoples of the world dancing around him. They looked like flowers...."Just taste this!" they called, holding out their most tempting dishes. "This is the hardest choice," said the woodcutter.

Some themes are not as explicit as Gerstein's.

We find that posing the question, "What is the story *really* about?" helps children build on each other's responses as they dig deeper to discover multiple themes in stories.

Point of View

The point of view is the vision of events of whoever is telling the story. The words must always reflect what that character or narrator knows and sees, otherwise we do not believe in the story. Susan Shreve sustains the boy's point of view in the five stories found in *Family Secrets*. Never are we outside of Sammy's mind. He thinks like a kid. "And to think I did it in cold blood ...mostly I wished I was dead," he says after he has cheated on a math test.

Mem Fox (1990) says about good stories:

> If we don't laugh, gasp, block our ears, sigh, vomit, giggle, curl our toes, sympathize, feel pain, weep, or shiver during the reading of a picture book, then surely the writer has wasted our time, our money and our precious trees. If I read a picture book and remain in the same emotional state I was in before I read it, then for me the book has failed. It's a here-today-and gone-tomorrow book.

PROVIDING AN ENVIRONMENT

Book discussions in the classroom, family, guidance room, or library are not just one more activity. The adult leader plans and arranges for discussions by selecting a group, or allowing children to self-select. While a group of six to twelve is ideal, there are some samples in this book (see Eleanor Estes, Helen Griffith, and Vera Williams) that were done in large classroom groups. Some of the guidance groups comprised children referred by the teacher to the counselor; some were self-selected. Other discussions in this book took place in remedial reading or special education groups. The discussion of *Miss Rumphius* took place in a family group.

Part of setting the stage is for the adult to use the information about the author, genre, and book format. Once the reading and discussion are underway, time can be allowed for the creation of meaning and making connections to other events, conditions, and curricula. The ideal book discussion in the classroom eventually incorporates many aspects of the curriculum.

You may be able to give the children choices among several books you like. It is possible, after children are accustomed to the process, to have more than one group discussion at a time in a classroom. Nevertheless, teachers will want to have read all the titles, and know ahead of time what may be important or necessary or useful to contribute to the discussion, such as information about the author, the year the story was written, and where the story takes place.

PRACTICING AND LEARNING FROM MISTAKES

Good teachers take risks and remain learners forever. We keep learning, changing, and experimenting with this process. Don't expect to have every session go well. When things do not go as we would like, we discuss the situation with the children. They share in the responsibility to create a good learning environment and often to choose the right books for worthwhile discussion.

GUIDING THE DISCUSSION

We do not tell children "this is the moral of the story." Messages or morals emerge through all those elements of story coming together around a theme. The authors and illustrators deliberately choose to put certain things in and leave other things out to assist readers in the process of finding meaning. Children will draw from the story what they are ready to hear and understand. Discussion leaders find their role easier if they are well grounded in the levels of cognitive, affective, and moral stages of development in children. Creating a receptive yet challenging discussion will give teachers opportunities to stimulate growth.

Prepared questions are a way for you to think about the book in myriad ways. You may find that you rarely need them, especially if you do a good job of attending and redirecting. While it is comforting to have discussion questions ready, we must not overlook our most important opportunity—building discussion on comments not answers to questions. Leaders develop skill in gradually changing overlapping responses into conversations. We do not wish for the children to talk just to us, but rather to share with others in the group. They make meaning about themselves, each other, and the world.

Encourage diverse opinions. Discussions are not guessing games to determine what the leader wants to hear. The thinking process is enhanced by hearing more than one interpretation of the topic at hand.

Allow time for thinking. Silent times are creative times. In the beginning you may suggest a quiet time to think about thoughts and feelings. When familiar with the freedom to do so, the children let you know when they are being thoughtful. *The Mountains of Tibet* elicits silence at the end. In contrast, *The Relatives Came* elicits response from everyone, all at the same time.

Ask for evidence from the story to corroborate opinions when there is disagreement. When using good literature, relish its artistic qualities. For example, in a discussion of *Sylvester and the Magic Pebble,* the children liked the phrase "stone dumb" and went back to the text to determine what it meant. As you read the story aloud at the beginning of a session, do not stop and explain or "do" vocabulary. Let the rich words and phrases be understood in the context of the story. In a discussion of *Mr. Gumpy's Outing,* one of the children corrected another about the difference between "bleating" and "bleeding." The child determined the meaning from the context. In the role play that followed another discussion of the same book, the children delighted in "mucking about" and "squabbling." The children continued to use the delicious words in conversations in the classroom for the very purpose of exploring their use and meaning.

High quality books or stories can be repeated. One way to do this is to use the book and then the video. Another is to look at a book from a different perspective. *A House for Hermit Crab* by Eric Carle can be a science lesson the second time around. One counselor borrowed a dreidel when she read Isaac Singer's "The Power of Light" and played her tape of Peter, Paul, and Mary singing "Don't Let the Light Go Out." One lesson expanded to three because the children wanted to know about the

Macabees, the Jewish people in Germany, Nazis, Jewish religious customs, the difference between the Old and New Testaments, and more.

Something tangible that represents an element of the story can be valuable. Some lupine seeds go well with *Miss Rumphius*, a jar of coins with *A Chair for My Mother*, and a bunch of bananas with *The Wretched Stone*.

Good discussions take time. We are in the real world of schedules, and we know that finding time is always a challenge. Time is important also in terms of learning how to discuss. Webs, charts, and other kinds of graphic organizers on story elements can initiate children in the skills of becoming critics and can lead to the freedom of expression they will cherish as they become more experienced.

The creation of meaning, as well as thinking about how ideas and events connect to one another, takes time. We know we have created ideal book discussions when eventually the discussion expands into all aspects of the curriculum.

LISTENING

Research on teacher behavior tells us over and over again that teacher-directed activities and teacher/student/teacher verbal exchanges are not consistent with how children learn. We use these behaviors as parents as well as teachers and they are hard to overcome.

Our goal was to overcome, but there are times when everyone is talking at once or "creative dramatics" go out of bounds and control seems needed. We find, however, that the more familiar students become with literature discussions the less the adult feels the need to use controlling behaviors. As the teacher becomes a learner with the children, children take charge of their own behavior. After one session, a teacher asked the students, "Does anyone want to hear what I think?" They answered, "Maybe tomorrow."

The real work of the adult in the group is to LISTEN, LISTEN, LISTEN. The children are working at creating meaning for themselves. By listening carefully, our own reflections can be carefully phrased to stimulate higher levels of thinking or at least more informed reflections. Sometimes we simply make connections between responses of different or differing children. The discussion of *Everett Anderson's Nine Month Long* by Lucille Clifton is an example. By connecting the comments of Laura and Shanin, the teacher encouraged communication between the two. At the end of that class, Laura left with tears in her eyes and Anthony went out the door shaking his head. Two weeks later the discussion was still influencing the behavior of Laura and Shanin.

PARTICIPATING

We know that modeling is one good way of teaching. Teachers who are learners model what children need to know, what we expect them to be. When we enter book discussions with children, it is with excitement and anticipation of learning. The children need to feel that we are glad to be there.

Every child needs to be assured of an opportunity to speak. Using friendly head shakes or a smiling look of expectation will often prompt a child to speak who would not otherwise. We try not to look at the children who are speaking, but, instead, to continually maintain eye contact with those who are not volunteering, and then we use supportive expressions to bring shy, reluctant children to the brink of saying something aloud.

We like these three initiating prompts to stimulate spontaneous responses: Talk about What You Notice; Talk about How the Story Makes You Feel; Talk about What the Story Reminds You of in Your Life. Children in our groups became used to this process and soon began asking us, "Well, what did you notice." One student enjoyed the process so much in a small group that he hurried back to the classroom with pencil and paper to copy the prompts off the board so his reading class could enjoy talking about a book in the same way he had just experienced.

Sometimes responses are physiological; we cry, laugh, or shiver. Children often find themselves expressing thoughts they didn't know they had. We have never discussed a book with a group of children without going away knowing something that we didn't know before. We may know more about individual children. We may know something about a book we had never thought of before. We may know something about ourselves that resulted from our comments or someone else's. We always know more about how to discuss books.

OTHER THINGS WE WANT TO SAY

Over a period of time stories reverberate in children's lives. Jacque Touchton's work with children with behavioral disabilities is done almost entirely through story, especially folktales. She notices that the references and metaphors of the stories seem to float around the room ready for the children to snatch when they need to make a connection. A study of *Why Mosquitos Buzz in People's Ears* made tattling behavior less effective in the class. Students reminded each other of the whining mosquito. The humor and the shared understanding defused tension.

There is a close relationship between talking, discussing, and writing. Sometimes writing seems a natural activity before or after the discussion. The Vera Williams and Shel Silverstein entries include writing. Written thoughts crystallize ideas that can then provide the basis for discussion. The same process can be used at the end of discussions, when the writing may be more extensive and purposeful.

REFERENCES

Aiken, Joan. (1976). "Writing for Enjoyment." pp. 15-26 in *Writers, Critics, and Children: Articles from Children's Literature in Education.* Edited by Geoff Fox, et al. Agathon.

Fox, Mem. (1990). "Writing Picture Books: A Love/Hate Relationship." *Horn Book* 45 (3): 288-96.

Vandergrift, Kay. (1980). *Child and Story: The Literary Connection.* Neal Schuman.

Book Entries

Molly Bang, *Delphine*

• •

Publisher and Date: Morrow, 1988
Illustrator: Molly Bang
Audience: Kindergarten and up
Main Theme: Fear
Other Possible Themes: Gifts, Imagination, Grandmothers,
    Bicycles
Values to Target: Courage, Coping with Fear and Worry

• •

ABOUT THE AUTHOR

Molly Garrett Bang was born December 29, 1943. She worked as a teacher of English in Kyoto, Japan, and as a translator and interpreter of Japanese in the United States. Most of the many children's books she has written are illustrated translations of Asian folktales. Her illustrations are distinctive for the unusual use of layout and color and for the portrayal of movement. Her experiences in other countries and knowledge of languages contribute to her success in retelling stories from many cultures. *Delphine* is an original work seemingly created to represent almost any culture. Bang lives in Woods Hole, Massachusetts (*SATA* v. 24, pp. 37-39).

ABOUT THE STORY

The mailman delivers a notice to Delphine that a box awaits her at the post office. She knows it is from Gram and even surmises what is in it.

However, she is worried, scared, even terrified about whether she is up to what will be expected of her. Her feelings of fear are related more in the intriguing pictures of Delphine than in the words that convey the plot. The story takes readers through Delphine's journey of anticipation, fear, courage, and eventual triumph.

We knew that feelings could be expressed in artistic ways, but Molly Bang has created especially exciting concrete images to represent Delphine's trepidation and fear at the thought of riding a bicycle. The pages of this book are not to be turned quickly. Each illustration needs to be experienced and interpreted as Delphine builds courage to take a ride. When the tigers and tightropes disappear, a self-confident Delphine remains. Bang's use of full page, primary colors, and interesting perspective and size relationships assists us in entering into Delphine's inner world.

DIALOGUE

Talk about What You Notice in the Story

• •

Since these children range in age from five to ten, multi-level response occurs. Rebecca and Jennifer immediately grasp Molly Bang's efforts to convey feelings in imaginative illustrations. Michael and Karen are viewing the illustrations more concretely because they are younger. Leslie raises the issue of perspective in the illustrations.

• •

Rebecca: She's going through hard times.
Kimberley: I think she's going to fall.
Jennifer: She worries too much. She worries about stuff when she doesn't even know what it is.
Michael: The tiger's on the bike.
Karen: How could she be that near a wolf?
Leslie: The mailman is so small.

Talk about How the Story Makes You Feel

• •

With no adult guidance, the children move the conversation to feeling. Almost every child mentions the word worry. When their conversations overlap, they name the degrees of fear. They obviously understood the author's intent.

• •

Jennifer:	She found out it was really easy. She was worrying about too many things.
Kimberley:	She worried about things in her imagination.
Rebecca:	She worried about what she would do with it.
Kimberley:	The pictures tell what she's thinking.
	[All together the children spontaneously recited all the words that described what Delphine was feeling: worried, afraid, scared, terrified.]
Rebecca:	Maybe it had happened before and she was thinking of what might happen again.
Kimberley:	Maybe she just imagined it.
Leslie:	*[Jennifer's younger sister]* How did she know it was a bike?
TEACHER:	MAYBE SHE HAD TOLD HER GRAM OR MOTHER THAT SHE WANTED A BIKE.
Leslie:	Maybe she was worried that it was something she didn't want, like she might go to the zoo and get a box and you wouldn't want that. We found a snake once, and we didn't want it. We put a basket over its head.

Talk about What the Story Reminds You of in Your Life

● ●

The children conclude with stories about their own fearful experiences. Rebecca is proud to tell of a fear she has overcome, like Delphine. Making such statements to a group is very affirming for children.

● ●

Michael:	She reminds me of my sister Christy. She rode my bike. But she wasn't afraid. But there's a boy in my class. He always says things like, "Is this too much?" "Do you think this will overflow?" and stuff like that. He's afraid of everything.
Jennifer:	I was afraid once. We were walking and came to this swinging bridge. It was like the one over Grandfather Mountain only not a real one. I sort of wanted to try it out. I wanted to see if I could do it. Before I knew it, I was walking on it.
Rebecca:	I used to be afraid of dogs. But now I know about dogs and why they do things. I'm bigger now. Like Delphine. Now she is grown up and proud.

TEACHER FOCUS

Visual Literacy: This discussion illustrates a lesson in visual literacy. The teacher was ready to ask about the size relationships and perspective, but the children "understood" the message of the visuals so well that she chose not to intrude in their responses.

Plot: The suspense is based on the fact that the readers do not know what Delphine is afraid of. To demonstrate this the teacher may ask for predictions after each paragraph. The children may apply what they discover about the surprise to their writing. (See writing activity in "Making Connections.")

COUNSELOR FOCUS

Naming and Sharing Feelings: In entering into Delphine's experience children can recognize their own feelings of fear and worry. Once a feeling is shared with the group, children will shed their feelings of loneliness and their conception that they are the only ones with such experiences. Re-experiencing the story through drawing and talking can create a new dimension to the identifying and sharing of common fears and worries. (See art activity in "Making Connections.")

MAKING CONNECTIONS

Writing: Children respond eagerly to the suggestion that they write their own stories of when they were afraid of something. The story is an excellent model for writing suspense. Children can be encouraged to analyze the surprise in the story, and to choose their own way of telling or writing a suspenseful story.

Art: The counselor or teacher may ask the children to do one of the following drawing exercises before sharing more with the group:

1. Draw your worries and fears as animals.
2. On a whole sheet of paper draw your head and shoulders. Instead of making your face, make symbols, drawings, or lines and colors to represent the worries on your mind.
3. Fold a paper in four sections. Make a cartoon sequence of yourself doing something very hard for the first time.

BOOKS FOR FOLLOW-UP LITERATURE STUDIES

Starred titles have full entries elsewhere in the book.

Babbitt, Natalie. (1970). *The Something.* Farrar, Straus & Giroux.
   "The Something" is terrifying, yet more humorous than the wild animals in *Delphine.*
Burningham, John. (1987). *John Patrick Norman McHennessy.* Crown Publishers.
   Burningham is visualizing any number of concepts in this story: imagination, adult-child relationships, schooling.
Prelutsky, Jack. (1976). *Nightmares: Poems to Trouble Your Sleep.* Illustrated by Arnold Lobel. Greenwillow Books.
   Twelve poems feature vampires, werewolves, ghouls, and monsters.
*Sendak, Maurice. (1963). *Where the Wild Things Are.* Harper and Row.
   Max is called a wild thing by his mother because he makes mischief. His journey to the land of the wild things and back home gives him power to tame the wild things within himself.
*Wood, Audrey. (1988). *Elbert's Bad Word.* Illustrated by Don Wood. Harcourt Brace Jovanovich.
   As with the illustrations in *Delphine,* Elbert's encounter with a bad word is made into a visual experience for the reader.

Judy Blume,
The Pain and the Great One

• •

Publisher and Date: Dell Yearling, 1984
Illustrator: Irene Trivas
Audience: Grades two to six
Main Theme: Sibling Rivalry
Other Possible Themes: Jealousy, Anger, Family Relations
Values to Target: Empathy, Reasons for Behavior

• •

ABOUT THE AUTHOR

Since her first book was published in 1969, Judy Blume's books have sold more than 30 million copies and have been translated into many different languages. Blume receives 2,000 letters every month from young readers, many seeking advice from an author they regard as a friend and confidante.

Blume explores the everyday lives of contemporary children and young adults. She was raised in suburban New Jersey and spent two of her childhood years in Miami Beach. She writes about people and places familiar to her, often basing stories on her own experiences or those of her children.

It took Blume over two years to find a publisher for her first book, *The One in the Middle Is a Green Kangaroo*. After its successful release her other books followed in rapid succession. *The Pain and the Great One* is dedicated "To the original Pain and the Great One with Love," her own children (*DLB* v. 52, pp. 30-38, and personal communication with Alice Naylor).

ABOUT THE STORY

This is a good read-aloud book because of the two voices, the Pain (the six-year-old little brother) and the Great One (the big sister). He is "a pain" to her. She is "the great one" to him. The Great One depicts her brother as a slowpoke who acts silly, makes messes, and bugs her while she's on the phone. The Pain maintains, "My sister thinks she's so great. She can play the piano, dial a phone number, open a can opener and baby sit." It appears to him that Mom and Dad must love *her* best. The reverse, of course, is true from The Great One's point of view. The amusing details of the events and facial expressions of the characters are expertly illustrated in water color.

Blume structured this book to place the reader in the shoes of one character at a time. The limited plot focuses on the alternate feelings of brother and sister, lending itself to a single issue theme. Even though children will enter into the role of the sibling most like themselves, the shape of the story draws them into the other point of view.

DIALOGUE

Talk about What You Notice in the Story

● ●

These fourth and fifth grade children are expressing delight at their recognition of circumstances in story which are so familiar in real life.

● ●

TEACHER: FROM YOUR REACTION I CAN TELL THAT THIS STORY HITS HOME WITH MANY OF YOU!

Cassie:	They were both telling the story. It was like the author had them taking turns.
TEACHER:	THAT'S REALLY GOOD, CASSIE. I WONDER WHY JUDY BLUME DECIDED TO WRITE THE BOOK THAT WAY?
Joseph:	Well, turn about is fair play!
Jennifer:	It's like we have to see both sides of the story.
Beth:	It was so funny when The Pain was singing that song. I know it got on her nerves. My little brother acts so stupid like that. And he's always doing dumb stuff when I'm on the phone. *[Energetic chorus of agreement]*
Joseph:	My little brother is all the time getting into my model paint, and he spilled some all over my airplane. I wish he'd leave my stuff alone.
Holly:	My little sister gets into my nail polish when I'm on the phone, or playing outside. It makes me so mad.
TEACHER:	THAT CAN BE INFURIATING!
Holly:	*[smiling]* Right!

Talk about How the Story Makes You Feel

● ●

The teacher's reflective statement leads into responses on the feeling level. The children begin by identifying with the character most like themselves, but the door is open for the consideration of another's point of view. Especially valuable in this discussion are the expressions of feelings of jealousy the children would never admit to without the support of The Pain and The Great One.

● ●

Robert:	Right! The Great One was pretty mad. I know all about that.
Cassie:	The main thing about the book was that both The Pain and The Great One thought the parents loved the other one best.
Haley:	*[with a sigh]* I know how that feels.
Cassie:	Right. I know they both really feel that way. But I know it's *not* true.
TEACHER:	IT'S NOT?
Cassie:	*[with certainty]* The mom and dad loved them *both* the same.
Matt:	They're just jealous of each other, that's it!
TEACHER:	HOW DOES JEALOUS FEEL?
Sarah:	I think it's mad and sad mixed together.

Chris:	It's like you need some attention and nobody is giving it to you.
Jennifer:	And then you get mad and try to get even or do something mean.
David:	That's like me, all right! *[Murmurs of agreement]*

Talk about *What the Story Reminds You of in Your Life*

• •

The children are beginning to objectify about their own experiences with sibling rivalry. Cassie understands that parents do love them both. Haley echoes a common need for attention.

• •

Teacher:	LOTS OF YOU AGREE WITH DAVID THAT THE STORY IS LIKE YOU.
Haley:	*Everything* that goes on in my house with me and my brother is *exactly* like this story.
Rob:	I know all about "Pains." We have one in our house too.
Jessie:	Sometimes it seems like parents always take up for the baby of the family.
David:	I don't know about that. My parents take up for my big sister. And she always bosses me around. I don't like having her in charge of me. She's always changing the channel away from what I want to watch on TV. Sometimes I get so mad at her, I make a trail out in the woods and think about how long I'd have to stay before somebody would miss me.
Beth:	I remember when I was little and I'd be jealous I used to go hide between the refrigerator and the wall. I'd be thinking, "They'll think I've run away. Then they'll be sorry!" *[laughter]*
Chris:	Hey, I've done stuff like that.
Haley:	After a while of pouting I usually get tired of being by myself.
Teacher:	THANKS FOR SHARING THAT, HALEY. I NOTICED THAT THE GREAT ONE ACTUALLY MISSED THE PAIN WHEN THEY PUT HIM TO BED EARLY.
Haley:	Right. She was just getting bored.
Denise:	I think sometimes little brothers or sisters would act nicer if we take some time for them.
Cassie:	It's like I said before, both of them just need attention.
Haley:	Let's face it. We all need attention.

TEACHER FOCUS

Point of View: How and why do The Pain and The Great One see things differently?

Discovering Implied Relationships: What is this story like from the parent's point of view?

Author's Intent: Why did Judy Blume choose to write the story from two perspectives instead of one?

COUNSELOR FOCUS

Reasons for Feelings and Reasons for Behavior: The story invites catharsis because feelings of siblings are so strong. Once children have identified their own common feelings with the characters they can be encouraged to see the relationship between feelings and behavior.

MAKING CONNECTIONS

The Empathy Game or Feeling Charades: For guidance lessons counselors or teachers may design cards with instructions for miming simple situations that exhibit varying feelings. Teachers first may clarify the difference between empathy and sympathy, using word roots. The game resembles charades. One at a time children draw a card, then act out the situation. The group first guesses the activity and then identifies several feeling words.

Below are some sample cue cards for the empathy game:

1. You are taking a very hard test. You haven't studied at all.
2. You have just picked up your spelling paper. You made 100.
3. You come into your room and find your little sister has been into all your stuff.
4. You get your plate of spaghetti. You drop it all over the floor in the cafeteria.
5. You are shooting an important free throw. You miss.
6. You lost your money for the movie.
7. Your favorite cookies are in the cookie jar.
8. Someone has called you a name.

Drawing: One mother reports that *The Pain and The Great One* is read over and over by her daughter, who enjoys drawing comparable scenes from their family life. In group work such drawings give further opportunities for writing or telling stories to go with the pictures. Children may write or tell a story from two points of view as Judy Blume did.

Reader's Theater: Choose a Pain and a Great One. Use hats for props. Re-experience the story as a dramatic interpretation.

Writing: Ask students to focus on an relationship between themselves and another sibling or friend. Choose an incident in the life of the two and write the story in two voices.

BOOKS FOR FOLLOW-UP LITERATURE STUDIES

Bulla, Clyde Robert. (1989). *The Christmas Coat*. Illustrated by Sylvia Wickstrom. Alfred A. Knopf.
> Two brothers who argue continually learn to cooperate after sharing responsibility for a thoughtless act.

Hederwick, Mairi. (1986). *Katie Morag and the Tiresome Ted*. Little, Brown.
> Younger children can identify with Katie who is so resentful of the new baby in her house that she throws her beloved teddy bear in the ocean. Older children will enjoy the fresh Scottish colloquialisms and may wish to learn more about the geography of the region in which the story is set.

Viorst, Judith. (1974). *Rosie and Michael*. Macmillan.
> This picture book depicts a relationship betweeen two "best friends." Viorst uses the same form of alternating points of view.

John Burningham,
Mr. Gumpy's Outing

• •

Publisher and Date: Holt and Company, 1971
Illustrator: John Burningham
Audience: Kindergarten and up
Main Themes: Recreation, Pleasure
Other Possible Themes: Manners
Values to Target: Sharing, Responsibility, Leisure

• •

ABOUT THE AUTHOR

After graduating from art school, John Burningham had a difficult time finding steady work as an illustrator. He taught part-time at an art school while drafting his first children's book. He won Great Britain's Kate Greenaway Medal for *Borka*, launching his successful career as an author. Since that time Burningham has written and illustrated more than 40 books. In addition to his own books, Burningham has illustrated several by other authors. When asked to illustrate Jules Verne's *Around the World in Eighty Days*, Burningham actually made the same trip described in the story. His books have won many awards and have been translated into numerous languages.

As much as he enjoys writing books, Burningham finds the process difficult. He might spend months or even years planning a book, and then make hundreds of sketches. Choosing the right words for a particular phrase may take hours. He has said that while his great pleasure is to do satisfying work, he often tends "to escape given any opportunity.... There are so many things that are more important to do than work" (p. 35). Mr. Gumpy indeed seems to exhibit the author's exuberance for life!

Burningham is married to author and illustrator Helen Oxenbury. They have three children and live in England (*SATA* v. 59, pp. 26-36).

ABOUT THE STORY

Mr. Gumpy is going on an outing down the river in his wooden boat. The children ask if they can come along. Mr. Gumpy readily agrees on one condition: "If you won't squabble!" A varied crew of animals join the fun, each agreeing in turn *not* to hop, chase, tease, bleat, flap, muck about, or kick! As one might predict, good intentions cannot prevent a chain reaction of activity that upsets the boat. The unflappable Mr. Gumpy leads his wet friends ashore and across the field to a tea party.

John Burningham is one of the select few writer-illustrators of children's books who presents children as living in the world with adults. Mr. Gumpy, perhaps his most interesting adult, is going about the leisurely business of life. After inviting others to join him, his expectations of the children (and animals) is that they will participate in the chores that present themselves. However, when they do not, Mr. Gumpy is unruffled and unchanged. He doesn't assume responsibility for their behavior nor does he judge, scold, lecture, or do their work. The effect is to empower the other characters (and readers) to be responsible for themselves. The illustrations and facial expressions reflect this feeling.

DIALOGUE

Talk about What You Notice in the Story

● ●

The vocabulary lesson for these children in a second grade reading class is "bleating" and "bleeding" because it is of interest to them.

Sonia is exhibiting thinking skills about animal behavior by connecting this story with another she has read. A teacher interested in assessing the ability to make predictions may note that Darcy, Bradley and David all describe their predictive thinking during the reading of the story.

● ●

TEACHER:	WOULD ANYONE LIKE TO BEGIN OUR CONVERSATION?
Bradley:	I noticed that there were a lot of words I didn't know.
TEACHER:	WHAT WORDS ARE WE TAKING ABOUT?
Bradley:	Like bleating.
Sonia:	Is it bleeding?
Darcie:	A sheep who was bleeding wouldn't be on a boat.
David:	I'm going to look it up. [returning] Bleating is the noise the sheep makes.
Sonia:	That makes sense. All the animals just did what they do when they got on the boat. *[Silence for a length of time]*
TEACHER:	WE ARE ALL QUIET. DID YOU NOTICE ANYTHING ELSE YOU WOULD LIKE TO COMMENT ON? DID YOU THINK ABOUT ANYTHING ELSE WHILE YOU WERE READING?
Sonia:	It's like *Who Sank the Boat* with all the animals on a boat.
Darcie:	I thought the same thing—so I knew the boat was going to tip over or something.
Bradley:	Every time there are a lot of animals on a boat it sinks!
David:	As soon as Mr. Gumpy said the animals could come but they couldn't do those things, I knew they were going to.
TEACHER:	HOW DID YOU KNOW?
David:	Because that's what they do.
Sonia:	Yeah, children wiggle. When we take a long trip my brother always wants to get out of his car seat—he just does, I can't stop him.
Darcie:	Mr. Gumpy probably knew it too.

Talk about How the Story Makes You Feel

● ●

The teacher prompts a discussion of Mr. Gumpy's character which extends to whether or not teachers "should" get mad. The discussion then is of the tone of the book ("But this is a fun book...") and therefore the children could predict that nothing bad could happen at the end.

● ●

TEACHER:	I NOTICED THAT MR. GUMPY DIDN'T SEEM ANGRY WHEN THE BOAT OVERTURNED. WERE YOU SURPRISED?
Sonia:	He shouldn't get mad.
Jason:	Teachers get mad when they shouldn't.
David:	After gym, I went to get a drink and I got yelled at—I ran and I was thirsty. Kids get thirsty.
TEACHER:	MR. GUMPY UNDERSTANDS WHAT THE DIFFERENT ANIMALS DO AND HE ACCEPTS AND EXPECTS THAT THESE THINGS WOULD HAPPEN. DO YOU THINK THAT'S WHY HE WASN'T ANGRY?
Sonia:	Yes, because he wasn't surprised at them.
Jason:	I think he had fun being in the water.
Darcie:	It would not have been fun if one of the animals or kids got drowned.
Bradley:	But this is a fun book, so they are not going to get drowned— they didn't.

Talk about What The Story Reminds You of in Your Life

• •

Jason compares himself to Mr. Gumpy. The other children project ideas about Mr. Gumpy which are not in the story. The teacher wisely recommends another book about him.

• •

TEACHER:	IF YOU WERE MR. GUMPY, WOULD YOU INVITE YOUR FRIENDS TO COME FOR A BOAT RIDE AGAIN?
David:	Did they ever get the boat out of the water?
Sonia:	Yes, here it is in the picture.
Jason:	Yeah, I would ask them again. Sometimes I ask Kevin over to play even though he's going to get in a fight with me. I just try not to fight with him.
Bradley:	Maybe Mr. Gumpy doesn't have other friends, so he has to ask them again.
Darcie:	Maybe he shouldn't put them in a boat next time. They could play a game or something.
TEACHER:	THERE IS ANOTHER MR. GUMPY BOOK, *MR. GUMPY'S MOTOR CAR*. WOULD ANY OF YOU BE INTERESTED IN READING IT?
Jason:	I would—I want to see his technique.
TEACHER:	WHAT TECHNIQUE?
Jason:	The illustrations.
Darcie:	I would like to see if the animals are the same.
Sonia:	Yeah, to see if Mr. Gumpy has the same friends.

TEACHER FOCUS

Tone: Use the story to make inferences about tone. How did we know that the story would turn out well for all in the end?

Predictions: During the reading, wait for or ask for predictions.

Language: Let the children know that Burningham is from England. Enjoy the verbs. Name synonyms from context cues.

Characterization: What do we expect pigs, sheep, children, etc., to do in a boat? What do you think of Mr. Gumpy? How is he different from many adults?

COUNSELOR FOCUS

Responsibility: If Mr. Gumpy takes his friends on a trip again what do you think will happen? Suppose Mr. Gumpy had scolded his friends. How would the story be different? How do we learn to be responsible?

Manners: Capitalize on the children's pure enjoyment of the polite interaction of the characters by allowing the children to create a role play and practice good manners. (See role play activity in "Making Connections.")

MAKING CONNECTIONS

Role Play: In small group guidance a counselor found this story ideal for role play with kindergarten through grade two. Children agreed upon the space for the river, the shore, the boat, the field, and the tea table. They made up a little sailing song for the peaceful part of the outing, and acted out all the flapping, bleating, and mucking about. (Of course, falling out was the most fun!) Bridget, who had noticed all the foods in the picture at Mr. Gumpy's tea party, presided at tea. "Please, pass the cherries. And now may I serve you some more tea?" Kenny, a kindergartner playing Mr. Gumpy, used the delicious sounding verbs to perfection in the role play and added them to classroom conversation for days. "Now don't squabble!" he advised his friends in the lunch line who broke into giggles instead of a scuffle.

BOOKS FOR FOLLOW-UP LITERATURE STUDIES

Burningham, John. (1983). *Mr. Gumpy's Motor Car.* Crowell Junior Books.
> Mr. Gumpy has the same friendliness and zest for living as ever!

Fitzhugh, Louise. (1964). *Harriet the Spy.* Dell.
> Ole Golly, her Nanny, and her father are extremely important in Harriet's life. A father who teaches a child how to play an onion in the school play can't be all bad. Use with fourth grade and up.

Magorian, Michelle. (1981). *Good Night, Mr. Tom*. Harper and Row.
Mr. Tom is just the kind of adult who is needed to overcome an abusive home and the horrors of World War II bombings of London. Use this with fifth and sixth graders.

Eric Carle,
A House for Hermit Crab

• •

Publisher and Date: Picture Book Studio, 1987
Illustrator: Eric Carle
Audience Level: Kindergarten and up
Main Theme: Growing and Changing
Other Possible Themes: Fear, Community, Friends, Uniqueness, Courage
Values to Target: Self-knowledge, Self-concept, Change

• •

ABOUT THE AUTHOR

In his recent and moving autobiography, Eric Carle, born in New York of German parents, remembers a childhood filled with joy in nature and curiosity about animals. He was always peeking under the bark of trees and under rocks, fascinated with the life cycles of small animals. He also describes a kindergarten room in New York that was full of sunlight, where his teacher provided him fat brushes and colorful paints. In 1935 his parents decided to move back to Germany to be near their relatives who assured them that life was good—Hitler had almost eliminated unemployment.

Eric said goodbye to Carleton Mayer, his best friend, and packed his Mickey Mouse comic books and a picture of George Washington to take to Germany. Although a cooperative little boy, he disliked school intensely. Even a good child was not exempt from raps on the hand with the ever-present bamboo stick.

When he was grown, Eric returned to the United States. Unannounced, he knocked on the door of his kindergarten friend, Carleton, who joyously recognized him. Later he was inspired by this friendship to write a book entitled, *Do You Want to Be My Friend?* He went on to illustrate *Brown Bear, Brown Bear* and to write *The Very Hungry Caterpillar*.

His books are printed in many languages. Mr. Carle says that he feels particularly fond of Hermit Crab, the hero of this book. (*SATAAS* v. 6, pp. 33-52, and personal communication with Sarah Borders.)

ABOUT THE STORY

Hermit Crab has grown too big for his shell, so he must find a new home. He is frightened but soon he is successful in finding a shell-house. However, it is too plain to feel much like a home. Happily, he encounters all kinds of lovely undersea neighbors who help him decorate his new dwelling and make it safe and tidy. Just when it is almost perfect, the inevitable happens: He is too big again! He steps aside for a smaller crab who promises to be good to his friends, and moves on to new possibilities.

Hermit Crab is a character children remember. He has an adventurous spirit, is industrious, pleasant to all he meets, and takes care of himself very well. The illustrations are to be relished. The inevitable joy and sadness of life are evident in this story of acceptance of change in spite of the attachments that must be broken.

DIALOGUE

Talk about What You Notice in the Story

• •

The teacher deliberately leads these second and third grade children back to the text to savor the exact words of the author. In the science lesson created here the children used the story as a concrete way of making meaning of the concept of time. Children are eager to hear the information provided about lanternfish in the book's concordance. Eric and Ricky see the author as a real person. Heather's comment to Ricky is the kind of affirmation that builds self-esteem.

• •

TEACHER: HERMIT CRAB HAS HIS SPECIAL WAY OF GREETING ALL THE SEA CREATURES. EACH TIME HE MET ONE OF THEM, HE NOTICED SOMETHING UNIQUE ABOUT THAT CREATURE. FOR EXAMPLE, WHEN HE MET THE SEA ANEMONES, HE SAID, "HOW BEAUTIFUL YOU ARE!" LET'S LOOK AGAIN AT THE TEXT TO SEE WHAT HE SAW AS SPECIAL ABOUT EACH CREATURE.

- The Coral—"How pretty you are."
- The Snails—"How tidy and hard-working you are."
- The Sea Urchins—"How fierce you are."
- The Lanternfish—"How bright you are."
- The Pebbles—"How smooth you are."

TEACHER:	NOW WE HAVE ALL THE CHARACTERS ON THE BOARD. WHO WANTS TO START?
Eric:	I have a question. Are those lanternfish like lightning bugs? I used to put lightning bugs in Mama's pocketbook.
Josh:	I'd like to put a lanternfish in my mama's pocketbook. She'd scream! *[laughter]*
Heather:	I like to put lightning bugs in a jar and turn out the lights and pretend it's my light bulb.
TEACHER:	IT SOUNDS LIKE YOU WANT TO KNOW MORE ABOUT THESE LANTERNFISH. ERIC CARLE HAS WRITTEN A SPECIAL SECTION OF THIS BOOK TO ANSWER YOUR QUESTIONS ABOUT THE SEA ANIMALS. WE CAN LOOK UP LANTERNFISH.
TEACHER:	*[AFTER SHARING INFORMATION]* NOW LET'S NOTICE HOW THE AUTHOR MARKED THE PASSING OF TIME IN THE STORY. I NOTICED IT STARTED IN JANUARY.
Josh:	*[beaming]* He met the starfish in my birthday month! It's April!
Jessica:	Mine is July. What was it in my month? *[After children noticed what was happening in Hermit Crab's life during the month of their birthday, a time line of Hermit's encounters was drawn on newsprint, with a parallel line for birthday months.]*
TEACHER:	SO, AS TIME PASSES, WHAT IS HAPPENING TO HERMIT CRAB?
Josh:	He's growing and growing. On every page he gets bigger and bigger and bigger. (A fast flip of the pages confirms Josh's observation of the artist's interpretation of growing.)
Chorus:	Bigger! Bigger! Bigger! Bigger!
Josh:	Finally he's so big he has outgrown his shell.
TEACHER:	HIS SHELL HAS BECOME TOO *SNUG*.
Ricky:	Like me! My sneakers got too snug. *[Enthusiastic snug sneaker, snug jacket, and snug shorts stories are invited within the time limit.]*
Eric:	You know what else I just noticed? I have the same name as Eric Carle!
Ricky:	That's cool! I wish there was an author named Ricky.
Heather:	Maybe *you* can be one someday!
TEACHER:	MAYBE YOU ALL ARE NOW! I KNOW ABOUT SOME BOOKS YOU HAVE BEEN WRITING. THAT MAKES YOU AN AUTHOR!

Talk about How the Story Makes You Feel

• •

Like Hermit Crab, children express times and places where they feel frightened, alone or "small." The teacher asks a question to move the conversation to ways of coping with these feelings.

• •

TEACHER:	HERMIT CRAB SAID, "IT WAS FRIGHTENING OUT THERE IN THE OPEN SEA WITHOUT A SHELL."
George:	He was scared!
Ricky:	He could get stung by an eel.
Heather:	*[shivering]* Or a jellyfish!
Joey:	Hermit crabs are pretty little compared to all those sharks and stuff.
TEACHER:	HAVE YOU EVER FELT LITTLE?
Eric:	I feel little on the school bus because we have a bunch of big kids who might poke people.
Kristina:	It's noisy on the bus.
Jessica:	I feel little at the mall when there are crowds of people walking every way.
TEACHER:	BEING ON THE BUS OR AT THE MALL IS LIKE HERMIT CRAB OUT OF HIS SHELL IN THE OPEN SEA. HERMIT WAS GOOD AT HELPING HIMSELF SURVIVE THOUGH.
Eric:	He got the spiny fish and the pebbles to make him more safe.
TEACHER:	CAN YOU HELP YOURSELF ON THE BUS WHEN YOU DON'T FEEL SO SAFE?
Eric:	I ask the bus driver if I can sit near the front with my friend.
Kristina:	Sometimes I just cover my ears like this when it gets on my nerves real bad!
TEACHER:	WELL, KRISTINA, YOU'RE PRETTY GOOD AT HELPING YOURSELF, LIKE HERMIT CRAB.

Talk about What the Story Reminds You of in Your Life

• •

The teacher nudges the children to think about the concept of community. The children report experiences that make it possible to assess their understanding of the concept.

• •

TEACHER:	HERMIT CRAB HAD WORKED HARD ON DECORATING HIS HOUSE. DOES THAT REMIND YOU OF ANYTHING IN YOUR LIFE?

Ricky:	Well, it got too snug! And he had to move again.
Heather:	So he had to start *all* over!
TEACHER:	*[RE-READING THE LAST PAGES ABOUT NEW POSSIBILITIES]* HERMIT CRAB WAS LOOKING AHEAD.
Jessica:	I've moved a whole bunch of times. I didn't want to go to Florida because I didn't know if I would like my new house or those people there.
TEACHER:	THAT WAS HARD FOR YOU.
Jessica:	Well, it wasn't so bad after a while. But then we had to move again. Now I'm here!
TEACHER:	LIKE HERMIT CRAB—YOU MOVED ON.
Jessica:	I try hard to make friends. *[with more energy]* I think we might stay here, because we are going to build a porch on our trailer.
TEACHER:	JESSICA HAS SHARED ABOUT MOVING AND MEETING NEW PEOPLE AS SHE MOVED. HERMIT CRAB WAS LIKE THAT. WOULD YOU LIKE TO FIND OUT MORE ABOUT HOW REAL HERMIT CRABS MEET AND LIVE WITH OTHER SEA ANIMALS? *[AGREEMENT]* LET'S TURN BACK TO THE CONCORDANCE. *[After sharing the information on symbiosis.]*
Ricky:	That is so *cool* that they eat the same food.
Heather:	Like a family.
Jerome:	We don't *really* eat the same food!
Kristina:	That's not polite to eat off of somebody's plate if you're a person! *[laughter]*
TEACHER:	THERE ARE WAYS WE CAN HELP EACH OTHER LIVE TOGETHER IN FAMILIES AND SCHOOLS.
Ricky:	I have a job to help at home. I feed my cat!
Jessica:	It's my turn to wipe tables in the cafeteria this week.
Eric:	When I'm bigger I might drive a school bus.
TEACHER:	FAMILIES ARE A COMMUNITY. SCHOOL IS A COMMUNITY. THERE IS A BIGGER COMMUNITY. WHAT IS IT?
Jessica:	The town.
TEACHER:	WHO DO WE COUNT ON TO WORK TOGETHER IN OUR TOWN?
Ricky:	Like fireman and the EMS.
Jerome:	And farmers.
TEACHER:	WE COULD GO ON AND ON, COULDN'T WE?

• •

Children and teachers may see, as Hermit Crab did, that there are many possibilities. As time and curriculum goals allow, children can contribute to a web of "School Helpers" and "Community Helpers" or go on to further social studies projects.

• •

TEACHER FOCUS

Science: This story is ideal for teaching about sea inhabitants, time, and symbiosis.

Oral Language: Note the greetings used by the characters. Examine our own style of meeting and greeting each other. Children might role play complimentary greetings.

Social Studies: Note how the latter part of this dialogue could introduce a unit on community.

Art: Children can name and use the media of collage. Compare this book to Eric Carle's other books. Can we recognize his style? (See the art projects in "Making Connections.")

COUNSELOR FOCUS

Growing and Changing: Children identify with Hermit Crab's perseverance and courage as he faces inevitable change. This change involves letting go of old familiar friends and venturing out alone to new possibilities. Counselors may wish to select this story early in the school year as students enter a new grade, or become part of a new student's group.

Self-Concept, Uniqueness: Each of Hermit Crab's friends had a special gift to offer.

MAKING CONNECTIONS

Role Play: The outline of greetings at the beginning of the Dialogue section may be adapted for a role play. Children choose roles they wish to play. The teacher urges Hermit Crab to get out of his snug shell, and show fear, then joy at finding a bigger shell. Greetings follow, with other characters lined up in the order of their appearance. Hermit Crab's encounters with coral, snail, and other characters can be narrated by a child or the teacher.

Art Project—Decorating a Room or a House: Mr. Carle now lives in Massachusetts. While he was working on his book about Hermit Crab, he was planning to move out of his secluded home in the mountains to a bigger house in Northampton which was empty, but full of possibilities. Children may wish to do an art project about home, starting with drawings of their own room or house and adding decorations as Hermit Crab did.

Art Project—Collage and Quills: Notice the spiral pattern on the shell of Hermit Crab. Spirals are an architectural motif symbolizing time, movement, and change. Children may notice that the patterns the author creates throughout the book are circles and vertical, except for the spiral of Hermit Crab's shell. For an art project children may quill Hermit Crab's shell and attach it with glue to a tempera painted underwater scene.

For the underwater scene, note that the end papers of the book are tempera. Mr. Carle does the lines representing moving water with the handle of his brush. Mix tempera colors to a cream consistency in baby food jars. Each child takes one color at a time so colors do not mix and become muddy. Make water lines with handle end of brush as the artist has done.

Follow the instructions given below for the quill hermit crab shell:

1. Cut strips of paper ¼" wide and 8½" long.
2. Roll strip around toothpick. Glue end to coil to keep it from unrolling.
3. Add quill shell with glue to Hermit Crab.
4. Add sea animals and Hermit Crab with collage to underwater scene.

Clay and Role Play: After noting the spiral and vertical lines in the story, one teacher decided to provide clay for a small group of second grade children to handle during the reading of the story. She only had to ask the children to observe the lines and shapes in the story and to fashion something from the story with their clay. Only the starfish and the urchin did not emerge spontaneously during the reading. The children did these co-operatively and then were ready to re-create the story with role play as described above, using their clay creations as props. Several discoveries were noted in this session. Clay has a calming effect on the children, and they *can* listen to the story while working. There is no finished art product to be evaluated, so it is very success oriented. Co-operation and sharing were evident and easy to achieve, allowing the children to experience one theme of the story.

Writing—Letter to the Author: Children can write a letter to Mr. Carle at Picture Book Studios, 10 Central St., Saxonville, MA 01701. He likes hearing from children. His wife, Barbara, is an educator, and takes a great interest in Eric's young fans whose letters fill the mailbox each day. She recently shared this one: "Dear Mr. Carle, Please write back quick and tell me that people don't eat Hermit Crabs."

Music: The following songs about leaving a familiar place were suggested by Brenda Allen, a school librarian in Springfield, Massachusetts, and Ruth Danckert of Picture Book Studio: "On the Road Again," "Leaving on a Jet Plane," and "Red River Valley."

BOOKS FOR FOLLOW-UP LITERATURE STUDIES

Starred titles have full entries elsewhere in the book.

Griffith, Helen. (1985). *Grandaddy's Place*. Illustrated by James Stevenson. Greenwillow Books.
> The country place in Georgia is strange to Janetta who adapts to the change, thanks to Grandaddy.

Hutchins, Pat. (1971). *Changes, Changes*. Bodley Head.
> This picture book gives children a visual experience with possibilties and change.

*Komaiko, Leah. (1987). *Annie Bananie*. Harper and Row.
> Annie Bananie is attached to her best friend who is moving away. Even though life must go on, she hopes she will never, ever be forgotten!

Martin, Bill Jr., and John Archambault. (1987). *Knots on a Counting Rope*. Illustrated by Ted Rand. Henry Holt.
> A blind Indian boy hears family stories from his grandfather that give him courage to go on with life on his own.

Beverly Cleary, "The Hard Boiled Egg Fad" from *Ramona Quimby, Age 8*

• •

Publisher and Date: William Morrow, 1981
Audience Level: Grades one and up
Main Theme: Peer Pressure, Fads,
Other Possible Themes: Imperfection, Siblings, Fears, Family Relations, Growing and Changing
Values to Target: Self-Awareness, Self-Acceptance, Perseverance

• •

ABOUT THE AUTHOR

Beverly Clearly was born in 1916 and spent a great deal of her childhood on a farm in Oregon. Despite her mother drilling her on the importance of books, reading, and libraries, Cleary had a difficult time learning to read. She remembers being in the "blackbird group," which was disgraceful. In the third grade, however, she finally started to read for pleasure, which greatly improved her reading skills.

During that time she also became very critical of books. She wanted "something to happen" on every page, preferably something funny. She also wanted stories about the kind of children she knew—plain, ordinary boys and girls.

The things Cleary desired in books when she was a young child have greatly influenced her work as an author. This is probably why she is so popular with children. Her books have received a long list of awards and honors, several of which are for the Ramona series (*SATA* v. 43, pp. 53-61).

ABOUT THE RAMONA SERIES

Ramona is sensitive, funny, eager to please, and determined. Cleary's selection of detail from the school environment is superb. There are the common lunch room routines and rituals, third grade characters such as Yard Ape, and teachers who are mostly nice, but also human beings with frailties. Ramona's family is typical for the copyright date of each book. Ramona calls it a "nice sticking-together family." Enjoy the many scenes of humor, discipline, forgiveness, frustration, and joy. These titles are literally a course in child development, as Ramona overcomes nighttime fears, jealousy, rejection, and insecurity in a loving family. There are possibilities for parent groups to enjoy reading and discussing Ramona books. Of course, it is better to read the whole book, but you will find that chapters are episodic and can stand alone for discussion purposes, if time does not allow reading the entire book. A teacher who is familiar with the series can readily find appropriate chapters for the school year. For example, Chapter 1 in *Ramona Quimby, Age 8* is entitled "The First Day of School." Chapter 7 in *Ramona and Her Father* is a good Christmas reading. Our reflections below explain our selection of "The Hard Boiled Egg Fad."

In "The Hard Boiled Egg Fad" Ramona, anxious to please and wanting to be included in the group, follows the current third grade fad of bringing a boiled egg in her lunch box. When she tries out the most popular way for cracking an egg (against the head) she finds that hers has *not* been hard boiled!

We selected this chapter for a discussion with third graders bearing in mind that they are ready to examine reasons for conformity, and to begin to recognize and empathize with frailties in themselves, and even the important adults in their lives.

The chapter also works well for identification of feelings, particularly embarrassment. It is crafted with sensory detail of the broken egg, which makes it humorous for a group reading together.

DIALOGUE

Talk about What You Notice in the Story

• •

By spring this third grade class had readers who felt that they "knew" Ramona and her family as if they were real people. Kayla summarizes the characteristics of well-meaning Ramona which endear her to her many fans. Jody and others respond to the sensory details as the story is read aloud. The teacher notices this and is intentional in re-reading the sensory language for pure enjoyment.

• •

TEACHER:	SOME OF YOU HAVE READ THE *RAMONA* BOOKS. WHAT CHARACTERS DO YOU REMEMBER?
Kayla:	Well, there's Ramona.
TEACHER:	CAN YOU SAY SOME MORE ABOUT HER?
Kayla:	She's always getting into maybe a little bit of trouble.
Jody:	Well, she's good, you know. She doesn't mean to be bad or anything.
TEACHER:	AND HER FAMILY?
Jessie:	Beezus is Ramona's sister. She's always using hair spray and stuff.
Leigh Ann:	She has a nice mom and dad.
TEACHER:	ANY CHARACTERS FROM SCHOOL?
Angie:	There's the Yard Ape. He is kind of goofy, and a little bit of a bully.
Jessie:	And she has nice teachers at school.
Kayla:	Oh, I know another one. There's this little girl who gets on her nerves where she has to go after school until her mom gets off work.
TEACHER:	*[RECORDING CHARACTER'S NAMES ON NEWSPRINT]* NOW WE ARE READY TO READ OUR CHAPTER. *[AFTER THE READING]* I CAN TELL YOU ENJOYED THE READING. WHO WANTS TO START? WHAT DID YOU NOTICE?
Jody:	*[with a shudder, hands on his hair, making faces]* All that egg in her hair!
TEACHER:	LET'S RE-READ A SENTENCE OR TWO. "SHE TRIED TO BRUSH THE YELLOW YOLK AND THE SLITHERY WHITE OUT OF HER HAIR … BUT SHE ONLY SUCCEEDED IN MAKING HER HANDS EGGY."
Ricky:	Pretty yucky!
	[Shivers and echoes of Ricky's remark]
Nikki:	And then she had to go to the office to get cleaned up!

Amanda:	Then she had to stick her head in that cold water.
Nikki:	And it was still all stiff.
Kayla:	And her face was all tight, like she could hardly smile.
	[Laughter]
TEACHER:	THOSE ARE GREAT COMMENTS. I CAN TELL BY YOUR FACES THAT THE AUTHOR'S WORDS ON THE PAGE CAN REALLY MAKE YOU FEEL SOMETHING. WHAT ELSE DO YOU NOTICE?
Jenna:	The secretary tried to cheer her up.
Brandon:	That's good. She needed that!
Paula:	And after that she was just sitting there on that cot all by herself.
Julie:	She was feeling pretty stupid!
Justin:	It was *very* embarrassing.
Kayla:	Really!
TEACHER:	WHAT WAS THE WORST THING ABOUT IT FOR RAMONA?
Jody:	Probably the children laughing.
Angie:	The Yard Ape laughed the most.
Kristy:	Then one girl was nice enough to help her.
Dana:	I think the worst part was when she was sitting in the office and nobody knew she was there, and the teachers talked about it.
Angie:	I remember from other Ramona books that she is always getting the idea that she is a pest.
TEACHER:	RAMONA WAS REALLY GETTING DOWN ON HERSELF. MAYBE YOU CAN SAY SOME MORE ABOUT THAT, ANGIE.
Angie:	Well, it's like she doesn't exactly mean to show off or anything, and then when she gets in a little trouble she's real sorry.
TEACHER:	WELL, SHE DID HEAR HER TEACHER USING THE WORD NUISANCE. DOES EVERYBODY KNOW WHAT THAT MEANS?
Julie:	I think it's sort of like a pain.
TEACHER:	DO YOU THINK MRS. WHALEY REALLY THOUGHT RAMONA WAS A NUISANCE?
Chorus:	No!
Angie:	I don't think teachers really think like that. Not about kids like Ramona.
Jessie:	It's kinda like it got bigger in her mind and all.
TEACHER:	SO YOU THINK IT IS A MISUNDERSTANDING.
Paula:	It's like it was more in her mind than the teacher's mind.
TEACHER:	WHAT ABOUT RAMONA'S MOTHER? REMEMBER HOW RAMONA WAS MAD AT HER FOR NOT BOILING THE EGG?

Heather:	Well, I don't think it was her mother's fault for not boiling the egg.
Elizabeth:	She wouldn't do it on purpose. She forgot.
Ricky:	Well, moms forget stuff sometimes.

Talk about How the Story Makes You Feel

●●

The children really had already moved the conversation to feelings. Since this was a large group, the teacher used a graphic organizer for identification of feelings and evidence from the story. The teacher recorded the children's ideas on newsprint.

●●

Talk about What the Story Reminds You of in Your Life

●●

The teacher calls attention to the title so that the children can recognize fads in their own life. Children are able to apply the story because they see how following a fad is motivated by wanting attention from their friends. Julie evaluates that some fads are dangerous. Then the discussion returns to shared feelings of embarrassment.

●●

TEACHER:	NOTICE THE WORD FAD IS IN THE TITLE? IT WAS A FAD TO BRING HARD BOILED EGGS TO SCHOOL. WHAT FADS HAVE YOU NOTICED IN OUR SCHOOL?
Brandon:	The boys like those railroad track haircuts.
Mandy:	For Christmas all the girls wanted the Minnie Mouse watch.
Jenna:	Girls wear headbands all the time.
TEACHER:	ANY LUNCHTIME FADS?
Jody:	People bring Jelly Bellies.
Paula:	But you're not supposed to eat them in class.
Justin:	Yeah, some people get in trouble.
TEACHER:	SO HARD BOILED EGGS ARE NOT OUR FAD RIGHT NOW?
Paula:	I'd rather have Jelly Bellies any day.
	[Laughter]
TEACHER:	SO WHAT DO YOU THING OF FADS?
Kayla:	If you have jelly bellies, you can share them with friends.

Josh:	If you have something to wear you can have somebody notice you on the bus. And you'll have something to show somebody.
TEACHER:	ANYTHING ELSE?
Julie:	Fads are cool, as long as they don't get you in bad trouble.
TEACHER:	CAN YOU SAY MORE ABOUT THAT?
Julie:	I mean like bringing something dangerous to school. Something that might hurt somebody. My mom won't get me a slap bracelet.
TEACHER:	HOW ABOUT SOME OTHER TIMES YOU HAVE FELT LIKE RAMONA?
Corey:	Once I dropped a whole plate of spaghetti in the cafeteria. It was all over the floor.
TEACHER:	HOW DID YOU FEEL?
Corey:	Bad! Embarrassed!

• •

This group had no scarcity of embarrassing moments to share. Sharing these and enjoying the ensuing laughter seemed bonding to the group.

• •

TEACHER FOCUS

Sensory Language: Analyze how Beverly Cleary's writing evokes a reader's emotional response.

Characterization and Critical Thinking: When a character has dimension children should be able to think of adjectives to describe the character. Students can make inferences about the kind of person Ramona is on the basis of her thoughts, actions, and experiences in this incident. When children read other books in the Ramona series, they will know her better. Beverly Cleary wrote the Ramona series over a long period of time. A large project would be to analyze changes in Ramona as she appears in various titles. Note that the copyright dates of the book may reflect the setting and events. Is Ramona still the same Ramona? Does she behave in ways you might expect? Watch the Ramona videos (available from Children's Circle-Weston Woods) and do similar comparisons.

COUNSELOR FOCUS

Imperfections: The school setting for this episode in which Ramona suffers from one embarrassment after another is a model for allowing children and adults to accept imperfections in each other.

Self-Awareness: In the scene where Ramona is waiting in the principal's office she hears her teacher's remark and interprets that she is a "nuisance." What can Ramona do about her bad feeling?

Embarrassment: Once feelings of embarrassment are expressed in a group, bonding takes place.

MAKING CONNECTIONS

Art and Storytelling: Examine the drawing of Ramona in the book. Consider how this helps to tell the story. Children can then draw their own embarrassed faces and write or tell the story of the incident that caused the feeling.

Vocabulary and Cooperative Learning: The boiled egg descriptions appeal to the sense of touch. The teacher may wish to bring objects to touch, taste, hear, or smell and play a game with identification of objects with eyes closed. Once the other senses are heightened by the game, children may brainstorm words that appeal to touch, sound, taste, and smell.

Writing: The class can collaborate on a dictionary of fads with illustrations and information. They can interview parents, grandparents, teachers, and older brothers and sisters about fads of their day to include in the dictionary.

BOOKS FOR FOLLOW-UP LITERATURE STUDIES

These children exhibit some "Ramona" characteristics:

Hurwitz, Johanna. (1989). *Russell and Elisa.* Illustrated by Lillian Hoban. Morrow Junior Books.
> Russell and his three-year-old sister Elisa have adventures in their apartment building.

Myers, Walter Dean. (1988). *Me, Mop and the Moondance Kid.* Illustrated by Rodney Pate. Delacourte.
> T.J. and his younger brother Moondance are in the orphanage. They involve themselves with their friend Mop's attempts to become adopted and to wreak revenge on their baseball rivals.

Spinelli, Jerry. (1990). *The Bathwater Gang.* Little, Brown.
> The similarity between this book and the Ramona books is in the supportive role of the adults in the lives of the children. The theme is boredom, and Grandma comes to the rescue.

Another book about fads in another genre:

Thompson, Peggy. (1978). *The King Has Horse's Ears.* Illustrated by David Small. Simon and Schuster.
> King Horace has an embarrassing secret: He has horse's ears. When his bride accepts him the way he is, horse's ears become a fad in the kingdom.

THE RAMONA SERIES

All titles published by William Morrow.
Ramona the Pest (1968)
Ramona the Brave (1975)
Ramona and Her Father (1977)
Ramona and Her Mother (1979)
Ramona Quimby, Age 8 (1981)

Lucille Clifton,
Everett Anderson's Nine Month Long

• •

Publisher and Date: Holt, Rinehart, Winston, 1978
Illustrator: Ann Grifalconi
Audience Level: Kindergarten through second grade
Main Theme: Siblings
Other Possible Themes: Jealousy, Families, Anger, Race
Values to Target: Caring

• •

ABOUT THE AUTHOR

Lucille Clifton was raised in and around Buffalo, New York. She won a full scholarship to Howard University and was the first person in her family to attend college. After two years she returned home. Back in Buffalo, Clifton became part of a group of African-American intellectuals. She started writing poetry and eventually published her first book in 1969. Since that time Clifton has written novels, poems, short stories, and children's books. Clifton's husband is also a writer, as well as an educator and artist. They have six children (*Junior Authors*, Third Book).

ABOUT THE ILLUSTRATOR

Ann Grifalconi began teaching after obtaining an art degree from Cooper Union Art School. Eventually she began to do illustration full time. She says she never illustrates a book she doesn't believe in. She grew up in the New York City area in a racially mixed neighborhood. She considers color "a note of grace" and a special sort of beauty. The books she has illustrated represent these views (from the book jacket).

ABOUT THE STORY

Everett Anderson has to adjust to changes in his life with his mother. She has married Mr. Perry, but Everett gets to keep his own name. Then a baby is on the way, and Everett isn't sure there is still room for him. In Clifton's poetic prose we hear how Mr. Perry and Everett talk about how love makes room for the baby and each other.

Children readily identify with Everett who seeks his place in a changing family. Clifton's portrayal of the establishment of the relationship between Everett and his stepfather is sensitive.

DIALOGUE

Talk about What You Notice in the Story

• •

This discussion is between second grade Chapter I students and a reading specialist. Because of the nature of this discussion, it is important to know that Cedric is an African-American male, Brandon and Anthony are white males, Laura is an African-American female, and Shanin is a white female. When Anthony wonders what is different about the book, the teacher allows him to wonder for a whole minute without interrupting. This decision allows Laura to express her explanation. The teacher resists any inclination to divert the discussion to safe ground. The result is that Shanin is also free to express herself on the subject. When all are aware of the fact that the characters in the book are black, they recognize that they have feelings about that.

• •

TEACHER:	EVERYONE HAS HAD A FEW MINUTES TO THINK. ARE WE READY TO SHARE OUR OBSERVATIONS AND THOUGHTS ON EVERETT ANDERSON?
Cedric:	I think it is a rhyming book.
Brandon:	There was a story just like this in *Springboards*.
TEACHER:	WHEN YOU SAY JUST LIKE THIS, DO YOU MEAN THE SAME STORY OR HOW WAS IT LIKE THIS STORY?
Brandon:	Everett Anderson was the boy in it.
Laura:	Yeah, I heard your group reading about him.

TEACHER:	THERE ARE SEVERAL BOOKS WRITTEN ABOUT EVERETT. PERHAPS THE SELECTION WAS TAKEN FROM ONE OF THE OTHER TITLES.
Anthony:	There's something different about this book. mmmmm, I don't know [About one minutes passes.]
Laura:	*[very quietly]* The boy is black—that's why it is different.
TEACHER:	HOW DOES THE CHARACTER OF EVERETT BEING BLACK MAKE THE STORY DIFFERENT? DIFFERENT FROM WHAT?
Laura:	Because there aren't books with black people in them.
Shanin:	*[jumping in very quickly]* I don't like to read books about black people. I want to choose books with white people. *[Laura looks at Shanin, Cedric looks away.]*

Talk about How the Story Makes You Feel

● ●

Here the teacher encourages interchange among the students and not between herself and the students. She nudges Shanin to examine her own statements in view of her actions, and encourages Laura to be assertive. The result is a sophisticated understanding expressed by Laura to Shanin.

● ●

TEACHER:	CEDRIC AND LAURA, HOW DOES SHANIN'S STATEMENT MAKE YOU FEEL? WHAT DO YOU THINK ABOUT IT?
Laura:	It makes me very sad.
Cedric:	I don't care. That's...
Shanin:	*[looking at Laura with incredulity]* Laura, are you sad? Really sad?
Laura:	Yes, how would you feel?
Shanin:	I don't know, but I don't read books with black people in them.
TEACHER:	LAURA, COULD YOU EXPLAIN WHY IT'S IMPORTANT TO YOU THAT EVERETT IS BLACK? SHANIN, I'M WONDERING WHY YOU DON'T READ BOOKS WITH BLACK CHARACTERS? HAVE YOU EVER ACTUALLY PUT A BOOK AWAY BECAUSE THE CHARACTER WAS BLACK?
Laura:	Because my best friend was Monica (begins to tear) and I had to move—now I don't have any black friends.
TEACHER:	SHANIN, HAVE YOU EVER DECIDED OR NOT DECIDED TO READ A BOOK BECAUSE OF A BLACK CHARACTER?
Shanin:	I don't think so, but I don't pick books with black people.
Anthony:	Reggie is black.

Cedric:	No, he's not.
Brandon:	Yeah, he's brown.
Cedric:	No, he's not because his dad is black, but his mom is white.
Brandon:	How do you know Everett is black?
Shanin:	Oh, come on, Brandon, look at the pictures.
Brandon:	Oh, yeah.
TEACHER:	LAURA, DO YOU READ OTHER BOOKS WITH BLACK CHARACTERS?
Laura:	I don't know any.
TEACHER:	HAVE YOU EVER ASKED A TEACHER OR LIBRARIAN TO HELP YOU FIND BOOKS?
Laura:	No.
Shanin:	I don't want to talk about being black anymore.
Laura:	We're not talking about being black. We're talking about the book and he's black.

Talk about What the Story Reminds You of in Your Life

● ●

With gentle questions the teacher begins to encourage the children to talk with each other about their thoughts and feelings. She is very careful to give equal time to each student, and even offers to participate in the discussion herself. Brandon's kind remark to Laura is another indication of the climate created by the teacher.

● ●

Anthony:	When my mommy was going to have a baby, she was weak, too.
Brandon:	I have an older sister, and she doesn't like me sometimes.
Cedric:	I can believe that! Sisters don't like their brothers.
TEACHER:	DO YOU THINK ALL BROTHERS AND SISTERS FEEL THAT WAY? WHY WERE EVERETT'S FEELINGS CHANGING?
Anthony:	Because his mom was acting different because she was tired, but then things were okay.
Brandon:	Yeah, sometimes I don't like it when my dad does things with my brothers.
TEACHER:	WHAT MAKES YOU FEEL BETTER?
Brandon:	When I get to do something or I get ... I don't know.
Shanin:	Everybody has sad feelings, mad feelings, happy feelings. We are just feelings.
TEACHER:	SHANIN, ARE YOU THINKING THAT YOU SEE SOME SIMILARITIES BETWEEN YOU AND EVERETT?
Shanin:	Oh, I guess.

Laura:	Everett could be ... don't know.
TEACHER:	LAURA, CAN I HELP YOU THINK ABOUT WHAT YOU WANT TO SAY? COULD ANYONE HERE HELP YOU?
Brandon:	Are you still sad about what Shanin said? I know another book that has a black character. I think it's on the shelf in our room.
Laura:	Okay.
TEACHER:	CEDRIC, YOU'VE BEEN QUIET. WOULD YOU LIKE SOME TIME TO SHARE SOMETHING?
Cedric:	I think, maybe, well, I liked the book.
TEACHER:	WHAT DID YOU ENJOY?
Cedric:	The rhyming. It's like rap.
Anthony:	We have to go.
TEACHER:	YES, I SEE TIME IS PASSING. WOULD ANYONE LIKE TO HEAR WHAT I NOTICED OR THOUGHT?
Shanin:	Maybe later, okay?
TEACHER:	OKAY. I'M NOT SURE WE'RE FINISHED.
Anthony:	We'll be back tomorrow.

TEACHER FOCUS

Poetry: Analyze to see what it is that makes the text poetic.

Point of View: What is it that Everett feels that his mother and Mr. Perry do not know?

Author Studies: The children in this discussion pointed out that they did not know of many books with black people in them. Why is this so? Librarians may be consulted to help children make connections between writers, their lives, their cultures, and their works.

COUNSELOR FOCUS

Racism: Everett Anderson's *Nine Month Long* was not chosen to "discuss racism," but the book serves as a model of a teacher's sensitivity and unwillingness to evade the issue when it arises.

Changes: Children may consider changes in their own families and share their feelings and ways of coping. These changes may or may not be as dramatic as getting a new stepfather. One first grade guidance group asked the counselor questions about the "nine months," giving her an opportunity to share information and guide a discussion about physical changes during pregnancy. As in the dialogue above, the children closed the discussion when their need for information was satisfied.

MAKING CONNECTIONS

It would be difficult to top the way in which this discussion made connections. When this group of children came back the next day, Cedric and Brandon didn't have any more to say on the subject. Laura asked if there were other books about Everett. Shanin replied that there may be some in the library. Why don't we look? They went to the library together, brought books back, and read together. Anthony worked on his own, as usual.

The next book the teacher used with the group was *The Hundred Penny Box* (Viking Press, 1975) by Sharon Bell Mathis. All the characters are African-American. Laura, who is very dramatic, suggested they do it as a play. Shanin played the mother, Laura was Aunt Dew, Cedric was Michael, and Brandon was the narrator.

Poetry: Stories told in rhyme are appealing to children at this age. Children can read more of Lucille Clifton's poetry, Eloise Greenfield also writes rap poetry: Some of her titles are mentioned in the bibliography at the end of the book. One class had a group recite Greenfield's poetry while another group mimed the poems. They videotaped their performance and sent a copy to Eloise Greenfield.

BOOKS FOR FOLLOW-UP LITERATURE STUDIES

Boyd, Candy Dawson. (1984). *Circle of Gold*. Scholastic.
> Twins Mattie and Matt learn to cope with the loss of their father and their mixed feelings toward their mother. This title is for middle grade students.

Greenfield, Eloise. (1974). *She Come Bringing Me That Little Baby Girl*. Illustrated by John Steptoe. Lippincott.
> In this picture book, a new baby causes jealousy until big brother realizes his importance to the baby.

Spinelli, Jerry. (1984). *Who Put That Hair in My Toothbrush?* Little, Brown.
> Upper elementary students will enjoy the story of Megin and her older brother Greg who have a big rivalry going with hilarious, and often disastrous, results.

Barbara Cooney, Miss Rumphius

• •

Publisher and Date: Viking, 1985
Illustrator: Barbara Cooney

Audience Level: Grades two and up
Main Theme: Life and Work
Other Possible Themes: Beauty, Young and Old, Dreams
Values to Target: Goal Setting, Beauty, Kindness

● ●

ABOUT THE AUTHOR

Barbara Cooney was born in 1917 in Brooklyn, New York. As a child, she spent summers in Maine where her grandmother had a home by the sea. She now lives in New York where she enjoys her roles as wife, gardener, gourmet cook, artist, mother, and grandmother. She has illustrated over 100 books. When she illustrates for other author's books, she usually travels to the locale in which her books are set. Cooney says she doesn't illustrate just for children but rather to communicate to anyone who will pay attention to her joy in perceiving beautiful, funny, and other evocative imagery in the world. She has won Caldecott Medals for *Chanticleer and the Fox* and *The Oxcart Man* by Brent Hall. Cooney reports that people often think she *is* Miss Rumphius. She replies, "Actually I do write about myself, but not only about myself. And I always tell the truth." *Miss Rumphius* truly has the ring of truth (*SATA* v. 59, pp. 47-55, and personal communication with Alice Naylor).

ABOUT THE STORY

A little girl named Alice narrates the story of her great aunt, also named Alice, who lived by the sea. The advice given to Miss Alice Rumphius by her grandfather when she was a child was, "You must do something to make the world more beautiful." Alice grows up to be "Miss Rumphius." She works as a librarian, travels to faraway places, and lives beside the sea, just as she had dreamed long ago. However, she doesn't forget her grandfather's advice. Years later she reminds her great niece Alice that she, too, must do something to make the world more beautiful. "I do not know yet what that can be," concludes this Alice.

For children this story stimulates concern about what they will do with their lives. The idea that whatever it is will contribute to making the world more beautiful is a happy thought for them. The illustrations are exquisitely peaceful. They give a sense of life continuing through generations of contributions from everyone. Adults also respond enthusiastically to this story because of the sheer beauty of the book itself.

DIALOGUE

Talk about What You Notice in the Story

● ●

This entry presents the shared reading experience of a family with four children of various ages. These responses were recorded during the family's nightly story time. The family includes John, age 3; Bill, age 6; Janey, age 9; and Laura, age 11. Notice the exuberance of John, the concrete observations of Bill, and the thoughtful reflections of the girls as each is gently guided by a parent who is willing to learn along with the children.

● ●

Janey:	What's lupine mean?
Laura:	I think it is a flower, a pink or blue flower. See the picture at the beginning.
Janey:	Oh, yes.
PARENT:	ISN'T THAT NEAT? SHE GETS TO PAINT IN THE SKIES!
Janey:	*[laughing]* My grandfather probably wouldn't trust me to paint in the skies.
Bill:	*[looking at the picture of the boats]* I'd climb up on that big thing and put my foot on it [as Miss Rumphius visits the tropical isle].
Janey:	What's mother of pearl?
PARENT:	IT'S LIKE A PEARL. IT HAS PRETTY COLORS.
Laura:	I wonder if the Bapa Raja's wife is jealous—about, you know, "You'll always remain in my heart."
PARENT:	I DON'T KNOW.
Laura:	I think it is like he loved her.
Janey:	Well, maybe it was not like a girlfriend thing, but she was special to him.
Janey:	What's a lotus?
PARENT:	PROBABLY A FLOWER. DO YOU WANT TO LOOK IT UP?
Laura:	No. Not now. Let's read more.
Bill:	Five bushels of lupine seeds—wow!
Janey:	Soon she'll be picking them.
John:	Mommy, Mommy, look at the bird.
PARENT:	YES, I SEE THE BIRD. WHAT ELSE ARE YOU LOOKING AT?
John:	Mommy, mommy look at the cat.
PARENT:	YES, WE SEE THE CAT, JOHN.
Janey:	That's neat. I didn't notice the cat. Good, John!

Talk about How the Story Makes You Feel

• •

The parent asks questions and makes statements about things that are important to her in the story. She asks the older children to explain or say more.

• •

PARENT: THAT'S A NEAT BOOK, DON'T YOU THINK? WHAT DID YOU LIKE BEST?

Bill: The flowers and everything.

Laura: I loved the story, but I didn't want her to get old.

PARENT: YOU DIDN'T WANT HER TO GET OLD.

Janey: Me neither. It seemed sad to get old.

Laura: I wanted her to get married.

PARENT: OH, YOU DID...

John: Mommy, look at these flowers.

PARENT: I *SEE.*

John: Mommy, look at *these* flowers.

Laura: *[patiently]* Yes, John, we see the pretty flowers.

PARENT: WHY DIDN'T YOU WANT HER TO GET OLD, JANEY?

Janey: Because she was so pretty when she was young.

PARENT: YOU DIDN'T THINK SHE WAS PRETTY WHEN SHE WAS OLD?

Janey: *[hesitating a minute]* Well, not really...

Laura: She had a cane and white hair when she was old. Can we go back and see how her face changed in the book?

Janey: *[comparing pages]* It's different, but it still looks like her. I think the artist made her face thinner because she was old.

PARENT: WHAT ABOUT THE THINGS SHE SAID AND DID WHEN SHE WAS OLD? WERE THOSE THINGS PRETTY?

Chorus: Uh hum... Sure!

PARENT: HOW WAS THAT?

Janey: Well, she made friends with a whole bunch of people and she changed their lives.

PARENT: SHE *DID* MAKE FRIENDS WITH A WHOLE BUNCH OF PEOPLE. ANYTHING ELSE?

Laura: Planting all those flowers.

PARENT: SHE WAS FOLLOWING THE ADVICE OF HER FATHER...

Laura: No, it was her grandfather.

PARENT: RIGHT! IT WAS HER GRANDFATHER.

Janey: I was wondering if him making things for boats and stuff was *his* way of making the world more beautiful.

PARENT: COULD BE...

Janey:	But I don't see how making Indians to stand outside of cigar stores would be making the world beautiful, because cigars are yucky.
Laura:	They were like works of art.
Janey:	Yeah, but they still didn't have to put them outside of cigar stores.
PARENT:	I GUESS THEY DIDN'T KNOW BACK THEN HOW CIGARS ARE NOT GOOD FOR YOU.
Laura:	That *was* a long time back, because Miss Rumphius was just a little girl then.
PARENT:	I WAS WONDERING IF YOU NOTICED HOW MISS RUMPHIUS HAD DIFFERENT KINDS OF NAMES IN THE STORY AT DIFFERENT TIMES IN HER LIFE.
Laura:	Her first name is Alice.
PARENT:	AND LATER SHE WAS CALLED SOMETHING DIFFERENT.
Chorus:	Miss Rumphius!
PARENT:	YES, SHE WAS MRS. RUMPHIUS...
Chorus:	No, it was *Miss*!
PARENT:	(LAUGHING) OH, YOU'RE RIGHT AGAIN. I SAID IT WRONG. I SHOULD HAVE KNOWN THAT.
Bill:	It's the title of the book.
Laura:	Yeah, she never got married.
PARENT:	ANYTHING ELSE SHE WAS CALLED?
Janey:	And she was the Lupine Lady.
Laura:	But before that she was the Crazy Old Lady.
	[Laughter]
PARENT:	CRAZY...WHY WAS THAT?
Janey:	She wasn't crazy...!
Laura:	They saw her coming down the road and sprinkling all those seeds everywhere, and they thought she was crazy.
PARENT:	THEY DIDN'T KNOW THAT SHE WAS DOING. WELL, WHAT DO YOU SUPPOSE THEY THOUGHT LATER, WHEN ALL THOSE FLOWERS STARTED COMING UP?
John:	I'll just run over to those flowers and I'll smell them.
Laura:	They thought she was *wonderful*!
PARENT:	DO YOU THINK THAT TEACHES ANYTHING?
Janey:	Yeah, you can't judge a book by its cover.
PARENT:	SO, THINGS ARE NOT ALWAYS WHAT THEY SEEM. WAS THERE ANOTHER NAME SHE WAS CALLED?
Laura:	Great Aunt Alice.
Bill:	*[echoing the words]* Great Aunt Alice...
PARENT:	WHICH ALICE IS TELLING THIS STORY?

Bill:	The little girl.
Laura:	Yeah... Alice, Junior. Miss Rumphius is Alice, Senior.
Janey:	The author is not Alice, is she?
Laura:	It's written by Barbara Cooney. I think she did the pictures for the book, *The Year of the Perfect Christmas Tree.* I liked that book. I *loved* the illustrations.
PARENT:	WHAT DO YOU THINK OF THESE ILLUSTRATIONS?
Chorus:	I love them!
PARENT:	WHAT DO YOU LIKE BEST ABOUT THE PICTURES?
Janey:	The way they express feelings. They look *real*.
PARENT:	SHOW US ONE THAT EXPRESSES FEELING.
Janey:	The picture of the Bapa Raja.
PARENT:	AND WHAT FEELING DO YOU NOTICE?
Laura:	It's happy. He's thanking her.
Janey:	And here, in the library she looks concentrated on her work. I like this picture of the library. It's so neat. I'd like to work in a place like that.

Talk about What the Story Reminds You of in Your Life.

• •

Laura recognizes the author's illustrations from another book. The discussion throughout reinforces the values that are important to the family, such as ways to make the world more beautiful. The older children express delight at the younger children's comments.

• •

PARENT:	I'VE BEEN THINKING ABOUT THE ADVICE HER GRANDFATHER GAVE HER.
Bill:	Always make the world pretty.
Janey:	If everybody did that, the world would be *wonderful*.
PARENT:	DO YOU THINK IT HAS TO BE SOMETHING PHYSICAL? LIKE PLANTING A FLOWER, OR PAINTING A PICTURE?
Janey:	No!
Laura:	Helping people? Action?
Janey:	Being kind...
PARENT:	ANYTHING ELSE?
Bill:	Helping people.
PARENT:	BILL, THERE'S SOMETHING YOU TALK TO ME ABOUT A LOT THIS YEAR, SOMETHING YOU WANT ME TO DO TO MAKE THE WORLD BEAUTIFUL...
Bill:	Oh yeah, Don't pollute!
Janey:	I think that if they would make everybody not be mean to each other, the world would be a happier and more

	beautiful place, and also if they wouldn't cut down all the trees to make paper and stuff. They could plant a tree after every tree they cut down, they wouldn't be taking any of the world's beauty.
Bill:	And they should fill up the big holes they dig in the earth.
PARENT:	DID YOU NOTICE WHAT HAPPENED TO THE SEEDS MISS RUMPHIUS PLANTED?
Bill:	They spread all over.
PARENT:	AND WHAT DOES THIS SAY TO US ABOUT BEAUTY?
Janey:	That it can spread.
Laura:	That if you start something, it will spread, spread, spread...
John:	And they run to the flowers and smell them.
PARENT:	AND THEY SMELL THEM AND IT MAKES THE CHILDREN HAPPY, DOESN'T IT, JOHN? DOES IT MAKE YOU HAPPY?
John:	It makes me *happy*!
PARENT:	DO YOU THINK WE HAVE TO WAIT UNTIL WE ARE OLD TO MAKE THE WORLD MORE BEAUTIFUL?
Chorus:	No!
Laura:	Well, John's only three, I don't know what he can do yet.
Janey:	He can do something.
Bill:	Yes!
John:	Yeah!
Laura:	John what would you do?
John:	I'd make some flowers.
PARENT:	AND BILL, WHAT DO YOU SEE OUTSIDE THE WINDOW THAT YOU HAVE ALREADY DONE TO MAKE THE WORLD BEAUTIFUL?
Bill:	The bird feeder. The birds come.
PARENT:	SO WE ALL ARE IN A WAY DOING SOMETHING. YOU KNOW MISS RUMPHIUS DID MORE THAN JUST PLANT FLOWERS.
Bill:	She traveled everywhere. She met people and she gave things to them and stuff.
John:	And she made dinosaurs and stuff...
Laura:	I don't think she did that, John. That was in another book. But maybe she might have painted something that looked like that when she was helping her grandfather.
PARENT:	DOES THIS BOOK MAKE YOU WANT TO DO ANYTHING?
Laura:	It makes me want to make the world better.
PARENT:	HOW ABOUT YOU, JANEY?
Janey:	This book makes me want to draw exactly like the person who drew it.
John:	And *there* are the flowers!

TEACHER FOCUS

Ecology: The metaphor of making the world beautiful has infinite possibilities with discussing and teaching about the planet and the environment.

Geography: Read more about Barbara Cooney as a young girl, and identify the setting for *Miss Rumphius*. Compare the settings to Cooney's other books, *Hattie and the Wild Waves* and *Island Boy*. Where, other than New England, do lupines grow? For a map study, find some real places like those Miss Rumphius visited—tropical isles, deserts, and mountains. The story never named the places. What might they be?

COUNSELOR FOCUS

Goal Setting: One teacher had her class draw a composite web of Miss Rumphius's ways of reaching her goal to make the world beautiful. Children were challenged to look beyond the concrete planting of flowers for a more abstract interpretation of beauty. They recalled Miss Rumphius' relationships with people, her work as a librarian, her travels, as well as her planting of the lupines. They were then asked to reflect about young Alice's words "I do not know yet what that may be" as they draw a web of specific dreams and goals for themselves for the future.

Family: Miss Rumphius never married, but she passed on her grandfather's advice to another generation. What are the important values or advice that children can identify as coming from their family? What advice will they want to give their own children? How do they picture themselves at other ages? 40? 50? As old as Miss Rumphius?

MAKING CONNECTIONS

Role Play: A counselor enjoyed giving her third grade guidance group a chance to role play the faraway places. Children volunteered to be Miss Rumphius, the Bapa Raja, his wife, the villagers, the cockatoos, and monkeys. They played out that great line, "You will always remain in my heart." Children recalled the line in the following weeks as a closing ritual for the group.

"Miss Rumphius Day": One reading teacher helped to organize a "Miss Rumphius Day" for seed planting. The children planted perennials and annuals. Using the line from the story, "I do not know yet what they may be," children talked about "generations of seeds." This concrete experience helped the children to see the larger metaphor of the story: The seed is like the ideas and traditions planted by one generation, renewed and relived in the next generation.

Research: Barbara Cooney dedicated the book to Saint Nicholas, the patron saint of children, maidens, and sailors. Children may want to research Nicholas (who was a real bishop in the early church according to some histories) and discover why this is an appropriate dedication. What does St. Nicholas have to do with Santa Claus?

Goal Setting: One professor reads this book to her graduate-level life and career planning course. Her students thoroughly enjoy the discovery of the metaphor and its applications, particularly the relationship of life and work.

Music: "The Garden Song" (sometimes known as "Inch by Inch") is a favorite of children and gives them a chance to dwell once more in the beauty of a metaphor about seeds. It takes "a rake and a hoe"—and loving care. (Words and chords available in *Winds of the People,* Sing Out Publications, 505 Eighth Ave., New York, NY 10018.)

Storytelling: This story is rich with meaning for older elementary children. Although the illustrations seem vital to the story, one school counselor discovered that the story stands alone very well. She has told it in sixth grade classes in an inner city school and notes varying, but always heartfelt responses. A sixth grade boy noted, "What I remember most about the story is that she keeps her promise to her grandfather. Most people I know don't keep their promises." Sixth graders are able to identify values that are passed down in families and are able to discuss the concept of work as beauty as well as find beauty in life beyond work.

BOOKS FOR FOLLOW-UP LITERATURE STUDIES

Bjork, Christina, and Lena Anderson. (1988). *Linea's Windowsill Garden.* Farrar, Straus & Giroux.
> This beautifully illustrated book combines a story about Linea with information about growing a garden.

Bulla, Clyde R. (1975). *One Poppy Seed.* Hale.
> Much like the lupines, poppies bloom all over the desert from a few seeds.

Cooney, Barbara. (1990). *Hattie and the Wild Waves.* Viking Press.
> Hattie loves beauty and has a sense of adventure, much like Alice Rumphius. The scenes depicted are from Barbara Cooney's childhood.

Lasky, Kathryn. (1987). *Sea Swan.* MacMillan.
> A zestful grandmother, Elzibah Swan, keeps her spirit of independence by learning to swim at age 75.

Lobel, Anita (1990). *Allison's Zinnia.* Greenwillow Books.
> Allison gives Beryl an amaryllis, and so on through the alphabet. A visual and verbal delight!

Carolyn Craven,
What the Mailman Brought

• •

Publisher and Date: Putnam, 1987
Illustrator: Tomie dePaola
Audience Level: Kindergarten and up
Main Theme: Illness
Other Possible Themes: Imagination, Creativity, Boredom,
    Loneliness, Self-control
Values to Target: Coping, Creativity, Self-reliance

• •

ABOUT THE AUTHOR

This book, Carolyn Craven's first, was selected as an outstanding book by Junior Literary Guild. Craven grew up in Middlebury, Vermont. She received her BA from Williams College and is currently working toward her doctorate in economics at Yale. She has worked as an art director for a New York publisher (from the book jacket).

ABOUT THE ILLUSTRATOR

Few children's authors have written or illustrated as many books as Tomie dePaola. Since his first book was published in 1966, dePaola has written more than 70 stories. During the same period he has illustrated more than 100 books by other authors.

DePaola had an active and eventful childhood in Meriden, Connecticut. One of his earliest loves was tap dancing, which he began at age six and continued until college. His other interest was drawing, and he decided as a child that he would be an artist when he grew up. He won a scholarship to Pratt Institute and graduated from there in 1956. After art school he spent six months in a Benedictine monastery in Vermont.

He has been an art teacher at various colleges. He lived in New York and California before settling in rural New Hampshire. DePaola writes and illustrates in the hope that his books will "touch the heart of some individual child and change that child's life for the better" (*SATA* v. 59, pp. 59-73. Note: This *SATA* entry has detailed descriptions of dePaola's school years, grade by grade, which may be of interest to the children in the corresponding grade.)

ABOUT THE STORY

William Beauregard, who has just moved to the city, is sick in bed. He stares out of the window wondering what he can possibly do during this, his second week in bed. He makes a sign saying "SICK OF THIS" and tapes it in the window facing out. The next morning he finds a mysterious package left for him by the mail carrier. As the week goes on, daily visits from the mail carrier become increasingly exciting.

The text and illustrations of this book by two different people are exquisitely combined. William is ill, bored, and lonely at home in bed. He counteracts his frustrations by relying on his imagination. The suspense of the plot enables the reader, like William, to feel a sense of control over seemingly uncontrollable circumstances.

DIALOGUE

Talk about What You Notice in the Story

• •

These second and third graders are totally absorbed in the visual experience with words and pictures. All eyes are glued to the page. Heather is totally "into" the story. She feels the "slowness" of the week ahead for William. Shari spontaneously shares the definition of the word fragile. Each child delights in the originality of the fantasy. They make a game of predicting, and enjoy it as sport. Whether they are right or wrong, they *love* predicting!

• •

Beth: I think the mailman is bringing William a letter from his other town.

Chase: Oh! It's a humongous box!

All Reading Together: *[with emphasis]* Sick—of—this.

Chase: I was sick last week. I ate all I could hold.

Shari: Home for another whole week. Oh no!

Heather: *[slowly, with emphasis on each syllable]* Mon-day, Tues-day, Wednes-day, Thurs-day, Fri-day... Oh, no! It's going to be a long week!

Ricky: The mailman must have read his sign! All right!

Beth: That was just what William wanted!

Josh: What? Mailmen don't waddle...

Chase: Oh, Man! It's a *duck!*

Shari: "Fragile." Fragile means it might break.

Ricky: How does the mailman know? Ducks can't read!

Heather: Oh! It's an *egg.*

• •

Children gleefully continued the guessing game celebrating both their accurate and inaccurate predictions for the arrival of the alligator, skunk, fish, and caterpillar mail carriers.

• •

Talk about How the Story Makes You Feel

• •

"Sick...of...This" becomes a byword among the group. There is obvious appreciation for the suspense in the story created by the art work. Rick and Shari seem to agree that it doesn't really matter whether the mailman was real or not. They simply delight in the power of William's imagination to combat the tedium of being sick.

• •

TEACHER:	SOUNDS LIKE YOU ALL KNOW HOW WILLIAM FEELS.
Shari:	William felt sick.
Josh:	And Sick of this!
	[Several echo: "Sick...of...this!"]
Heather:	When I was sick, I couldn't get out of bed. I had shots. I couldn't get my arm to move to open the door.
Chase:	I got sick and I had to grab a chair to walk.
TEACHER:	WHAT ABOUT "SICK OF THIS"? HOW DOES THAT FEEL?
Jeremy:	Oh, he was tired of lying around and doing nothing. When I was sick, I was so bored I rolled out of the bed and went out the door. I forget it was raining. The rain was cold on my head.
Josh:	The story was fun, but strange because every time there was a *new* mailman.
TEACHER:	I NOTICED AT THE END MRS. BEAUREGARD SAID THE MAILMAN HAD BEEN SICK ALL WEEK.
Patrick:	Well, maybe the boy imagined all those things and drew those pictures out of his head with water paint and his palette.
TEACHER:	DOES IT MATTER WHETHER IT WAS REAL OR NOT?
Ricky:	Not really. The little boy saw the mailman—the alligator and duck and all. That's what counts.
Shari:	And his parents think, "Crazy again!"
TEACHER:	DO YOU THINK HE'S CRAZY?
Chorus:	"No!" "He's cool." "He's a good painter." "He liked imagining everything."

Talk about What the Story Reminds You of in Your Life

• •

Shari has already invented an interesting diversion when she is sick. Josh and Ricky learn from William that their own imaginations may be better than TV.

• •

Josh: I like putting signs on the door of my room for people to read. I say NO TRESPASSING—KEEP OUT—SHAMOO.

Patrick: It reminds me of the time I had the chicken pox and I had to stay home.

Shari: When I have to stay in the bed, I make mountains. I push my knees up under the sheets. Then I pretend there are little skiers going up and down the hills.

Heather: Have you ever made a tent with your knees under the cover? I pretend it is a circus tent in my bed.

Chase: I have a TV in my room. Something good about being sick is staying in bed and watching TV.

Ricky: TV's boring!

Josh: Well, it's a good thing William didn't watch TV or he never would have all those visits from the mailman!

Teacher: GOOD POINT, JOSH!

Ricky: Yeah, being sick and all, what he did was a whole lot funner than TV.

TEACHER FOCUS

Art: What is the importance of art to William while he is sick? What is the purpose of art in our lives?

Suspension of Disbelief: This book is different in its approach to fantasy, because there is such a fine line between real and unreal. All of this *could* be William's imagination except the presents. How do we explain that? What other well-known stories are make-believe?

Community Helpers: The book can introduce the mail carrier!

COUNSELOR FOCUS

Illness/Wellness: This book uniquely addresses the all-too-common experience of being sick, and the tedium and boredom that the children readily identify.

Empathy: Take time to talk about what prompted William to write "Sick" and then "of this."

Self-Reliance: A discussion can lead children who identify with William to consider how he relies upon himself and his imagination to survive his illness.

MAKING CONNECTIONS

Art: A group can reflect about whether William Beauregard might be very much like Tomie dePaola, the illustrator of the book. Children can speculate about what they'd like their mail carrier to be. Chase (grade three) decided on a dinosaur, as depicted in the illustration.

Music: Pete Seeger popularized the song "Mail Myself to You" in his children's concerts. This is now a favorite in John McCutcheon's concerts and is recorded on John's award-winning children's tape: *Mail Myself to You* (Appalseed Productions, 1025 Locust Ave., Charlottesville, VA 22901, 804-977-6321).

BOOKS FOR FOLLOW-UP LITERATURE STUDIES

Hamilton, Virginia. (1967). *Zeely*. Macmillan.
> Zeely's imagination helps her to understand herself. Use this with fourth grade and up.

Heide, Florence Parry. (1971). *The Shrinking of Treehorn*. Illustrated by Edward Gorey. Holiday House.
> The mood of this story is similar to that in *What the Mailman Brought* in that the boy feels "invisible" to his parents.

Levoy, Myron. (1977). *Alan and Naomi*. Harper & Row.
> Alan's mother insists that he be responsible for Naomi after school. Naomi is a victim of the Holocaust who has recently come to the United States. For grades five and up.

Slepian, Jan. (1980). *The Alfred Summer*. Macmillan.
> Four preteens who are either left out or disabled work together to build a boat. Use with older elementary children.

Eleanor Estes,
The Hundred Dresses

• •

Publisher and Date: Harcourt, 1942
Audience Level: Grades four and up
Main Theme: Prejudice

Other Possible Themes: Cruelty, Peer Pressure, Forgiveness,
Stereotyping, Poverty
Values to Target: Empathy, Kindness

● ●

ABOUT THE AUTHOR

Eleanor Estes was born in 1906 in West Haven, Connecticut, the
setting of many of her books. In town there were two schools, a small
wooden one and an ivy covered brick school, which may be recognizable
in *The Hundred Dresses.* She was also well-known for *Ginger Pye,* which
won the Newbery Award, and for The Moffats series. Estes wrote, "I like
to make children laugh or cry, or be moved in some way. I like to feel that
I am holding up a mirror and I hope that what is reflected is the true image
of childhood." Eleanor Estes died in July 1988. (*SATA* v. 7, p. 80).

ABOUT THE STORY

One day Wanda Petronski, a poor immigrant girl who wore the same
faded blue dress to school every day, approached a crowd of girls who
were admiring someone's dress. "I've got a hundred dresses home," she
said quietly to Peggy, the most popular girl in the class. "What?" Peggy
asked incredulously. This was the beginning of a teasing game the girls
played every day with Wanda. Maddie, who was poor herself, felt bad
about the ridiculing and wished they would stop. However, she couldn't
risk losing Peggy's friendship and was afraid to speak up. Set in the 1940s,
the story invites projection into all three characters: Peggy, who led the
crowd to choose Wanda as a scapegoat; Maddie, who went along with the
game in spite of her guilt feelings; and Wanda, the target for unkind
actions who still maintains her pride and acts with graciousness and
courage.

Parents and teachers of fourth and fifth graders typically notice that
pressure to conform to the group intensifies in the upper elementary years.
The desire to be included often prompts cruel actions that cause hurt
feelings among children. This story offers children the opportunity to
empathize with Wanda, Maddie, or Peggy. Children are inclined to
identify with the character most like themselves.

This short chapter book requires at least three 30-minute sessions of
oral reading, followed by response time and a final session for discussion.
The responses to the first prompt given below were recorded from
discussions during the reading. The later responses were made after the
book was finished.

DIALOGUE

Talk about What You Notice in the Story

• •

This is an old and widely read book, but the role of the teacher is crucial in leading children to make meaning together. Here she helps these 4th and 5th graders look at why there is such a thing as a "cut down" and provides information that diffuses reasons for prejudice.

• •

Regina: My mother came to school right here when she was a little girl. I wonder if our school was ever like Wanda's school back then. I like learning about things "back then."

TEACHER: WELL, BACK THEN, FOR ONE THING, WE WORE DRESSES.
[Amazed exclamations]

Lashonda: Always dresses?

TEACHER: RIGHT. WE WORE JEANS ON SATURDAYS MAYBE, BUT NEVER TO SCHOOL.
[The teacher allowed for a few more minutes of sharing details of how school has changed over the years.]

TEACHER: WE HAVE NOTICED LOTS OF DETAILS ABOUT SCHOOL BACK THEN. WHAT ELSE DID YOU NOTICE?

Lashonda: I mostly noticed how Wanda was left out. She had that funny name. They always called her Wanda Petronski, not just Wanda.

Haley: Well we do that, like if we have two Jennifers.

Jessie: This was different though. There wasn't another Wanda.

TEACHER: SO YOU NOTICE A "CUT DOWN." THEY ALWAYS CALLED HER "WANDA PETRONSKI."

Jerome: *[with indignation]* It's not her fault what her name is!

Raymond: What kind of name is that anyway?

Tyrone: It's Polish.

Raymond: What's so bad about that? What's Polish mean?

Danica: It's the country. It's on the map.
[Children located Poland on the map of Europe, and took the opportunity to share information and to clarify some misinformation.]

TEACHER: ACTUALLY MANY FAMOUS PEOPLE ARE POLISH. CHOPIN, THE MUSICIAN IS ONE. MADAME CURIE WAS POLISH.

Tyrone: Those names don't end with "ski."

TEACHER: GOOD POINT, TYRONE. ONLY SOME POLISH NAMES END WITH "SKI." IT MEANS SON—LIKE JOHNSON OR PETERSON.

64 / Eleanor Estes

Tyrone:	That's cool.
TEACHER:	ANYTHING ELSE YOU NOTICE?
Summer:	They're just picking on her name and it's some kind of excuse they use to make her feel left out.
Sharon:	Everybody just let Peggy be the boss all the time.
Kim:	She's popular, that's why.
TEACHER:	WHAT ABOUT MADDIE?
Summer:	Really, I don't think she liked it, but she's afraid that she'll be left out unless she goes along with it.
Dana:	It's not right! But she's scared she won't have any friends.

● ●

In the earlier chapters the class enjoyed anticipating what might happen: Would Maddie change her mind and stick up for Wanda? Would Wanda get angry and fight back in some way? How long could this go on? Many expressed anger toward Wanda, because after all it wasn't right to lie about dresses. The feeling dissipated into sadness with the receiving of Mr. Petronski's letter. Then there was the surprise on the day of the art contest. Chris discovered a key theme of the book, exclaiming "We thought she was lying. In a way, she wasn't lying at all. She *did* have a hundred dresses!"

● ●

Talk about How the Story Makes You Feel

● ●

This conversation occurred after the reading of the book was complete. The empathy the children feel is put to good use by the teacher who helps to resolve a conflict in the classroom.

● ●

P.J.:	I felt very sad for Wanda.
Jessie:	I was even *mad* about the way Peggy acted all the time!
Haley:	Yeah, just because somebody's not as good looking or doesn't have the right clothes or isn't popular, they get made fun of.
Chris:	That's really for no good reason at all.
TEACHER:	IT REALLY DOESN'T MAKE MUCH SENSE, DOES IT?
Chad:	I guess picking on one person makes those doing it feel like they're big or something.
Haley:	Well, it's pretty rotten if you're the one left out.
Jessie:	In our class it's not always the same one who gets left out. It's kinda' like one day you're in, another day you might

	have somebody mad and talking in the bathroom about you, telling somebody else not to be your friend.
Holly:	Right! Why can't three people be best friends?
Jessie:	I don't understand that either!
Beth:	'Cause somebody's always getting jealous.
TEACHER:	JEALOUS?
Beth:	Really! Sometimes people act like they own their best friends.
TEACHER:	SO LOTS OF YOU KNOW HOW WANDA FEELS BECAUSE YOU HAVE FELT THAT WAY.
Chris:	Boys are like that too except they just fight it out and get it over quicker. Chad and I were in a fight yesterday.
TEACHER:	AND DO YOU HAVE SOMETHING TO SAY TO EACH OTHER TODAY?
Chris:	*[with a laugh]* Yeah, man. I'm sorry about that!

Talk about What the Story Reminds You of in Your Life

• •

These are written responses the children recorded in journals. The teacher responded to each in writing. Names are changed here to protect confidentiality. The hundred dresses became a metaphor for discrimination in this class for the entire year. Reminders of "Wanda Petronski" expedited the talking out of many difficulties among friends. The larger issue of ethnic prejudice in the story is overshadowed by the children's personal experiences with feeling left out.

• •

Summer:	I just thought the whole story was really sad. Wanda was nice to them even though they were mean to her, and then she had to leave and never did get to have a friend there. Sometimes people are mean to me when I try to be nice.
Alicia:	It reminds me of being new here this year. Everybody said my shoes were from the dollar store. I wondered if I would ever have a friend.
Shenitra:	One time the whole class ganged up on me and it was terrible.
Jerry:	This story reminds me of my first day at school when I thought I would miss something and everybody would laugh at me all the time.
Latoya:	Sometimes my cousin will be boss and leave me out. Then sometimes I leave her out too. I don't know exactly why we do that.

Latasha: *[with a drawing of Wanda with tears in her eyes]* I will *never* forget Wanda Petronski!

TEACHER FOCUS

Prejudice: The literary transaction can have a stronger impact on classroom behavior than rules and instructions. The teacher's task is to be in touch with her or his own ethnocentricity and how to get beyond it.

Kindness: Reading this book at the beginning of a school year can set the stage for creating a community of caring and for weakening the formation of cliques.

COUNSELOR FOCUS

Friendship: Issues of popularity and being left out are topics for consideration after an experience with the story. This book can be a "unit" for classroom or small group guidance.

Empathy: Children can practice being in the shoes of Wanda, Peggy, and Maddie. They can look for feelings, thoughts, and behaviors of these characters that have parallels in their lives.

MAKING CONNECTIONS

Art: As a reminder of Wanda Petronski, one teacher's reading classes decorated their classroom doors and walls with the hundred dresses, all different designs colored with crayon.

Social Studies: Bring old school yearbooks and memorabilia to class. Children may then be inspired to have conversations or even to tape interviews with their parents and other adults about school days in the past. Allow children to collaborate on preparing open-ended questions for the interviews. Evaluate in a role play which questions elicit the most interesting kinds of information.

BOOKS FOR FOLLOW-UP LITERATURE STUDIES

Blume, Judy. (1971). *Freckle Juice.* Illustrated by Sonia O. Lisker. Four Winds Press.
    A teacher helps a boy understand that all children do not have to be the same.
Cohen, Barbara. (1983). *Molly's Pilgrim.* Illustrated by Michael Derany. Lothrop, Lee and Shepard.
    Molly's Jewish mother helps Molly dress her pilgrim doll in a costume of old Russia. Molly is very embarrassed until she realizes that her pilgrim is unique. This picture book can be used with younger children.

Sachs, Marilyn. (1981). *Hello, Wrong Number.* Illustrated by Pamela Johnson. Dutton.

> A boy and a girl who converse with each other on the phone because of a wrong number find that appearances are not so important in real friendships.

Mem Fox, *Wilfrid Gordon McDonald Partridge*

• •

Publisher and Date: Kane/ Miller, 1985
Illustrator: Julie Vivas
Audience Level: Grades two and up
Main Theme: Compassion
Other Possible Themes: Friendship of Young and Old, Creativity, Memory, Competence, People in the Neighborhood
Values to Target: Empathy, Competence

• •

ABOUT THE AUTHOR

Mem Fox was born in Melbourne, Australia, but spent much of her early life in Zimbabwe where her parents were missionaries. Her father's name was Wilfrid Gordon McDonald Partridge. She writes that her parents were very supportive of the African move for independence. As a school girl, she describes herself as a tomboy who loved climbing trees and playing football. After high school she went to England to study drama. She returned to Australia in 1970 with her husband. She now lives near Adelaide, and teaches language arts and literature at the South Australian College of Advanced Education. She has several other highly acclaimed picture books, including *Possum Magic, Koala Lou, Hattie and the Fox,* and *Night Noises* (*SATA* v. 51, pp. 65-70).

ABOUT THE ILLUSTRATOR

Julie Vivas is one of Australia's most accomplished illustrators. Her works include *The Train to Bondi Beach, The Nativity,* and *The Very Best of Friends*. She illustrated another Mem Fox favorite *Possum Magic*. She lives in Sydney with her husband and two children (from the book jacket).

ABOUT THE STORY

A small boy who is "not very old either" has special friends at the retirement home next door. When he hears his father saying that his favorite friend, Miss Nancy Allison Delacourt Cooper, has "lost her memory," he sets out to find it for her. He begins by asking the residents, "What is a memory?" Wilfrid searches around the hen house, his yard, and his house until he finds some special objects to match each definition of memory. He places his unusual collection in a basket and delivers the gifts to Miss Nancy. As she touches each gift, a wonderful memory returns. They smile together because Miss Nancy's memory has been found. Mem Fox's gift for rhythmic language and Julie Vivas' detailed and humorous illustrations of characters in motion combine for a memorable experience.

Without sentimentality Mem Fox creates a sensitive story of an intergenerational friendship. The story structure has a clear beginning (the introduction of the characters), middle (looking for memories), and end (Miss Nancy's memories). The finely structured plot engages both the thinking and feeling parts of the reader. Rhythmic language such as "Something from long ago, my lad, something from long ago," encourages younger audiences to join in the refrain and to savor the tangible items Wilfrid collects for Miss Nancy.

DIALOGUE

Talk about What You Notice in the Story

• •

The teacher follows the superficial responses of these second and third graders to the art work with a specific request to look at the language of the story and the story structure.

• •

TEACHER:	I NOTICED YOU LAUGHED AT THE ILLUSTRATIONS BY JULIE VIVAS, THE ILLUSTRATOR.
Shari:	*[laughing]* She makes Wilfrid's shirt come up above his tummy. I can see his belly button. *[More giggles]*
Adam:	*[making balancing motion]* He's skateboarding just right.
Keetha:	It was so funny when Miss Nancy's dress blew up.

Shari:	And she wore that funny thing for a bathing suit when she was young. You could *not* get a sun tan in that.
Jeremy:	I like the picture with the chairs lined up. The old people are all different looking.
TEACHER:	WILFRID GORDON KNEW ALL THESE PEOPLE WHO LIVED AT THE OLD PEOPLE'S HOME. HE LIKED THEM ALL FOR DIFFERENT REASONS. LET'S FIND WHAT WAS SPECIAL ABOUT EACH ONE. *[A double page depicts all the characters. Children enjoy re-reading the lines about each for pure pleasure, e.g., "Mr. Tippett who was crazy about cricket."]*
TEACHER:	I NOTICED THAT WILFRID'S PARENTS REFER TO MISS NANCY AS A "POOR OLD THING."
Chorus:	She had lost her memory.
TEACHER:	DO YOU THINK SHE WAS A "POOR OLD THING?"
Jason:	No. She's 96. I think she may live to be 100!
TEACHER:	WILFRID WENT TO THE REST HOME TO FIND A DEFINITION OF A "MEMORY." ARE ANY OF THE DEFINITIONS RIGHT OR WRONG?
Jeremy:	A memory is different for everyone. *[Children recall and read in chorus the definitions of memory.]*
TEACHER:	LET'S SEE IF WE CAN REMEMBER NOW WHAT WILFRID FOUND FOR EACH DEFINITION OF MEMORY.

• •

The following represents the final order of matching gifts to definitions as compiled by the children on the newsprint:

- Something from long ago—a shoe box of shells
- Something to make you laugh—a puppet on strings
- Something to make you cry—a medal
- Something as precious as gold—the football
- Something warm—the egg

• •

TEACHER:	I NOTICED THAT THE FIRST PART OF THE STORY HAS TO DO WITH FINDING OUT WHAT A MEMORY IS. THE SECOND PART IS FINDING OBJECTS TO HELP MISS NANCY REMEMBER. WHAT IS THE THIRD PART?
Shari:	It's what Miss Nancy remembered! *[Children enjoyed putting the entire structure of the story together using the newsprint as reference.]*

Talk about How the Story Makes You Feel

• •

Children literally bask in the feeling of caring which is more evident in tone and body language than in words.

• •

Shari: I felt so happy when she remembered.

TEACHER: MISS NANCY WHOM EVERYBODY KNEW HAD "LOST HER MEMORY" DID REMEMBER AGAIN.

Chase: It was because Wilfrid brought her the basket.

Beth: It was when she touched those real things and held them right there in her hand

Keetha: This is a really nice story.

Talk about What the Story Reminds You of in Your Life

• •

The teacher deliberately structures a sensory activity to get children in touch with the concept of memory. The children are quiet and reflective during this conversation.

• •

TEACHER: TOUCHING THINGS DOES HELP US REMEMBER. NOW EVERYONE SIT VERY STILL AND CLOSE YOUR EYES. HOLD YOUR HANDS TOGETHER AND RELAX. TAKE A MINUTE—DON'T RUSH NOW—AND IMAGINE THAT THERE IS SOMETHING IN YOUR HAND. IT CAN BE SOMETHING AROUND YOUR HOUSE. IT CAN BE SOMETHING WARM. IT MIGHT BE SOMETHING FROM LONG AGO. IT MIGHT BE SOMETHING THAT MAKES YOU CRY. IT MIGHT BE SOMETHING TO MAKE YOU LAUGH, OR, IT MIGHT EVEN BE PRECIOUS AS GOLD. IN A FEW MINUTES WE'LL OPEN OUR EYES AND TELL THE GROUP WHAT IS IN OUR HAND.

April: What I have in my hand is my soft warm pillow. It's special because it's just mine. I've had it since I was three.

Andy: Mine is something warm. It's my little fluffy kitten.

Adam: Mine is something warm, too. It's my puppy.

Brandon: I'm thinking about this this funny cowboy hat I got in Texas. It feels smooth.

Keetha: I have something as precious as gold. It's the little glass unicorn my mother gave me.

Shari: Mine is something to make me laugh. It's my little toy monkey.

Chris:	Mine is something to make me cry. It's the picture of my daddy in a frame. He played a guitar. My daddy died when I was six.
TEACHER:	(AFTER SOME SILENCE) YOU MAY OPEN YOUR EYES NOW. I WANT TO THANK YOU FOR SHARING YOUR MEMORIES AND THANK YOU FOR LISTENING TO EACH OTHER.

[The counselor who lead the group whose dialogue is recorded above was not aware that Chris's father had died. The children in the group already knew, and were quietly supportive.]

TEACHER FOCUS

Language: The sounds of the beautiful language are worth reciting together. Children will relish the opportunity to read in chorus.

Vocabulary: Children may wish to know about cricket, which can lead into a comparison of the different games in the United States and Australia, the home of the author. The familiar folksong "Waltzing Matilda" about a swagman who camped by a billabong contains colorful language of Austrailia and is widely anthologized in folk music collections.

Story Structure: Children can be led to analyze the predictive quality of the story structure. How did we know that there would be an object and a memory for every definition acquired by young Wilfrid?

COUNSELOR FOCUS

Caring: This book never fails to offer a positive emotional experience for groups and individuals of all ages.

Grief: If memories shared depict unfinished grief, a counselor or teacher will sense that a child may need an invitation for one-to-one counseling.

Work, Competence: Wilfrid's diligence and total absorption in his task helps him to forget the barriers that exist between the old people and the rest of the population. His pride in accomplishment is evident. A topic for story sharing may be "A Time I Kept Trying Until I Succeeded."

MAKING CONNECTIONS

Art: A simple but effective way of gathering responses from younger children is to have them fold a sheet of paper in fourths and draw four memories. They may wish to draw "something warm," "something precious as gold," etc.

Storytelling: The topic "Something I Like to Remember" can be used in dyads or small groups.

Service Projects: This story was used with a middle school group before their visit to a nursing home to sing Christmas carols. They were good sports about being read a picture book and noted how they felt better prepared for their visit as a result of it. Two outstanding films, *Close Harmony* and *Peege,* can expand on the theme of intergenerational friendships for grades 6 and up. The films are available at state libraries or from ECUFILM, 810 12th Ave., Nashville, TN 37203.

BOOKS FOR FOLLOW-UP LITERATURE STUDIES

Starred titles have full entries elsewhere in the book.

dePaola, Tomie. (1980). *Now One Foot, Now the Other.* Putnam.
> When his grandfather has a stroke, Bobby has a chance to return the kindness he has been shown.

Greenfield, Eloise. (1980). *Grandmama's Joy.* Illustrated by Carole Byard. Collins.
> Grandmama is not rich with money, but feels that life is rich because she has Randy, her "joy."

* Rylant, Cynthia. (1983). *Miss Maggie.* Dutton.
> Nat listens to his heart and befriends Miss Maggie.

Whitman, Sally. (1978). *A Special Trade.* Illustrated by Karen Gundersheimer. Harper and Row.
> Bartholomew takes care of Nelly when she is a baby. Nelly is able to reciprocate when Bartholomew is in a wheel chair.

Zolotow, Charlotte. (1984). *I Know a Lady.* Illustrated by James Stevenson. Greenwillow Books.
> Sally enjoys an old lady in the neighborhood who is thoughtful of children.

Mordicai Gerstein,
The Mountains of Tibet

• •

Publisher and Date: Harper and Row Publishers, 1987
Audience Level: Grades three and up
Main Theme: Choices
Other Possible Themes: Gender, Diversity
Values to Target: Possibilities of Life, Diversity

• •

ABOUT THE AUTHOR

Author and illustrator Mordicai Gerstein was surrounded with books and art as a child. His mother bought books for him and took him to the library. Through these experiences he developed a love for fairy tales, myths, and fantasy. Even as a child he illustrated his favorite stories and songs.

Gerstein's first career was in film. He has also worked as a sculptor. More recently he started illustrating books for other authors. Eventually he began writing and illustrating his own books on a full time basis. Like many illustrators for children, Gerstein is in tune with his own childhood as well as the world of color. Gerstein believed that childhood is "the well we draw upon—it is the source of everything" (p. 86) (*SATA*, v. 47, pp. 79-86).

ABOUT THE STORY

A woodcutter lives out his life on the "craggy mountains" of Tibet all the time longing to see other people, countries, even planets. When he dies a voice offers him choices for another life. He sees all those people, countries and planets he always wanted to see. His choices are familiar ones, but startling nonetheless. The beautiful pictures carry out the theme and view of life as eternal possibilities.

The author told us the story of waking up on the first morning after a change in his life and remembering the Tibetan Book of the Dead. Intrigued with how making choices had been important in his life, he based this story on his feelings about his own experience and the Hindu concept of carefully preparing yourself for the choices you have to make to create another life. Reincarnation becomes a metaphor for choice. The beauty of the illustrations and text sustain the interest of both primary grade children and adults. The fact that the woodcutter dies never having fulfilled his dreams has a powerful influence on many young people. One college student said, "I want those choices now!" The surprise ending also stirs strong reactions, from "It doesn't make any difference" to astonishment and disbelief. One student said the book was boring because it was so predictable. Another felt that the choice at the end was not believable—who would choose to be a girl if they could be a boy? The issues raised here are provocative for all ages, but expect different reactions from each age group.

DIALOGUE

Talk about What You Notice in the Story

● ●

The children in this neighborhood group "story hour" are in grades 3 to 6. They notice the pictures, the choices, the issues, and the specifics. They give each other things to think about. The teacher does not feel the need to belabor any of it.

● ●

James:	The pictures were good.
Murray:	It told a lesson that you always have to make choices in your life.
Agnes:	I agree.
Joan:	It seems like you can only go so far and then you have to tell the truth.
Jan:	I noticed that the man liked to fly kites and then when he died and became a girl he still liked to fly kites.
Lisa:	And when the little girl was born on the mountain, she loved to fly kites too.
Lisa:	You can never accomplish what you want to in life.
Christopher:	I thought it was funny he chose to be a girl.

Talk about How the Story Makes You Feel

● ●

Judging by the responses of the children this book at first seems more a book to wonder and think about than to feel about. Then Lori, with great feeling, speaks about the child touching the woodcutter's heart.

● ●

Sarah:	I liked the images the book gives. It gave me a light-hearted, happy feeling, like anything can happen.
Murray:	I think the book was good.
Melony:	I think one thing that I liked is that you always have to make choices.
Jennifer:	I'd have a hard time choosing.
Stephanie:	I wish it was true...that we could choose.
Jan:	I agree with Melony that you always have to make choices whether you die and are up in heaven. You have to make choices everywhere.
Joan:	You do?

Karen:	Not in heaven you don't.
Jan:	Yes you do.
Karen:	How do you know?
Jennifer:	You have to make choices right now.
Michelle:	His first life wasn't really so bad.
Megan:	I wonder why the end was like it was. It's hard to understand for me.
Lori:	A child touched his heart.

Talk about What the Story Reminds You of in Your Life

• •

Lori's remark strikes a deep chord in Kimberley. The teacher encourages the children to talk more about the things they bring up, such as being reminded of the Bible and the difference between being a boy and a girl. Jenny understands that reincarnation is a metaphor for making us think about the one life we have to live. Melony has a response about death not being so frightening.

• •

Kimberley:	It relates to the Bible.
TEACHER:	HOW DOES IT DO THAT?
Kimberley:	Because its about love.
Michelle:	I was surprised. The last part was good. Michael wanted him to be a boy. We wanted him to be a girl.
TEACHER:	DOES IT MATTER?
Michael:	No, it doesn't matter who you are or what you are.
Rebecca:	Yes it does. Like it decides how you're going to dress, and stuff like that.
Karen:	I never knew my great, great, great Grandpa, but I did know my great, great, great Grandma.
Kimberley:	*[Karen's sister]* What does that have to do with it?
Karen:	They fought about what I would be before I was born, a boy or a girl.
Rebecca:	How do you know?
Karen:	'Cause they told me.
Jenny:	We should learn to be happy with our own lives because not everyone has a chance to relive their life.
Lori:	It gave me a safe feeling about death.
Melony:	The book was warm and friendly. For the first time death seemed like a pleasant thing. Nothing about it was frightening. It felt good and right to be in this place called heaven.

The book concentrated on afterlife and merely mentions the death of the woodcutter.

Michelle: It gave me the chills.

Stephanie: The place where I was born will always be special to myself.

TEACHER FOCUS

Metaphor: The beauty of the book is that while Gerstein uses the metaphor of reincarnation, readers perceive that their choices are here and now in this life.

Research: A good way to develop alternate perspectives is to research Hindu beliefs and Tibetan culture.

Visual Literacy: The illustrations add new dimensions to the telling of the story.

COUNSELOR FOCUS

Choices: This is a "What is life all about?" book. Allow children time to hear the story, reflect, draw, and talk, and conversation will become more filled with meaning. The story has sufficient depth to warrant repeated use.

MAKING CONNECTIONS

Art: Gerstein has used the mandala (circular patterns or images) in the illustrations. In old Buddhist Eastern temples mandalas represented life from origin to end. Children may notice the circle and square patterns that depict inner and outer aspects of life. They may recall seeing kaleidoscopes; some may have had the experience of making mandala patterns with compasses. An art project may begin with an 8" square piece of colored paper with a circle cut out and a white paper underneath. Children may fill their circle with half dark and half light, half suns and half moons, half boys and half girls. Color with crayon or pencils.

BOOKS FOR FOLLOW-UP LITERATURE STUDIES

Starred titles have full entries elsewhere in the book.

*Cooney, Barbara. (1985). *Miss Rumphius*. Viking Press.
    Miss Rumphius was given a powerful structure for making choices. The reader is moved by an individual's responsibility for the world.

Gerstein, Mordicai. (1983). *Arnold of the Ducks*. Harper and Row.
    Mistaken for a fish, Arnold is picked up and cared for by a family of ducks. Later he is returned to his human family, but recognizes his other mother as she flies by.

Gerstein, Mordicai. (1984). *The Room*. Harper and Row.

     This book gives a kaleidoscope view of a room that shows how it changed with each renter over the years. Now the room is for rent again.

———. (1986). *Seal Mother*. Dial Books.

     A seal sheds her skin, becomes human, marries, and bears a son. After the son is grown the seal longs to return to the sea.

Graham, Bob. (1987). *Charlotte and Henry*. Viking Penguin Inc.

     In this primary-level chapter book with beautiful illustrations, Henry worries about and nurtures Charlotte who goes through her daring-dos unfettered by fear or worry.

Houston, Gloria. (1992). *My Great Aunt Arizona*. Illustrated by Susan Condie Lamb. Harper and Row.

     Arizona knew what her choices would be, but never had the opportunity to make them. She passed the longing on to her students.

Yorinks, Arthur. (1990). *Ugh*. Illustrated by Richard Egielski. Farrar, Straus & Giroux.

     Ugh invents the bicycle before humankind knows of the wheel.

Patricia Reilly Giff, *Today Was a Terrible Day*

• •

Publisher and Date: Viking, 1980
Illustrator: Susanna Natti
Audience Level: Grade one and up
Main Theme: Stereotyping
Other Possible Themes: Fear of Failure, Name Calling, Kindness, Learning, Rejection
Values to Target: Empathy

• •

ABOUT THE AUTHOR

Patricia Reilly Giff still lives in her native New York. She reports always having a book in her hand when she was young. After she read everything on the children's shelves in the library, she started with the adult books. Her father read all of *Evangeline* to her aloud when she was quite young.

She married a detective and they have three grown children. She always wanted to write, but pursued a career in education first. She taught in grades three through six and then became a reading specialist. She says that she has known so many children who had "hard lives and unhappy faces." She wanted to say something to these children. Other books by Patricia Giff include *Fourth Grade Celebrity, Next Year I'll Be Special, Have you Seen Hyacinth Macaw?,* and *The Winter Worm* (*SATA* v. 33, pp. 83-85).

ABOUT THE ILLUSTRATOR

The daughter of a school principal and an author, Susanna Natti grew up in Massachusetts. She reports that she knew by age eight that she wanted to be an illustrator. She and her favorite cousin spent much time drawing and making books just for the fun of it. She began art lessons when she was ten. Her first teacher taught her how to express motion and feeling in her drawings by quickly sketching the whole shape with the pencil before adding any detail. She still uses this method when she draws figures for such books as the Ronald Morgan series. She likes to use black and white line drawings and water color. She still resides in Massachusetts with her husband who is an electrical engineer. She does volunteer work in a high school classes for exceptional students (*SATA* v. 32, pp. 141-42).

ABOUT THE STORY

Ronald Morgan's bad day begins when he drops his pencil, crawls under the desk, and earns the name "Snakey" from his classmates. He eats the wrong lunch, goofs on his reading, and misses a catch for an easy out in the baseball game. He can't even be successful as plant monitor—he knocks over the teacher's favorite plant. Fortunately, he has a sensitive teacher, Miss Tyler, who gives him a most extraordinary note to take home. Susanna Natti's illustrations have characters with wonderful facial expressions and postures. The yellow pad reproduction of the note from the teacher works exceptionally well.

In this era of "pullouts" and special programs for "low kids" or "slower students," opportunities for expression of children's feelings are welcome. In classroom guidance, counselors find that children are *relieved* to be able to talk openly about ability grouping. The practice is glossed over by parents and teachers who don't wish to hurt children's feelings. "But *we* know who's in the low group anyway…" report the children who know just how Ronald Morgan feels.

DIALOGUE

Talk About What You Notice in the Story

● ●

This is an excellent reading lesson. For a start the teacher helps these second and third grade children recall the events of the story. Brandon notices the illustration and content of the teacher's note. Since the children ask for turns reading aloud, the teacher is able to simply pass the book around and allow the children to celebrate their success.

The teacher asked the students to recall what happened in the story to see how the author helped them to want to keep reading.

The children enjoyed assisting in re-constructing the story line on newsprint, and noting the feelings and thoughts of Ronald. They noted the following events in Ronald's day:

- Drops his pencil—Is called Snakey
- Signs his own homework—Children laugh
- Eats Jimmy's lunch by mistake
- Asks for help—Is insulted by Rosemary
- Shoots water on Joy Farley's dress
- Drops the ball in center field
- Has no lunch
- Makes a mistake in reading
- Knocks over the plant
- Gets the note
- Reads the note
- Brings a plant for Miss Tyler

● ●

TEACHER: THE FIRST PART OF RONALD'S DAY IS TERRIBLE!
Brandon: They're always laughing at Ronald and calling him Snakey.
Kristy: I don't like nicknames like that.
Beth: My daddy gave me a nickname. It's "Boo."
TEACHER: IS THAT DIFFERENT FROM RONALD'S BEING CALLED SNAKEY?
Beth: Sure. My daddy wasn't making fun of me.
Paula: The kids *are* making fun of Ronald Morgan.
Kristy: Rosemary wasn't nice at all.
Christopher: Neither were the guys playing baseball.
Teacher: What were you thinking when Miss Tyler first handed him the note?
Christopher: I thought, "Problems, problems!"
Brandon: I thought, "Oh no!"

Paula:	Me, too. I just *knew* it would be bad.
Eric:	I thought she was giving him extra reading sentences.
Kevin:	I thought his mama was going to have to come to school.
Christopher:	Right! Most times notes are *not* good.
TEACHER:	[REFERRING TO NEWSPRINT] WHERE DID YOU FEEL THE MOST EXCITED DURING THE READING?
Tiffany:	It turned from sad to happy when he read the note.
Brandon:	Hey! Can we see that page with the note again?
TEACHER:	SURE!
Eric:	I can read that!
TEACHER:	GREAT! READ IT SO WE CAN ALL HEAR IT NOW!
	[After Eric's reading there is spontaneous applause. Children wait with extraordinary patience as each child is given a turn to read the note. The group continues the applause in a celebrative manner.]

Talk about How the Story Makes You Feel

• •

In this Chapter I reading class, the children feel free enough to talk about their discomfort with school. The teacher recognizes that talk alone helps them to feel better about themselves.

• •

TEACHER:	HOW DO YOU SUPPOSE IT FEELS TO BE IN A GROUP LIKE THE ROCKETS INSTEAD OF THE MARINERS?
Paula:	Ronald Morgan felt sad. And he wasn't even very good for a Rocket.
Kristy:	I'd feel sort of embarrassed to be a Rocket.
Eric:	Some people have to go to special classes.
Paula:	And some go to "A.G." They're smarter. They think they're better.
	(In this school system A. G. is the abbreviation for academically gifted.)
TEACHER:	DOES "A.G." MEAN THEY CAN DO EVERYTHING BETTER?
Paula:	No, not everything.
Christopher:	Just some things like reading.
Eric:	If you're "A.G" you might not even be good at kick ball.
TEACHER:	RONALD MORGAN WASN'T "A.G.".
Paula:	Oh, I know *just* how Ronald Morgan felt. When I first came to second grade I was scared to come to school because I thought I couldn't remember how to read. I cried before school every day.

Tiffany:	Me, too. In the first grade I felt that way all the time. Some days Mama couldn't even make me get on the bus. I'd be sick.
TEACHER:	IT SEEMS TO ME THAT ALL OF YOU FEEL BETTER THAN THAT NOW.
M. J.:	I still sometimes feel like there's this big pile of work and I can't do it fast enough.
TEACHER:	IT GETS PRETTY HARD SOMETIMES. HOW DID RONALD HANDLE HIS SAD FEELINGS?
Tiffany:	Well, Miss Tyler helped him. She was nice.
TEACHER:	DO YOU THINK HE HELPED HIMSELF, TOO?
Tiffany:	After the good note he called his friend and told him he could read.
TEACHER:	SHARING GOOD NEWS HELPS.
Kristy:	Yeah. I tell my mom good stuff.
Christopher:	And Ronald Morgan brought Miss Tyler a plant for her birthday. *[laughing]* She needed one.
Paula:	That was nice of him!

Talk about What the Story Reminds You of in Your Life

• •

The teacher takes the lead in making children aware of how language is used to hurt and to help others. While children easily recognize hurtful words, they need help in re-constructing language that is helpful to others.

• •

TEACHER:	I NOTICED HOW RONALD ASKED ROSEMARY FOR HELP. WHO REMEMBERS HER EXACT REPLY? CAN YOU SAY IT THE WAY SHE DID?
Paula:	*[making a face and hamming it up]* "Ronald Morgan, you will never get to the third grade because *you* can't read. Some Rocket you are!"

• •

The children enjoyed dramatizing "put downs." It seemed to be very cathartic. In the role play, even a *nice* kid gets a chance to say something mean! After a good laugh at the all-too-familiar words and tones, these children were ready to brainstorm kinder words.

• •

TEACHER:	YOU ARE ALL SO GOOD AT IMITATING PUT DOWNS. YOU MUST HAVE HEARD SUCH REMARKS BEFORE SOMEWHERE.
Christopher:	Oh, we hear a bunch of stuff like that every day.

TEACHER:	WE KNOW WE DON'T WANT TO BE LIKE ROSEMARY OR BILLY. LET'S TAKE THE EXAMPLE ON THE BASEBALL FIELD AND THINK OF DIFFERENT WORDS TO SAY. HERE IS THE HURTFUL REMARK: "YOU LOST THE GAME, SNAKEY!" WHO CAN SAY IT LIKE A PUT DOWN?
Christopher:	*[with sarcasm]* "You just lost the game, Snakey!"
TEACHER:	DID HE HAVE TO SAY THAT?
Kristy:	No. Ronald felt bad enough already!
Eric:	He could have said, "Shake it off!"
M.J.:	Or, "That's O K. You'll get it next time."
TEACHER:	THE AUTHOR OF THIS STORY, PATRICIA GIFF, IS A TEACHER. WHAT WOULD YOU LIKE TO SAY TO HER IF SHE WERE HERE?
Paula:	I'd say, "You wrote it good."
Christopher:	I'd tell her Happy Birthday—if it was her birthday! If it's not, I'd ask her when it is.

TEACHER FOCUS

Plot: Outlining the events of the story demonstrates how the writer creates the story line with a "surprise" at what Miss Tyler's note said.

Writing and Punctuating Dialogue: Children can write conversations using the story as a model. (See activity in "Making Connections.")

Language: Ronald is in the "Rockets." Explore how language in used to categorize and define people.

COUNSELOR FOCUS

Empathy: The story is so sensitively portrayed that children quickly identify with Ronald's feelings. Ronald's awareness of his own capabilities may inspire children to use their own.

Stereotyping: Children have real feelings about being labeled that need to be addressed.

Name Calling: Ronald is hurt by name calling. The counselor can focus on preventing hurt feelings from both sides of painful exchanges. What are better ways to express anger than calling names? How can one who receives painful words handle it? (See activity in "Making Connections.")

MAKING CONNECTIONS

Writing or Role Play: This story demonstrates the power of "encouraging words" and "hurtful words." Older students may choose to write short incidents from school life that end with a hurtful put-down. The baseball game at recess (p. 12-13) could serve as a model for original stories. Encouraging words can be substituted in a version with a happier ending.

Children will often come up with what they perceive to be encouragement, with such words as, "You could do better if you would just practice more." The difference between this and an empathetic response is subtle, but important. If we already feel bad, we do not need a lecture. At that time we need to hear, "It's O.K., Don't worry, Tough luck!" Later we can be reminded to practice more.

Appreciation Time or Message Board: One sixth grade teacher did an appreciation time with her fifth/sixth grade class as a response to this story. This exercise expanded into a message board for appreciative notes in her classroom. (The yellow note pad in the book makes a great model for a bulletin board.)

BOOKS FOR FOLLOW-UP LITERATURE STUDIES

Giff, Patricia Reilly. (1984). *The Beast in Ms. Rooney's Room*. Dell.
   In this short chapter book for primary grades, Richard Best is "left back" in the second grade. He overcomes his feelings of inadequacy.
———. (1988). *Happy Birthday, Ronald Morgan*. Illustrated by Susanna Natti. Penguin.
   Ronald Morgan is not sure anyone, even his best friend, will remember his birthday. Children will enjoy knowing the same characters from *Today Was a Terrible Day*.
———. (1986). *Watch Out, Ronald Morgan*. Illustrated by Susanna Natti. Penguin.
   Ronald needs glasses, and overcomes his self-conscious feelings with help from peers and adults.
Korschunow, Irina. (1986). *Adam Draws Himself a Dragon*. Harper and Row.
   Adam draws a dragon who becomes a friendly listener. This is another short episodic chapter book for primary grades.
Smith, Janice Lee. (1988). *The Show and Tell War*. Illustrated by Dick Gackenbach. Harper.
   Adam Joshua worries about his baby sister and his dog, and is afraid of Elliot Banks, the school's worst bully. He has many misadventures such as stealing a book from the library, pretending to be sick so he can stay home from school, and getting upstaged at show-and-tell time. Any of the five episodic chapters can stand alone for a single reading.
Viorst, Judith. (1972). *Alexander and the Terrible, Horrible, No Good Very Bad Day*. Antheneum.
   Everything goes wrong for Alexander who decides maybe it's better to move to Australia.

Helen Griffith,
Grandaddy's Place

● ●

Publisher and Date: Greenwillow, 1987
Illustrator: James Stevenson
Audience Level: Grades one and up
Main Theme: Extended Family Relationships
Other Possible Themes: Shyness, Kindness, Aging, Nature, Farm
 Life
Values to Target: Self-Awareness, Self-Knowledge, Empathy

● ●

ABOUT THE AUTHOR

Helen Griffith lives in Wilmington, Delaware, the town where she grew up. She always liked to write when she was a young girl, but her first career was a secretary for a building products company. She began writing nonfiction for magazines. At age 40 she started writing for children. She especially loves all kinds of animals. Her first children's series was *Alex and the Cat.* Her hobby is bird watching (*SATA* v. 39, p. 97).

ABOUT THE ILLUSTRATOR

James Stevenson grew up in several small towns in New York state. He loved movies and comic books as a child, and began drawing at a very early age. He graduated from Yale and became an officer in the Marine Corps. After his military duty he became a reporter for *Life* Magazine, and later joined the staff of *The New Yorker* where he created cartoon ideas. In the past twenty years he has written and illustrated numerous picture books. He also illustrates for other authors like Helen Griffith, Jack Prelutsky, and Charlotte Zolotow (*SATA* v.42, pp. 180-83).

ABOUT THE STORY

Janetta arrives with her mother on the train from Baltimore to meet her Grandaddy. A city girl, she is shy at first of him and the animals and the place. "I don't want to stay here!" she firmly announces. Her mother frets about Janetta's behavior. "Let her be," says Grandaddy. Shyness turns to real fear as the mule makes strange noises and the wasps buzz around the porch. She runs into the house for safety. "Nothing here likes me!" At night they all sit under the stars on the front steps and Grandaddy, with just the right touches of humor, uses his gift as a storyteller to make friends with Janetta. Soon she is laughing at the mule story. Her comfort with the place grows. Grandaddy takes her fishing. She makes friends with the cat, even the mule. On another star-filled evening as they sit on the front steps, Janetta starts thinking of names for the animals. Then we know the bonding has begun.

The author balances the point of view of Janetta and her grandaddy. The effect is a process of developing accommodation between characters. Stevenson's delightful illustrations enhance the text, helping to demonstrate how the relationship builds slowly through the sharing of experiences.

DIALOGUE

Talk about What You Notice in the Story

• •

Frequently children such as Larry make comments about whether a story is true or real. The teacher asks if Larry wants to say more, but doesn't make a judgment call. These third grade children then work out together how fantasy is used to understand real things. Heather sums it up succinctly. The teacher's comments about the chapters is worth noting because the chapters correspond to the change in Janetta and therefore help the children understand the character development.

• •

TEACHER:	I COULD TELL BY YOUR FACES YOU ENJOYED THE STORY. THINK FOR A MINUTE AND DECIDE WHAT YOU REMEMBER BEST RIGHT NOW.
Larry:	Before we start, is this story for real?
TEACHER:	CAN YOU SAY MORE ABOUT WHAT YOU MEAN BY THAT, LARRY?
Larry:	What I mean is you can't talk to a star!
Heather:	Well, of course not, but that doesn't mean the story is not for real. It *is*!
Larry:	*[pausing, reflecting]* Yes... I guess that's what I was thinking.
Kayla:	Grandaddy is just playing with her! You can tell that easy.
Kristy:	Well, a star *can* fall out of the sky anyway.
Larry:	I know it, but a mule can't jump up in the sky and let a star get on his back.
TEACHER:	WE HAVE A GOOD CONVERSATION GOING NOW.

Justin:	Well, you were right, Larry, that you can't talk to a star. I think this is kind of like a bedtime story.
TEACHER:	A BEDTIME STORY...
Justin:	Bedtime stories don't have to be all real.
Heather:	*[with finality]* So, it's like I said. It's for real. The whole story is real and there are tall tales in the story.
Kayla:	Well, what I think is that Grandaddy was just telling fibs, but in a good kind of way.
TEACHER:	YOU ARE MAKING SOME GREAT COMMENTS. WHO HAS SOMETHING ELSE YOU NOTICE?
Heather:	The house did not look good to her. It was an old broken down shack. And it had the wasps' nest.
Paula:	I think she was scared of the wasps and all because she was from the city and didn't know any better.
M.J.:	I noticed that it must have been a while back in time since the girl and her mother rode a train.
Jonathan:	I've *never* ridden a train in my life. *[M.J. shared information about trains that run through the local area.]*
Brandon:	*[who lives on a farm]* I thought it was funny that she was afraid of all the animals, even the chickens!
Jonathan:	She didn't even know what the mule was! I thought everybody knew about mules.
Paula:	Well, she was from the city and the place looked weird to her.
Kristy:	She didn't even know her grandaddy. Mine lives right across the street from me!
TEACHER:	KRISTY, I THINK YOU ARE LUCKY!
Paula:	The little girl in the story was lucky too because her grandaddy was fun!
Marcus:	The best part was when Grandaddy talked to the fish.
Julie:	I liked that picture of the star falling.
TEACHER:	YOU HAVE NOTICED DIFFERENT PARTS OF THE STORY. NOW LET'S THINK ABOUT HOW THE STORY HAS SEVERAL CHAPTERS—A BEGINNING, MIDDLE, AND END. WHAT DO YOU NOTICE ABOUT THE STRUCTURE OF THE STORY?
Douglas:	It was kinda' like in the beginning when she said, "I don't even like the place"—and she ended up liking it. It's like saying you can't judge a book by it's cover.
TEACHER:	SO, JANETTA CHANGED FROM THE BEGINNING OF THE STORY TO THE END.

Leigh Ann:	It was like Grandaddy wanted to tell all those stories and make her feel important.
Heather:	Well, what I really thought was that he was trying to help her have a little fun.
Douglas:	It was when she started naming the animals, then we knew she liked them and she liked the place.

Talk about How the Story Makes You Feel

• •

The teacher values Justin's offer to use body language for communicating feeling and then requests words to do the same thing.

• •

TEACHER:	SEVERAL OF YOU NOTICED HOW JANETTA WAS AFRAID. THE AUTHOR, HELEN GRIFFITH, USED THE EXPRESSION THAT JANETTA IS SHY OF THE PLACE. SOME OF YOU KNOW HOW THAT FEELS.
Brandon:	It's a little bit scared feeling.
Justin:	I can show you "shy."
TEACHER:	GREAT! DO YOU MIND STANDING UP SO WE CAN SEE? *[Justin does body language for shy which is followed by enthusiastic responses of "Oh, yeah," "I've felt that way," "Can I do it too?"]*
TEACHER:	THAT'S GREAT BODY LANGUAGE. NOW WHO CAN SAY MORE IN WORDS ABOUT BEING SHY?
Jackie:	Whenever I get shy or scared it is weird. I feel my toes start to wrinkle up.
Paula:	My daddy knows some people and I don't know them. When I talk to them, I get shy.
Jody:	Yeah, I might be shy at somebody's house when I don't know the people.
Kristy:	I might be shy at the grocery store, especially if I didn't know where the soup was and my mom told me to get it.
Corey:	I was at McDonald's and I went out on the playground. A girl said "hey" to me and I ran back in through the door. *[laughter]*
TEACHER:	THESE "SHY" STORIES ARE FUN. OF COURSE, THERE'S MORE TO THE STORY THAN JANETTA BEING SHY. CAN YOU SAY MORE ABOUT HOW YOU FEEL ABOUT THE STORY?
Tonetta:	It is a good and happy feeling story.
TEACHER:	CAN YOU SAY MORE ABOUT THAT?
Tonetta:	Grandaddy just let Janetta be. He didn't get upset or nothing like that.

TEACHER:	SO YOU LIKED HOW HE LET HER BE?
Tonetta:	Well, if he had been grouchy all the time she would never have liked the farm or felt any better.

Talk about What the Story Reminds You of in Your Life

• •

The teacher's comments lead the children to view aging as positive. Shania is already beyond that and wants to be a grandma.

• •

TEACHER:	I SUPPOSE OUR GRANDPARENTS AND OTHER RELATIVES ARE IMPORTANT PEOPLE TO ALL OF US.
Jonathan:	This story reminds me of how my grandaddy pretends like he's pulling a nickel out of his ear.
Paula:	They say it's lucky to pull a nickel out of your ear. Except I don't think you can really do it.
Kayla:	It's a trick!
TEACHER:	SO GETTING OLDER DOESN'T MEAN ALWAYS THERE'S NO FUN.
Tonetta:	Some people think of getting old as bad, but Grandaddy shows that even old people can keep some fun in life.
Miranda:	My most favorite place of all is Grandma's house.
Shania:	*[proudly]* I'm going to be a grandma when I grow up.
Miranda:	I guess grandparents can be more relaxed than parents.
Douglas:	Well, I guess it's harder for parents since they are in charge of us mostly every day.

TEACHER FOCUS

Family: The story depicts an extended family relationship between young and old. Grandaddy makes the bonding happen with his patience, humor, and acceptance. The relationship then becomes reciprocal. If the book *Georgia Music* is also used, children can follow the character development.

Ageism: Tonetta recognized the positive view of older people. Children can do a web of positive characteristics of Grandaddy with evidence to support each adjective.

Transportation: Passenger trains have changed since the time of this story. In what ways? Children may be inspired to research the history of railroads. Most communities have railroad "fans" or retired railroad workers who are delighted to share information and stories about trains.

COUNSELOR FOCUS

Shyness: Children feel comforted to share with a group stories of their own shyness. By so doing they learn that such feelings are common to all.

Naming: A discussion of naming is fruitful in helping children to understand that naming is an archetypal symbol of power and inclusion. When Janetta began to name the animals, she gave up her fear and began to care for them. A related counseling activity can be to share how each of us were named by people who cared for us. Children enjoy telling the story of how they were named.

Nonverbal Communication: Although this was not the counselor's agenda in the lesson above, Justin's idea of depicting shyness led the group to new awareness of body language.

MAKING CONNECTIONS

Music: A lively grandma is depicted in the title song on Kathy Fink's tape, "Grandma Slid Down the Mountain" (Rounder Records, One Camp St., Cambridge, MA 02140). "She'll Be Comin' Round the Mountain" will do fine too!

BOOKS FOR FOLLOW-UP LITERATURE STUDIES

Greenfield, Eloise. (1988). *Grandpa's Face.* Illustrated by Floyd Cooper. Philomel.
> Tamika is frightened when she discovers her grandfather in his stage make-up, which is unlike his usual loving face.

Griffith, Helen. (1985). *Georgia Music.* Illustrated by James Stevenson. Greenwillow Books.
> Children who enjoyed the story will welcome the sequel to *Grandaddy's Place.* The little girl and her mother come back to Georgia every year. There is music in the air—cricket chirps, tree frog trills, and the sassy mockingbird's song. Janetta and her grandfather work in the garden and sit on the porch where he makes music on the mouth organ. One summer, however, is not the same. "I'm not sick," says Grandaddy, "just mighty tired." They take him back to Baltimore, where he still feels tired. The little girl gets out the old mouth organ and practices until she can play the "Georgia Music." She makes him smile. The two books make a good sequence because the children love the fact that Grandaddy reappears and that the relationship can be reciprocal.

Howard, Elizabeth. (1991). *Aunt Flossie's Hats (and Crab Cakes Later).* Illustrated by James Ransome. Clarion.
> Aunt Flossie shares stories of the past and lets her granddaughters play dress up in her old hats as a Sunday afternoon ritual.

Schwartz, Amy. (1987). *Oma and Bobo.* Bradbury.
> Alice loves her dog but her grandmother is more than indifferent, until, of course, Oma (Grandmother) and Bobo become bonded.

Stolz, Mary. (1988). *Storm in the Night.* Illustrated by Pat Cummings. Harper and Row.

> Sitting with his grandfather during a thunderstorm, Thomas hears stories about the time his grandfather was afraid of storms.

Ezra Jack Keats,
Whistle for Willie

• •

Publisher and Date: Viking, 1964
Illustrator: Ezra Jack Keats
Audience Level: Kindergarten and up
Main Theme: Perseverance
Other Possible Themes: Diligence, Patience, Celebration of
 Sensory Experience
Values to Target: Learning

• •

ABOUT THE AUTHOR

Ezra Jack Keats grew up poor, in a Brooklyn, New York, tenement house. He began painting and drawing at age four. His mother was proud of her son's talent, but his disapproving father was convinced that Keats would never be able to support himself as an artist.

Keats won three scholarships to art schools, but could not afford to attend. His first job as an artist was painting murals for the government-funded Works Project Administration. He decided to become an illustrator after serving as a camouflage expert in World War II.

Keats illustrated books by other authors for nine years before writing and illustrating his own stories. His books most often feature African-Americans with whom he shared the common experiences of childhood. Keats uses a variety of art media in his books, including painting and collage.

Before his death in 1983, he wrote and illustrated 21 children's books. He won the Caldecott Medal in 1963 for *The Snowy Day* (*SATA* v. 57, pp. 77-87).

ABOUT THE STORY

Peter wishes he could whistle for his dog, Willie. But each time he puckers his lips, nothing happens. So, he makes himself content doing things he *can* do. He can twirl, crawl in a box, play dress up in his father's hat, and run from his shadow. Finally, he scrambles under a carton to hide from Willie and tries the whistle one more time.

The basic ingredients of self-esteem are feeling lovable and capable. There are many celebrations of "I can do that!" in the life of a young child. *Whistle for Willie* not only celebrates the pride that Peter experiences after his diligent effort, but also his ability to happily engage in other pastimes, diversions, and discoveries while he is trying!

DIALOGUE

Talk about What You Notice in the Story

• •

The pacing of the story is important in allowing the responses that come along the way to become part of the story telling. Actually experiencing the whistle enables these 6- and 7-year-old children to feel like Peter.

• •

[These spontaneous remarks and squeals of delight accompany the reading:]

"Look at the stoplight! What happened?"
"It just looks like that to Peter."
"He's dizzy!"
"What's that red and white pole for?"
"Oh, it's a barbershop..."
"Somebody wrote and drew all over the wall with paint!"
"Oh look! The hat is *big*!"
"That looks like real wallpaper!"
"Can we make a book with wallpaper like that?"
"He can walk to the store! I can't do that. It's too far to the store."
"Oh look! Willie doesn't know that's Peter in the box."
"Willie *likes* the whistle."
"Can we whistle now?"
"Let's read it again!"

TEACHER: WELL, WE CAN DO BOTH. WE CAN WHISTLE AND WE CAN READ IT AGAIN. I CAN TELL YOU ALL REALLY WANT TO TRY A WHISTLE RIGHT NOW. YOU HAVE ALL WAITED PATIENTLY LIKE PETER. OKAY, LET'S ALL

HAVE A TURN TRYING A WHISTLE. ONE AT A TIME, SO YOU CAN HEAR
YOURSELVES!

Talk about How the Story Makes You Feel

● ●

The teacher leads the children to understand the sequence of the
story, to be physically involved, and to be conscious of the language.

A review of the illustrations helps children construct a sequence
of what Peter *can* do. They record the following on newsprint:

● He can twirl around
● He can crawl in a box
● He can run from his shadow
● He can draw a chalk line
● He can talk like his daddy
● He can whistle

● ●

Holly:	I can twirl. When I twirled around I thought the living room was turning. I said, "Mama, why are you doing that to the living room?"
Carol:	I was twirling outside and I fell down. The trees were looking down at me.
Malea:	*[with a giggle]* I *love* that part when he puts on his daddy's hat.
TEACHER:	*[CREATING A SPONTANEOUS ROLE PLAY]* WHAT WOULD YOU SAY TO THE MIRROR IF YOU DRESSED UP IN YOUR DADDY'S HAT?
Malea:	*[in a deep voice]* I'd say, "Hi, Honey. I'm home." *[All deep voices now...]*
Chad:	I'd say, "What's for dinner?"
Johnny:	"How's your day? Where's Johnny?"
Nicholas:	"I'm worn out!"
Trent:	"I'm going out to drive the tractor."
TEACHER:	I LIKE YOUR FUNNY VOICES. LET'S LOOK BACK AT PETER. HOW IS HE FEELING?
Kenny:	He's having fun! And *we're* having fun!
Kristina:	Happy that he can play and happy that he can whistle.
Tyrone:	Proud!
TEACHER:	LEARNING TO WHISTLE WASN'T ALL THAT EASY FOR PETER.
Kenny:	No. It took a long time.
Tyrone:	*[unable to resist lip puckering once more]* It is hard! I can do it!

[More whistles!]

TEACHER: I AM IMPRESSED WITH ALL THESE WHISTLES. I BELIEVE ALL OF YOU ARE PROUD!

Talk about What the Story Reminds You of in Your Life

• •

The concept of theme is introduced as the children identify similar experiences to Peter's.

• •

TEACHER: KENNY JUST SAID IT WAS HARD FOR PETER. WHAT IS SOMETHING YOU CAN DO THAT WAS HARD, OR TOOK A LONG TIME TO LEARN?

A Chorus: "Tying my shoes." "Blowing bubbles." "Riding a bicycle without training wheels."

TEACHER: ADAM, HOW DID YOU FEEL?

Adam: I fell off my bike 16 times and I cried. Now that was after training wheels were off.

TEACHER: I'M GUESSING THAT NOW YOU CAN RIDE A BIKE.

Adam: Ye-es! It's *easy*!

TEACHER: AND JUSTIN—ABOUT THE BUBBLES...

Justin: Well, I got gum *all* on my face and in my ears.
[laughter]

TEACHER: LET'S FINISH BY DRAWING WHAT WE CAN DO AND JUST ENJOY OUR PROUD FEELINGS.

TEACHER FOCUS

Story Structure: As the teacher involves young children physically by role playing the things Peter *can* do, she is also teaching the basics of the story structure.

Comparison: See connecting activity with *The Very Quiet Cricket* in "Making Connections."

Theme: For younger children sharing experiences like the character in the story is an introduction to theme.

Cities: Ezra Jack Keats grew up in a poor section of New York. What can we learn about the city from this story and other stories by the author? Children can infer what else a city looks like. This may lead to Map Study. Find New York on the map. How do we infer from a map about the size of a city? Discover why and how cities grow.

COUNSELOR FOCUS

Sensory Awareness/Role Play: Role play the story to demonstrate how all the senses help us know what is around us. What senses are we using? Other books by Keats, such as *The Snowy Day,* invite similar experiences.

Patience/Perseverance: Invite children's understanding that mastering new tasks doesn't occur instantly. This can be accomplished through group sharing of experiences about learning something new or art activities to stimulate discussion on the topic. Did Peter get frustrated in learning something new? Talk more about this negative feeling and how to manage it, relating back to experiences children identify.

MAKING CONNECTIONS

Comparing the Language of Stories: The children in one reading class made a spontaneous connection. When the teacher read the words, "He blew till his cheeks were tired. But nothing happened...," several children added in a chorus, "Not a sound." They looked at each other, amazed at their own reaction. These words were not on the page! One child exclaimed, "That's from the cricket book! This book is like the cricket book." The group then was prompted to examine the similarities between this story and *The Very Quiet Cricket* by Eric Carle. They were able to discuss the similarities of theme in the two stories: "They both were tired of waiting." "Peter kept on trying." "He *was* like the very quiet cricket." "Finally, in both stories, something happened!"

Music: The happy tone of the story can be re-experienced by singing the title song from the Ella Jenkins recording "You Sing a Song." The children have a chance to mime different instruments and to try humming and clapping to the beat, as well as whistling.

Art: Children notice Keats' collage and are very attracted to his use of multimedia. A class can create a book with a page to celebrate what each child *can* do. Children can examine the illustrations and make suggestions for supplies for the collage pages. Silhouettes of children's profiles in the style of Keats can be cut from dark paper for the foreground of each child's page.

Poetry/ Choral Reading: Jack Prelutsky's poem "Whistling" connects well with the story. Children enjoyed a choral reading. (The poem can be found in *The Big Book of Poetry*, Steck Vaughn Reading Links Series.)

BOOKS FOR FOLLOW-UP LITERATURE STUDIES

A Companion Book

Keats, Ezra Jack. (1967). *Peter's Chair*. Harper and Row.
>Peter has to be quiet because there's a new baby in the house. What's more, his parents are even planning to paint his old high chair and crib for his little sister. Peter decides to take his dog, Willy, and the chair with him when he runs away. He tries out the chair and finds that it's much too small for him.

Other Titles

Brown, Marcia. (1961). *Once A Mouse*. Scribner.
>This is a fable from India with a little lesson about a mouse whose sense of accomplishment goes to his head.

Carlstrom, Nancy White. (1987). *The Moon Came Too*. Illustrated by Stella Ormai. MacMillan.
>A young child takes charge and happily plans exactly what to pack to go to grandma's house. She chooses what is important to her, including the moon!

Greenfield, Eloise. (1988). *Nathaniel Talking*. Illustrated by Jan Spivey Gilchrist. Black Butterfly Children's Books.
>Among children today learning rap may be as important as learning to whistle. Nathaniel shows us how.

Leah Komaiko, *Annie Bananie*

• •

Publisher and Date: Harper and Row, 1987
Illustrator: Laura Cornell
Audience Level: Kindergarten through second grade
Main Theme: Separation
Other Possible Themes: Friendship, Imaginary Play, Sadness
Values to Target: Connection

• •

ABOUT THE AUTHOR

Among other things, Leah Komaiko has been a stand-up comedian. She was born in Chicago and was writing poetry by age eight. Her college degree is in creative writing, and she has written for films and magazines. She now resides in both New York and Los Angeles (from book jacket).

ABOUT THE ILLUSTRATOR

Laura Cornell was born and grew up in California; she planned to go to medical school but then decided to fulfill a childhood dream and become an illustrator. She lives in New York City (from book jacket).

ABOUT THE STORY

The rhyming text is in the voice of the child narrator who has discovered that her friend, Ann, is moving away. The pictures relate all the wonderful times they have had together in the past. At first the narrator expresses anger at the thought of losing her best friend. Then, when Annie Bananie cries, she comforts her, and in the end they look forward to a different kind of relationship.

The zany adventures remembered by these best friends are totally captivating. We never tire of the pictures and rhyming text. The power of the book lies in the thoroughly satisfying emotional journey the two experience, going from anger to sadness, to acceptance, and finally to a new kind of relationship that allows for other friends as well. The legendary nature of their remembrances are in perfect contrast to the realistic sadness of their pending separation. The author has put the good times in pictures and the sadness into words.

DIALOGUE

• •

Six second grade students met with their teacher in the reading resource room. Darcie, having become familiar with the process, started the discussion.

• •

Talk about What You Notice in the Story

• •

When David makes a judgment comment (i.e., the title is weird), the teacher offers information and requests clarification of terms. The value of her contribution is that David and Sonia are on the verge of understanding why the author used exaggeration. The discussion might have taken a different turn if the teacher had chosen to respond to Bradley's remark about his parents' divorce.

• •

Darcie:	Who is going to start?
TEACHER:	PERHAPS PEOPLE WOULD LIKE A FEW MINUTES TO THINK BEFORE WE BEGIN.
Bradley:	The pictures help you follow along.
Jason:	I didn't need any help—the words were easy.
David:	Annie Bananie is a weird title. Is it a real name?
Sonia:	No, it's like a game you play with names.
TEACHER:	THERE WAS A SONG CALLED THE "NAME GAME" THAT WAS POPULAR IN THE SIXTIES THAT PUT ENDINGS ON TO NAMES IN RHYME.
Michael:	That was a long time ago. How old are you?
TEACHER:	I'M THIRTY-NINE YEARS OLD.
Darcie:	Jason said the title was weird.
Jason:	No, I didn't say it. David said it was weird.
Darcie:	Okay, whoever, but Annie was weird, and her friend didn't mind it.
Jason:	They were both weird.
TEACHER:	WHAT DO YOU MEAN BY WEIRD?
Michael:	They did some weird stuff. Look at the pictures.
Bradley:	Yeah, read some of the stuff, brushing teeth with mud, tying a brother to a tree, now that's weird.
TEACHER:	HAVE YOU EVER DONE "WEIRD STUFF" WITH A FRIEND?
All:	Yeah!
Sonia:	I think it was sad that Annie was moving away.
Darcie:	But we don't know how far she's moving.
Michael:	Maybe they can still see each other.
Bradley:	We don't know why they are moving. Maybe their parents are getting a divorce. I had to move when my parents got a divorce.
TEACHER:	COULD WE GO BACK FOR A MINUTE TO THE WEIRD STUFF AGAIN? DO YOU THINK THEY ACTUALLY DID ALL THAT OR WERE THEY EXAGGERAT-ING?
David:	Probably, because your mother wouldn't let you tie up your brother.
Sonia:	They are making it up so other people think they are great friends.

Talk about How the Story Makes You Feel

• •

The teacher makes the children conscious of the narrator's role. This helps the children see the differences in the feelings of the two characters. Darcie is very insightful about the relationship of hurt and anger. Jason follows with another wise comment about the feeling of guilt and "acting angry."

• •

TEACHER: SONIA, EARLIER YOU SAID THE BOOK WAS SAD. WHAT WAS THE NARRATOR FEELING IN THE BEGINNING OF THE STORY?

Michael: Who's the narrator?

Darcie: Annie's friend. She was mad because Annie was moving away.

David: It wasn't her fault. She shouldn't be mad.

Darcie: Well, her feelings were hurt so she was acting mad.

TEACHER: YOU DON'T THINK SHE WAS ANGRY?

Jason: Yes, she was angry, but it's like when you do something wrong at home and you get in trouble and your mom yells and shouts at you. You act mad at your mother but really I get mad at myself because I did it.

TEACHER: HAVE ANY OF YOU HAD THE SAME EXPERIENCE?

Bradley: Yeah.

Sonia: I don't think so.

TEACHER: WAS THERE ANY PLACE IN THE STORY WHERE THE NARRATOR'S FEELINGS CHANGED?

Michael: Well, she felt bad when Annie started to cry.

Darcie: She wasn't thinking about Annie. Annie is going to miss her too.

Michael: They decide they can make new friends.

Sonia: You can make new friends when you move.

Jason: It's not easy.

David: It is for me.

Talk about What the Story Reminds You of in Your Life

• •

These children are experienced book discussers. They talk about genre, format, and make comparisons to other titles. The teacher respects the opinions of the children, and shows that she doesn't forget what they say. She catches Bradley in an interesting contradiction.

• •

Bradley: Do we have to read any more books like this?

TEACHER: DO YOU WANT TO?

Bradley: No, I want to read chapter books! This was babyish.

Sonia:	No, it isn't; there just isn't enough details.
Darcie:	Sometimes short books are good when you don't have much time.
Jason:	I think I like nonfiction, not fiction.
TEACHER:	SO AM I HEARING CORRECTLY THAT NOT MANY OF YOU LIKED THIS BOOK?
Michael:	It was okay.
Darcie:	I liked the pictures.
Bradley:	I think it's a girl's book.
TEACHER:	BUT YOU DID SAY IT REMINDED YOU OF YOUR OWN LIFE.
Bradley:	Yeah, I guess so, but I like *The Boxcar Children* books.
Sonia:	I think it was okay. We talked about it so it was okay.
TEACHER:	THANK YOU.
Darcie:	Did you like it?
TEACHER:	YES, I ENJOYED IT.

TEACHER FOCUS

Language: The poetry of the story can be relished for both sound and meaning.

Exaggeration and Humor: The author's literary device of exaggeration can be connected to other kinds of humor children understand in tall tales, jokes, or common expressions in everyday language.

COUNSELOR FOCUS

Change and Loss: *Annie Bananie* can be a good introduction to a new student or friendship group because it addresses both the good times friends have together and the inevitable changes and transitions.

Naming: A successful icebreaker for the group may be to use rhyming words or alliteration to make a "funny name" for each group member. Examples for rhyming words: "Andy Dandy, Heather Feather." Examples for alliterative words: "Jennifer Jellybean," "Miranda Moonlight." Children can draw pictures of themselves incorporating the theme of the "funny name."

MAKING CONNECTIONS

Letter Writing: A good follow-up activity is to write letters to the Annies in the children's lives who have gone away. The pain of separation is often followed by forgetting about friends and even relatives who have moved away. The book reminds children of the pain of separation, and the emotion prompts the desire to communicate with someone once close to you.

BOOKS FOR FOLLOW-UP LITERATURE STUDIES

Henkes, Kevin. (1988). *Chester's Way*. Greenwillow Books.
>Chester and Wilson are the best of friends because they are so much alike. Along comes Lilly who isn't like them at all. She upsets their lives for awhile, but then adds interest.

MacLachlan, Patricia. (1986). *Sarah Plain and Tall*. Caedmon.
>Life on the plains in the early United States was difficult without a wife and mother. Sarah answers the newspaper advertisement for a mother. Father and children write letters to Sarah hoping she will say "yes" to joining them.

Waber, Bernard. (1988). *Ira Says Goodbye*. Houghton Mifflin.
>Ira is heartbroken at the news that Reggie is moving. Reggie, on the other hand, seems to be excited about moving and not sad about leaving Ira. Accommodation is reached.

Leo Lionni,
Frederick

• •

Publisher and Date: Pantheon, 1967
Illustrator: Leo Lionni
Audience Level: Kindergarten and up
Main Theme: Beauty
Other Possible Themes: Work, Art, Fairness, Sharing, Fables, Poetry
Values to Target: Aesthetics, Fairness

• •

ABOUT THE AUTHOR

Leo Lionni is an accomplished filmmaker, sculptor, painter, graphic artist, designer, and children's book author. He was born in Holland, became an American citizen in 1945, and later moved to Italy. Lionni has two sons but does not claim any special insights into the psychology of children. Leonni says that he writes "for that part of us, of myself and of my friends, which has never changed, which is still a child." Lionni creates fables that focus on individuality, self-reliance, and aesthetic value. *Little*

Blue and Little Yellow was written for his grandchildren and started his career in children's books. He would like to be appreciated for the coherence of form and content in his books. He says that sometimes pictures form first in his mind and sometimes text. He is particularly fond of birds and has several of his own (*CLR* v. 7, pp. 119-21).

ABOUT THE STORY

Frederick is one of several books in which Lionni poses moral dilemmas. Frederick is a part of a mouse community busily hunting down nuts, berries, and grain to store for winter. As the other mice rush hither and yon, they pass Frederick who seems to be doing nothing. They ask him what he is doing and he responds with a description of his work: "I am gathering colors, warmth from the sun, words, all to help us get through the winter." When the food runs out, they call upon Frederick for the fruits of his labor.

This story, like *The Giving Tree,* stirs strong responses and delicious discussions. The debate is usually between those who consider art and beauty a basic necessity of life and those who believe that food and security come first. The book poses for consideration a viewpoint that children may not hold themselves. At the same time, in a culture where the value of art and beauty is considered more a commodity than basic to human need, this book serves to stimulate thought.

DIALOGUE

Talk about What You Notice in the Story

● ●

This first discussion of Frederick is with a group of young adults. The first concern of these young adults is fairness. It is okay for Frederick to be different, but is it fair for him to eat the fruits of the labor of others? Lee, however, thinks positively and wants to think in terms of Frederick's contribution to the community. Notice the reference to a comparable folktale.

● ●

Donda: Did Frederick eat the food gathered by the others?
Stephanie: He had to. Maybe he was able to live off his imagination.
Monica: He fed the other ones.
Julie: Do you think he was going without eating?
Lee: Why ask?

Bob: It's human nature—if we gathered the food you can't eat. Like the *Little Red Hen.*

Lee: It doesn't matter if he ate. Focus on what he *did* contribute.

Talk about How the Story Makes You Feel

● ●

The students become divided into two camps. Christopher is disparaging of the "razzle dazzle" while Lee considers the story a spiritual experience.

● ●

Vicki: Is that enough for you?

Lee: What he did was important. He didn't gather his stuff without eating. It's like a second grade trade-off. Both are equally important.

Bob: If he had hauled some food, it would have lasted longer.

Nicholas: It wasn't fair that he didn't help.

Michelle: People need more than the basics.

Donda: It doesn't show him eating. It's up to the reader to decide.

Lee: It's spiritual.

Vicki: But they would have a little bit more if . . .

Bob: They would have come into my house and eaten my cereal and rice.

Julie: If they didn't have colors and words they would have survived just the same.

Christopher: That stuff is just a lot of razzle dazzle.

Julie: They could have killed each other. Colors and words wouldn't make up for food.

Janice: My five-year-old brother said that this story made him so sad he wanted to cry. I'm not sure why.

Michelle: Is it fair?

Lee: He worked hard at what he did.

Talk about What the Story Reminds You of in Your Life

● ●

The discussion takes a philosophical turn. What is to be valued in work—reward or dignity? Donda's question stimulates the examination of personal belief systems.

● ●

TEACHER:	THINK ABOUT YOUR COMMUNITY. SOME PEOPLE DO ONE THING, OTHERS ANOTHER. IS ONE JOB MORE IMPORTANT THAN ANOTHER?
Christopher:	Some sit around and let other people feed them.
Bob:	Everyone likes music. They say musicians work, I have trouble with that. Work is using your muscles, being dirty and sweating. But I don't like to think what life would be like without music.
TEACHER:	SOME PEOPLE THINK TEACHING ISN'T WORK.
Donda:	There are good ways of teaching and not good.
TEACHER:	IS THERE A RELATIONSHIP BETWEEN FREDERICK AND TEACHING?
Christopher:	Is it work to read a poem?
Michelle:	Work is a negative thing, its physical, and we always say we "go to work."
Janice:	A career is not work.
Bob:	Work is labor.
Julie:	Everyone has their own job.
Monica:	Everyone should put their share in.
Vicki:	Look at basketball players, they make millions.
TEACHER:	DOES THAT BOTHER YOU? WOULD IT BOTHER YOU IF YOU WERE MAKING MILLIONS?
Donda:	There should be dignity no matter what you do.
Bob:	A student can drop out of school and make more money than a teacher.
Janice:	Society places the responsibility for children on teachers.
Bob:	You can't blame parents. Teachers don't become teachers for the money.
Lee:	What parents think teachers do and what they really do doesn't cause me a problem.

Talk about What You Notice in the Story

• •

This second discussion of Frederick is with a group of first graders. The younger students are equally concerned with fairness, but they stay in the story much longer than the older students. They notice the specifics of the illustrations.

• •

TEACHER:	WHAT DO YOU THINK OF FREDERICK?
Trent:	I think he's kinda cute.
Nicholas:	Did Frederick eat?
Trent:	I don't think so. He just held the flower.

Jonathan:	And he blushed.
Ikey:	Yes he *did* eat. I saw it in the book.
TEACHER:	LET'S LOOK AGAIN AT THE BOOK AND SEE.
Chorus:	Look at him. I think he's eating!

Talk about How the Story Makes You Feel

• •

The discussion of fairness continues. Nicholas, Jonathan, and Trent enjoy retelling parts of the story and then they collaborate to define a poet because the teacher doesn't jump in with her definition.

• •

Nicholas:	It wasn't fair that he didn't help.
Jonathan:	And he got to eat.
Trent:	I think he should help so he could eat. If he didn't eat, he would die and drink water.
TEACHER:	FREDERICK DID SOME OTHER THINGS BESIDES EATING.
Nicholas:	He said "close your eyes" and it got warmer and warmer. He said "close your eyes again" and they saw the colors and all that stuff.
Jonathan:	My very favorite part of the story was when they closed their eyes.
TEACHER:	SO DID FREDERICK HELP IN SOME WAY EVEN THOUGH HE DIDN'T CARRY FOOD?
Nicholas:	Yes! But he still shouldn't eat.
TEACHER:	(REREADING) "FREDERICK, YOU'RE A POET!"
Nicholas:	A poet is when you blush.
Jonathan:	No, a poet is a type of story.
Trent:	I know! It's something that rhymes.

Talk about What the Story Reminds You of in Your Life

• •

Trent and Jonathan become poets—what more can we ask?

• •

TEACHER:	YES, THE POET IS THE ONE WHO MAKES THE RHYMES. ARE YOU A POET?
Trent:	I'm a poet. I want to sing it in a song. *[Trent's song about Frederick was spontaneous and sung into a toy microphone in the guidance room.]*

Frederick, Frederick, you're so fine
I like the way you look,

I like the way you smile,
I like the way you feel,
That's all.

The Pebble Song as sung by Jonathan was also spontaneous.

Pebbles. Pebbles.
I like you because you make a nice wall.
You're so pretty, you're so strong.
That's all of my song.

TEACHER: NOW WHO'S A POET?
Nicholas and Jonathan: We are!
TEACHER: I KNOW IT.
Nicholas: I know it.
Chorus: I know it!

TEACHER FOCUS

Fairness: In the classroom community, fairness is always an issue. This book provides a means by which the belief that everybody contributes in their own way can be discussed with Frederick as the immediate concern.

Community: The mouse community works together to meet the needs of all, serving as a model of how the classroom or larger society can do the same.

Nature: The change of seasons and its effect on animal life and feeding patterns can be connected to science.

Genre: This is an ideal book to begin the study of poetry. It also is a modern fable and can be used along with Aesop and Arnold Lobel's *Fables*.

COUNSELOR FOCUS

Moral Dilemmas: The unresolved dilemma is based on whether one believes that food is more important than art. Was Frederick contributing equally? Is equality always a criteria?

Cooperation: The visual aspect of the book celebrates the cooperative community in which Frederick lives.

Individuality: Frederick is so endearing that this story provides a good introduction to acceptance of people who are different from us.

MAKING CONNECTIONS

Classroom Environment: The "razzle dazzle" comment from one of her university students made the instructor conscious of the lack of emphasis on beauty in the classroom. After spring break her class added curtains, paper flowers, table cloths, plants, a music corner, and poetry on the bulletin board. The student who made the comment about razzle dazzle objected to making paper flowers but was pleased with the result. Classrooms for younger children typically abound with color and "razzle dazzle." Using children's work to contribute to the beauty can give them insight into this story. Drawing children's attention to the choices they are making in the clothes they wear and the color of the pencils they write with may be a beginning for those who do not value art in their lives.

BOOKS FOR FOLLOW-UP LITERATURE STUDIES

dePaola, Tomi. (1989). *The Art Lesson.* Putnam.
> Tommy's desire to be creative is foiled by a teacher-directed art class in school.

Leaf, Munro. (c.1936). *The Story of Ferdinand.* Illustrated by Robert Lawson. Viking Press.
> Ferdinand prefers the beauty of flowers to fighting in the ring. This is quite unusual for a bull!

Lionni, Leo. (1985). *Frederick's Fables: A Leo Lionni Treasury of Favorite Stories.* Pantheon.
> These animal fables are warm and wise. All celebrate individuality and entice children to look at themselves and the world in refreshing ways. This collection includes the best of the Lionni fables. The introduction by Bruno Bettelheim is also helpful. *Swimmy* is about courage and community. *Cornelius* is a comment on conformity. *It's Mine* addresses greed as a metaphor. *Fish is Fish* is about self-discovery. These titles are also available individually. Five titles, including *Frederick*, are available on video. (Contact Chinaberry Book Service at 1-800-776-2242.)

Maxner, Joyce. (1989). *Nicholas Cricket.* Harper and Row.
> The Bug-a-Wug Cricket Band engages an orchestra to make music in the night.

Williams, Vera B. (1984). *Music, Music for Everyone.* Greenwillow Books.
> Rosa plays the accordion to help her mother earn money and support the family while her grandmother is ill.

Arnold Lobel,
Fables

● ●

Publisher and Date: Harper and Row, 1980
Illustrator: Arnold Lobel
Audience Level: Second grade and up
Main Theme: Foolish and Wise Behavior
Other Possible Themes: Acceptance, Humor, Choices
Values to Target: Self-Awareness, Diversity in Perspective,
   Problem Solving

● ●

ABOUT THE AUTHOR

Books and reading were a joyful part of Arnold Lobel's otherwise unhappy childhood. He decided at a young age to become an artist and graduated from the Pratt Institute in 1955. While in art school Lobel decided to specialize in book illustration.

Lobel began his career in advertising and then pursued his desire to illustrate books. He illustrated his first book in 1958. Four years later Lobel began writing and illustrating his own books while continuing to illustrate those by other authors. At the time of his death in 1987, Lobel had illustrated 33 of his own books. He wrote four others that were illustrated by his wife, Anita Lobel. During this same time he illustrated 68 books by other authors.

Until the mid-1960s, Lobel found his illustrations overly cartoon-like. By 1970 he had developed his own characteristic style. Lobel found illustrating easier than writing (*SATA* v. 89, pp. 89-107).

ABOUT THE BOOK

Lobel was asked by his publisher to illustrate Aesop's fables. After trying for two years he gave up but told his editor that he would feel comfortable illustrating his own fables. That's what he did, and the illustrations won the Caldecott Medal.

Lobel's 20 animal stories are longer, more elaborate, and funnier than Aesop's *Fables*. Likewise, the morals are unexpected, adding to the fun. Each fable stands on its own in terms of situations and conclusions. However, one can discuss Lobel's style of art and language as consistent throughout the book. His animal characters vibrate with vitality. The text is predominantly dialogue between the two characters in each fable. The dialogue illuminates human tendencies toward conceit, foolishness, pride, stupidity and humility.

DIALOGUE

"The Baboon's Umbrella"

Talk about What You Notice in the Story

• •

These fourth grade children collaborate to suggest wiser alternatives than the one chosen by Baboon.

• •

TEACHER:	WHAT DO YOU NOTICE?
Lily:	In the picture I could tell it was going to start raining. There are dark clouds.
Jared:	He should have thought before he cut those holes because he should have known it might rain.
Beige:	It did rain.
Lee:	He shouldn't have done it because that isn't what umbrellas are for.
Lily:	One thing he could have done, he could have held the umbrella behind him.
Vali:	He could have leaned it on his shoulder.
Lee:	What is a gibbon?
TEACHER:	IT'S AN APE, IN THE MONKEY FAMILY.

Talk about How the Story Makes You Feel

• •

Fables stimulate thinking more than feeling. The children continue to suggest improvements on the response of Baboon.

• •

TEACHER:	WHAT DO YOU THINK OF THE MORAL? ADVICE FROM FRIENDS IS SOMETIMES GOOD, SOMETIMES BAD.
Jennifer:	You should listen to your friends.
Brooks:	I would think about the advice and what would happen if you took it.
Jared:	You should think before you take advice.

Lily:	If you couldn't patch up the holes very well, when you can't undo what you did . . .
Jared:	Sometimes you should think before you take advice.
Lily:	And if you can undo it okay, but she couldn't patch up the holes, and that's something you can't undo. Only do something you can undo.
Lee:	Sometimes you should think after you get advice.
Jennifer:	If you didn't think it was going to rain, okay, but he carried the umbrella because it might rain, so he should have stopped to think.
Lily:	She was trying to be helpful.
Catherine:	If it hadn't rained, that might have been a good way to get the sun to shine on you.
Jared:	Why didn't he take it by the handle and put it in the house?
Beige:	He should have had a raincoat on.
Jennifer:	I don't see why he didn't just take the umbrella and put it in his house.
Lee:	That's right. Friends' advice is like the weather. I think that's true.
Jared:	I'd take advice from my own head. *[Several students say, Yeah!]*
Vali:	My head is hard. *[Lots of laughter]*
TEACHER:	SO IF A GIBBON CAME ALONG AND TOLD YOU TO PUT HOLES IN YOUR UMBRELLA, YOU'D DO IT?
Vali:	Maybe.
Lily:	That's stupid.

Talk about What the Story Reminds You of in Your Life

● ●

The teacher repeats Lobel's moral. The children leave Baboon's bad decision making behind and discuss the moral itself.

● ●

TEACHER:	HAVE ANY OF YOU HAD SOMETHING LIKE THAT HAPPEN TO YOU? ADVICE IS LIKE THE WEATHER, SOME IS GOOD, SOME IS BAD.
Brooks:	Yeah. I have. *[The others giggle]*
TEACHER:	LET'S HEAR IT.
Brooks:	Today I put on shorts because I thought it would be warm, and it's cold.

Lily:	I didn't take advice from my mother. She told me to put the horse in the barn. I thought the horse was too old to be frisky, but she wasn't. Mom had gone to work. (Everyone shouted, "Come on, Lily! Show her! Show her! Show her!" Her teeth were knocked out. Lily proceeded to remove her two front teeth.)
TEACHER:	THAT'S KIND OF THE OPPOSITE OF THE MORAL, ISN'T IT? YOU SHOULD HAVE FOLLOWED YOUR MOTHER'S ADVICE.
Lily:	That was one of my chores.
TEACHER:	SHOULD WE TRY ANOTHER ONE?

"The Camel Dances"

• •

Lots of giggles occur during the telling of this fable. Catherine and Lily enter into the character of the camel.

• •

Jared:	How come it said that the camel's feet was blistered, when camels have hoofs?
Jennifer:	She doesn't care if people don't like the way she dances.
Beige:	It's like an animal can't be another one, like a bird can't be a camel.
Vali:	She kept trying and trying until she pleased herself.
Lily:	I think it was just the opposite of the Baboon because she didn't take advice; well it wasn't really advice but she didn't do what the other camels said. She ended up pleasing herself.
Jared:	She didn't care what other people thought.
Catherine:	I would just say if I was the camel I would say to the audience, "If you want to dance like that you try to please yourself as much as I do."
Lily:	I'd tell the critic to go and try to dance himself.
Chorus:	"Yeah." "Go on!" "Try!"
TEACHER:	NOW HAVE ANY OF YOU EVER TRIED TO PLEASE YOURSELF EVEN THOUGH EVERYONE SAID YOU WERE "HUMPY AND LUMPY AND BAGGY AND BUMPY."
Lee:	Yesterday I had a friend over and we went on this long hike, okay? We were on a flat piece of land and we were going to go back. I wanted to go up the hill and they kept saying, "No, you're wrong. If you go on the road you'll get to the right place." I kept going up the hill and I got home and there

was a phone call, and my friend and my brother were calling home and they were lost.

Jennifer: Once we were doing fairy tales, and we were deciding whether to either write or to draw. This one person said, "I'm a better drawer than you are, so you can't do it." The teacher came by and she said, "You both draw really good, and neither of you draws better than the other."

TEACHER: COULD YOU HAVE COME TO THAT CONCLUSION WITHOUT THE TEACHER, OR DID YOU FEEL BAD?

Jennifer: Well, she was hurting my feelings.

TEACHER: THE CAMEL DIDN'T HAVE HER FEELINGS HURT, SHE JUST SAID, THAT'S TOO BAD, I'M GOING TO DANCE ANYHOW.

Lily: The people who called her names and stuff. I would just say try a little harder.

Catherine: I was trying to say something. There was a friend over. She kept saying to put this thing we had together one way. When we got it all put together my way worked. The way she put it together wouldn't have worked.

TEACHER: DID YOU FEEL LIKE THE CAMEL? I KNOW I'M RIGHT AND I DON'T CARE WHAT YOU THINK.

Lily: Sometimes I do things that I'm really proud of. One time I tried to make a bird's nest, and I thought it was really good, and I showed it to my sister, and she said, "That's not so good." And really it didn't look like a bird's nest but at the time I was really proud of it.

● ●

The teacher emphasizes that the camel pleased herself, but these fourth graders are very much concerned with pleasing others. Talk about the humpy, lumpy, baggy, bumpy camel gives them language with which to recall the independent camel.

● ●

TEACHER: IT'S HARD TO STICK UP FOR YOURSELF. WE'RE ALWAYS INFLUENCED BY WHAT OTHER PEOPLE THINK. JUST REMEMBER THAT EVEN THOUGH YOU ARE HUMPY AND LUMPY AND BAGGY AND BUMPY YOU CAN DO FOR YOURSELF WHATEVER YOU WANT.

"The Hen and the Apple Tree"

••

The teacher takes Jared's interest in real wolves to make distinctions in genre—fairy tales and fable. She compares the characters in the various fables.

••

TEACHER:	ONE MORE, ABOUT A WOLF. LET'S SEE IF THIS WOLF LIVES UP TO ITS REPUTATION. WHY DID YOU CHOOSE A WOLF, JARED?
Chorus:	"He loves wolves." "Wolves are wonderful."
Lee:	"It's his favorite animal."
TEACHER:	DO YOU LIKE WOLVES IN FAIRY TALES OR REAL WOLVES? REAL WOLVES ARE VERY . . .
All Students:	Complicated!
TEACHER:	COMPLICATED, YES. WOLVES IN FAIRY TALES ARE NOT COMPLICATED AT ALL. THEY'RE ALWAYS OUT TO GET YOU. *[At the end of the story, the teacher asks for a prediction about the moral.]*
Lily:	Stick up for yourself.
Jennifer:	It's difficult to outsmart somebody.
Jared:	I don't know.
Cathy:	Think before you try to outsmart someone.
Teacher:	Here's what Arnold Lobel thought the moral was: "It's always difficult to pose as something one is not." How does that compare to the humpy, lumpy camel? What's different between the camel and the wolf in the way they behaved?
Brooks:	The camel kept on trying and the wolf didn't.
Lily:	The wolf could easily think of another plan and outsmart the hen.
Lee:	The wolf gave up.
Jared:	He could call up his uncle the big bad wolf and get him to help . . . and blow the house down.

TEACHER FOCUS

Critical Thinking: Fables are perfect for making predictions about what the moral might be. The author's choice may not be the only one.

Human Character: Fables are a subject in themselves, but their chief characteristic is to humorously portray human foibles. The result of reading fables is that we become more tolerant of our own foibles as well as those of others.

COUNSELOR FOCUS

Tolerance: The nonjudgmental nature of fables builds tolerance in readers.

Humor: Once the acceptance takes place children begin to laugh kindly with others and at themselves.

MAKING CONNECTIONS

Genre Study: From this discussion, we could begin a study of the differences between real animals and their fairy tale and fable counter-parts.

Another interesting comparison is between Aesop and Lobel. Students are always interested in knowing that there was no such person as Aesop. It is believed that a name was given to a fictitous person in order to cumulate all the fables in the Greek folk culture of the sixth century B.C.

Wolves: With a student like Jared in the class, it was obvious that everyone became interested in wolves. They read together Jean George's *Julie of the Wolves* (Harper and Row, 1972).

BOOKS FOR FOLLOW-UP LITERATURE STUDIES

Anno, Mitsumasa. (1989). *Anno's Aesop: A Book of Fables.* Orchard Books.
　　An illustrated version of the traditional fables with an interpreter giving a
　　different perspective on the morals.
Bierhorst, John. (1987). *Doctor Coyote: A Native American Aesop's Fables.*
Macmillan.
　　These fables bear the least resemblance to what the Western mind is used to.
　　The tales have a special Native American structure.
Paxton, Tom. (1990). *Belling the Cat and Other Aesop's Fables.* Morrow Junior Books.
　　Paxton retells several of Aesop's fables in poetry form with beautiful illustra-
　　tions by Robert Rayevsky.

Evaline Ness,
Sam, Bangs and Moonshine

● ●

Publisher and Date: Holt, 1966
Illustrator: Evaline Ness
Audience Level: Grades three and up

Main Theme: Coping With Sadness
Other Possible Themes: Truth, Fantasy and Reality
Values to Target: Empathy

• •

ABOUT THE AUTHOR

Evaline Ness, born in Union City, Ohio, in 1911, began illustrating her sister Josephine's stories when she was in grade school. Her interest in art continued through high school, but she received little acknowledgement of her talent. She attended the Chicago Art Institute, bussing dishes in a cafeteria, working in a library, and modeling for artists to support herself. After two impoverished years she quit art school to work as a fashion illustrator. Ness resumed her study of art seven years later and became an accomplished painter. She was a highly successful commercial illustrator but eventually tired of the pressure and pace.

She illustrated her first children's book at age 43. Since then Ness has illustrated over 30 books by other authors and has written more than 15 of her own. Ness won the Caldecott Medal in 1967 for *Sam, Bangs and Moonshine*. Three of her other books have been Caldecott runners-up (*SATAAS* v. 1, pp. 223-31).

ABOUT THE STORY

The "Moonshine" in the story is a metaphor for a world of make-believe into which "Sam" retreats after her mother dies. The daughter of a fisherman, Sam is known for a "reckless habit of lying." The lying includes stories that her mother is a mermaid and that she has a fierce lion and a baby kangaroo at home for pets. The truth is that Sam's mother is dead and that her only pet is a cat named Bangs. One day Sam's stories prove to be dangerous for her younger friend, Thomas, and for her beloved cat as well.

This story is often indexed as one to teach the difference between reality and truth. But the heartfelt response to the sadness in the story is more compelling, and discussions should not be limited to listing reasons for "why we should not escape from reality." The plot is not so much about overcoming "Moonshine" as it is about Samantha's recognition that she shares inevitable sadness with others. At the end of the story she sees Thomas and her father in a new light and recognizes the difference between good and bad "Moonshine."

A SUGGESTION FOR TEACHERS WITH LARGE GROUPS

When doing this story with a large group, intimate conversation is usually not possible and it is best to start the group with an organizing activity. Each child draws from a box the name of Sam, her father, or Thomas. Then instruct the group as follows:

1. Listen to the whole story as if you were that character.
2. Note how you were feeling during the story.
3. After reading the story reflect about why you behaved in the manner you did in the story.

Small groups collaborate for each character's "story," and contribute to the final discussion. This approach serves to involve all the children and to obtain more insightful responses in a limited amount of time.

DIALOGUE

Talk about What You Notice in the Story

• •

For the following discussion with a group of fifth and sixth graders, the teacher openly acknowledges learning from the children about a deeper meaning to the title, and then adds a connection of her own. Note that Malinda is beyond superficial didacticism as an interpretation of this story. She understands the deep motivation for Sam's behavior, and does not simply criticize lying.

• •

Jennifer:	I was wondering what the title meant. I thought it was about a boy.
Nathan:	And I thought moonshine was bootleg whiskey! *[laughter]*
TEACHER:	MAYBE THERE IS A CONNECTION. MOONSHINE IS REAL STUFF!
Holly:	Well, I guess you would say bootleg whiskey is real whiskey.
Nathan:	But it is fake, in a way. It might not be clean. *I* wouldn't drink it! *[more laughter]*
TEACHER:	MOONSHINE CAN ALSO MEAN BY THE LIGHT OF THE MOON.
C.J.:	Well the moon really doesn't have a light of its own. It's the sun's light.
TEACHER:	SO THE LIGHT IS NOT TRULY THE MOON'S. MOONSHINE MAY BE A WELL-CHOSEN WORD FOR THE TITLE.

Chris:	Well it's easy to remember. And the definition of moonshine makes sense.
TEACHER:	THAT'S A GOOD POINT. WAS SAM BAD? A LIAR? ON PAGE ONE IT SAYS "SHE HAD THE RECKLESS HABIT OF LYING."
Malinda:	Oh, no . . . she was just wishing her mother was still around and she made up a story about the mermaid to get attention and make herself feel better.

Talk about How the Story Makes You Feel

● ●

This is a story heavy with feelings. The teacher is successful in having the children take on the perspectives of one or another of the characters, who have different reasons for feeling sad and different ways of responding to their sadness. Chris at first believes that Thomas is a spoiled brat, and then changes his mind when he understands through the discussion that Thomas, too, is lonely.

● ●

TEACHER:	[READING FROM THE TEXT] "REAL WAS NO MOTHER AT ALL."
Malinda:	Sam was lonely. And sad.
TEACHER:	WHAT ARE SOME OTHER WAYS SHE BEHAVES BECAUSE SHE'S SAD?
Brooke:	She made up stories about her mermaid mother.
Jennifer:	And she talked to her cat.
Nathan:	She was always out for impressing Thomas. She made him do all kinds of things.
Jennifer:	It was like a game.
TEACHER:	WOULD YOU CALL IT A MEAN GAME?
Malinda:	I don't think she meant to be mean at first, but it was sure a terrible mistake to send Thomas out looking for a mermaid in the cave.
Brooke:	That picture of Thomas with his bicycle is my favorite in the whole book!
Chris:	He lived in a big house and had a jungle gym. Maybe he was a spoiled brat. He was younger than Sam.
Jessie:	He must have been an only child.
Chris:	I think he was lonely, too.
TEACHER:	ALL THREE CHARACTERS HAVE SOME FEELINGS IN COMMON.
Jennifer:	It never said that Sam's father was lonely. But he must have been sad too.
TEACHER:	HE HAS SOME REASON TO BE SAD.
Malinda:	[thoughtfully] After all, it was his wife who died.

Brooke:	And a fisherman is alone most of the time.
Casey:	That explains why Sam was lonely too. Her father was gone a lot.
TEACHER:	DID HER FATHER DO WHAT YOU WANTED HIM TO?
Malinda:	Yes. He was calm. He talked to her about good and bad moonshine.
Chris:	And he brought her the little kangaroo rat off the banana boat.
TEACHER:	AND SHE GAVE IT AWAY!
Casey:	She asked her father and he left it to her. It must have been hard to give her new real kangaroo rat away.
Jennifer:	She had changed in her attitude toward Thomas.
TEACHER:	SO SAM HAS LEARNED SOME THINGS.
Brooke:	About understanding how Thomas feels. And about good and bad moonshine. *[smiling]* She said she'd keep the chariot.
TEACHER:	I LIKE THAT! NOW, WHAT ABOUT HER SADNESS?
Jennifer:	It will be there a long time.
Malinda:	Well, it will, but at least she has a friend.

Talk about What the Story Reminds You of in Your Life

• •

The teacher participates in the admission to moonshine in her life, and then brings the children back to the sadness in the story. This results in the heartfelt statements of Brooke and Jennifer. The statements about differences in perceptions of boys and girls could be pursued.

• •

TEACHER:	IS IT POSSIBLE TO LIVE WITHOUT SOME MOONSHINE?
Jennifer:	I hope we can all have *some*. I talk to my cat all the time.
Malinda:	And we all have some kinds of chariots
Jessie:	My sisters and I used to pretend to be *The Borrowers*. That was good moonshine.
TEACHER:	AND I WAS NANCY DREW! WHAT KINDS OF BAD MOONSHINE DO YOU NOTICE AT SCHOOL?
Several Girls:	*[in unison]* Gossip! That's the worst! Spreading rumors.
Jessie:	I can remember when the bad moonshine was about *me*!
Nathan:	I don't think boys are as bad as girls about spreading rumors.
Brooke:	But you fight!

Alan:	I think boys brag about stuff that's not true. That could be moonshine too.
TEACHER:	I REALLY LIKE THE WAY YOU RECOGNIZE EVERYDAY MOONSHINE. WHAT CAN WE DO ABOUT IT?
Haley:	Well, if you hear a rumor in the restroom, you can just not repeat it.
Jessie:	You can just go and tell whoever it's about.
Brooke:	I don't think that always helps.
Beth:	Well if you tell Mrs. Borders or your teacher, they can help get it straight. They'll make you talk it out face to face.
Chorus:	Right!
TEACHER:	SOUNDS LIKE A GOOD CURE FOR BAD MOONSHINE TO ME. WE'VE TALKED ABOUT MOONSHINE IN OUR LIVES. WHAT ABOUT SADNESS?
Brooke:	People keep telling me that other kids feel sad, too, and I'm not the only one. But it sure doesn't seem that way, sometimes. It seems like it's only me.
Jennifer:	But that's what friends are for. You have to remember that.

TEACHER FOCUS

Death: This story handles the subject of death differently than many in that we don't know the character who has died. We only know the resulting sadness. Classroom communities can become havens for the expression and sharing of grief.

Safety: The danger of allowing self-interest to influence our behavior can lead to dangerous results. Sam was fortunate, but the suspense in the story will assist children in recognizing that luck isn't always on our side. Water safety is the particular issue in this story.

Pets: The role of Bangs in this story is particularly poignant. Without the pet Sam's pain would have been intolerable.

Author's Craft: The literary devices in this story are executed with great skill. The archetypal use of naming (what is moonshine) serves as metaphor for Sam's need to name her grief. The illustrations are impressionistic rather than realistic in keeping with the conceptual nature of the theme.

COUNSELOR FOCUS

Lying: There are always reasons behind the lying that children do. When discussing this story, students may be able to recognize their own reasons for lying.

Grief: The story makes clear that grief is a lonely state to be in. Sam needed friends and family to help her through.

MAKING CONNECTIONS

The metaphor of moonshine reverberated for days in several classes that read this book. The main connection was the word itself which everyone now understood. "Bad Moonshine" (particularly the rumor variety) is pervasive in relationships in fifth and sixth grade classes. The use of the word moonshine reminded children to be sensitive to feelings of the victims of rumors or manipulation.

The story also has uses in individual counseling with children who are experiencing sadness.

BOOKS FOR FOLLOW-UP LITERATURE STUDIES

Alexander, Sue. (1983). *Nadia, the Willful*. Pantheon.
> Although she is told not to speak the name of the one who dies, Nadia refuses to avoid her sadness at her brother's death.

Keats, Ezra Jack.(1981). *Regards to the Man in the Moon*. Four Winds.
> Jennifer, in the preceding discussion, called the group's attention to this familiar picture book as an example of "Good Moonshine." In the story she remembered how neighborhood kids played "Outer Space" using discarded boxes and junk. "This was like Sam's dragon and chariot," she noted.

Lowry, Lois. (1977). *A Summer to Die*. Houghton-Mifflin.
> In this full-length novel, Molly is dying and her sister Meg must come to terms with birth, death, youth, and aging.

Zolotow, Charlotte. (1974). *My Grandson Lew*. Illustrated by William Pene du Bois. Greenwillow.
> When mother and child remember Grandpa, it is with sadness tempered by pleasure in wonderful memories. The simple text makes this book appropriate for young children.

Cynthia Rylant, *Miss Maggie*

• •

Publisher and Date: Dutton, 1983
Illustrator: Thomas DiGrazia
Audience Level: Grades four and up
Main Theme: Prejudice, Misjudgment

Other Possible Themes: Friendship, Relationships of Young and
      Old, Kindness, Courage
Values to Target: Empathy, Age, Choices

• •

ABOUT THE AUTHOR

Cynthia Rylant is a prolific and versatile writer of picture books, novels, and poetry. She has published over 35 books, a number of which have won awards. Her characters and themes are drawn from her experiences growing up in West Virginia where she lived with her grandparents in a coal mining community.

Rylant was a good student with many friends. She participated in nearly every available activity in high school and held leadership positions. Like many of her girlfriends, her extracurricular interests included boys, the Beatles, and reading comic books.

She didn't consider writing books until she began working in the children's room of a public library. She read boxload after boxload of the children's books she was supposed to be shelving in the library. She penned her first book in one hour, mailed it off without revisions, and two months later *When I Was Young in the Mountains* was accepted for publication. Most of Rylant's other books have been written with similar speed and precision. She now lives in Ohio with her son and their pets. Every summer they visit her childhood home in West Virginia (*SATA* v. 13, p. 155, and personal communication with Alice Naylor).

ABOUT THE ILLUSTRATOR

Thomas Di Grazia was a versatile studio artist, designer and illustrator. His captivating drawings can also be seen in several books by Lucille Clifton, including *Amifika*. He died just before the publication of *Miss Maggie* (from the book jacket).

ABOUT THE STORY

Cynthia Rylant reports that as a child she once knew a real "Miss Maggie" who lived in a log house on the mountain. Nat Crawford, the boy in the story, is fascinated by what folks tell about this classic mountain character—especially the tale about the black snake. He is afraid to get too close to Miss Maggie, and is ashamed to be seen with her when he and his grandfather take her to town. But one morning he notices from a distance that Miss Maggie's chimney isn't puffing. What happens after that, as the author notes, is a "story worth telling."

Children are able to feel empathy and to think about right and wrong before they develop the will to act on their feelings. This story is compelling in that it depicts a young character who makes a moral choice, listening "to his heart, not his feet."

DIALOGUE

Talk about What You Notice in the Story

• •

The first responses listed below occurred during the reading. The fifth grade children were so engrossed with the suspenseful plot, they spontaneously made predictions and shared reactions to both text and illustrations.

• •

"Oh no! Something has happened to Miss Maggie!"
"Maybe she's just sick."
"He's going to see that snake!'
"Do you think he'll go in the house?"
"I wouldn't!"
"I think he'll go get his grandpa."
"Turn the page!"
"Oh, she doesn't have her bonnet on and she looks like she might die."
"Who is Henry?"
"I wonder if Henry is her husband or son who has died."
"Oh, she looks better now. Like she feels better."

TEACHER:	I NOTICED THAT YOU WERE VERY ENGROSSED IN THE STORY. HOW DOES CYNTHIA RYLANT CREATE SUSPENSE?
Erin:	Well, when he looked across the field and there was no smoke coming from the chimney, I thought for sure Miss Maggie was dead.
Scott:	Then he got to her door and he didn't hear her lips smacking on her snuff like usual.
TEACHER:	[REFERRING TO TEXT] "AND HIS THROAT FROZE UP ON HIM . . ."
Denise:	Oh yeah! I know how that feels. Mine felt that way this morning.
Scott:	Really?
Denise:	Remember, I had to read the announcements today on the intercom.

Erin: Oh! Me, too. I know what you mean.

Talk about How the Story Makes You Feel

• •

Although Jessica and Erin make evaluation comments about the story, the rest of the discussion is reliving the feelings of the story. The teacher rereads memorable passages and unobtrusively introduces the quality of the author's language.

• •

TEACHER:	DENISE RECOGNIZED A FEELING MOST OF US HAVE HAD. ARE THERE ANY OTHER FEELINGS ABOUT THE STORY?
Jessica:	It's a good story.
Erin:	It's a *sad* story.
Chris:	I was sad that Miss Maggie was sad.
Erin:	All she had in life was a bird!
Holly:	Right! Until Nat brought her the snake at the end. He was Henry. That was cool.
Valerie:	It is really a good thing Nat didn't run away from there.
Chad:	Well, Nat wasn't the only one who was scared of her. Miss Maggie had a reputation for being real strange. Most people wouldn't do any of what he did.
Scott:	Folks were always saying she was weird.
Erin:	*If* he believed what folks say . . .
Denise:	But the folks didn't even *know* her. They were not in contact with her.
TEACHER:	SO THEY TALK ABOUT HER, BUT THEY DON'T EVEN KNOW HER . . . THAT'S A GOOD POINT.
	[nods of agreement]
Angela:	Sometimes people really do misjudge other people by what folks say, or by the way they look and dress or something like that.
Haley:	Right. I know all about it. You can miss out on making a friend if you judge a person too soon.
Alan:	Well, Nat's family must not have believed what folks said, because his grandmother was always sending him over to help Miss Maggie.
TEACHER:	MAYBE THAT TELLS US SOMETHING ABOUT NAT'S GRANDPARENTS.
Jody:	They made up their own minds what to believe.
Jeremy:	And they were kind.
Jeff:	They took her to town with them. Most people wouldn't go out of their way like that.

Chris:	Right. If Nat had never been sent over there to her house with the buttermilk he would not have been that close to her.
Chad:	Then the next time he came to the porch was really scary.
TEACHER:	[CALLING ATTENTION TO THE TEXT] THERE IS A SENTENCE OR TWO THAT STANDS OUT IN MY MIND. "IF HIS FEET HAD LISTENED TO HIS HEAD, NAT WOULD HAVE BOUNDED OUT OF THAT HOUSE IN A FLASH. BUT HIS FEET WEREN'T LISTENING. ONLY HIS HEART."
Erin:	I think she might really have died if he hadn't come.
Denise:	Even if she didn't die, he would never have found out how she really was. He would not have had her for a friend.
TEACHER:	SO HIS LISTENING TO HIS HEART WAS VERY IMPORTANT.
Denise:	Really!

Talk about What the Story Reminds You of in Your Life

• •

The discussion of feelings helps the children remember incidents in their own lives. The teacher relates their stories to similar feelings and choices in the story, connecting their lives with those of Nat and Miss Maggie.

• •

Erin:	It reminds me of a woman we pick up on our way to church. She's blind in one eye, and I used to be scared of the way she looks. But I found out she really can be funny and nice.
TEACHER:	SOMETIMES PEOPLE ARE MISJUDGED BECAUSE OF THEIR LOOKS.
Holly:	Even at school people are misjudged on their looks.
Denise:	Sometimes people just don't even try to get to know somebody when they're new at school or something.
TEACHER:	I WONDER WHY.
Casey:	They are in their little groups.
Denise:	Maybe they just don't care!
Haley:	They're just thinking about themselves, and they're happy because they've got some friends.
Erin:	There's always one or two people who go out of their way to care. But not everybody.
TEACHER:	SO THIS STORY MAKES YOU THINK ABOUT CARING.
Alan:	Right. I think Nat was caring.
Denise:	And brave. I could never have done it myself!
Erin:	You might! You might be surprised at what you could do. If you *had* to . . .
Scott:	[hesitantly] I *might* have done it. I'm not sure.

Valerie:	I think I would probably have gone to get my grandfather first before I went in. I couldn't do it by myself.
TEACHER:	SUPPOSE NAT HAD DONE THAT. WOULD IT MAKE A DIFFERENCE?
Jeremy:	Maybe not.
Erin:	I don't agree with that. She could have died while he was gone.
Scott:	And if his grandfather were there too, Miss Maggie may not ever have told him about Henry. The grandfather might have rushed in and all that.
TEACHER:	SO THE FRIENDSHIP BETWEEN NAT AND MISS MAGGIE DEPENDED ON HIS DOING JUST WHAT HE DID.
Chris:	Yes. They gave gifts to each other. He took her the snake and named it Henry.
TEACHER:	THE ARTIST HAS A FINAL INTERPRETATION OF THAT. NOTICE THE END PAGE HERE WITH THE COFFEE CAN AND THE SNAKE. APPARENTLY HE SEES THE GIFTS AS AN IMPORTANT SYMBOL TOO.
Jeremy:	That's cool!
TEACHER:	WHAT QUESTION WOULD YOU ASK IF THE AUTHOR WERE HERE?
Denise:	I'd like to know how much the real Miss Maggie is like the one in the story. Does the author change the name?
Erin:	I'd like to know if the real Miss Maggie is alive.
Rick:	I'd like to know who the artist saw to help him draw Miss Maggie.

TEACHER FOCUS

Appalachia: The setting of this story is integral to the story and well delineated. The book gives the sense of place and also serves as a model for writing about a place.

Ageism: Many children will feel the same about an old person as Nat did about Miss Maggie. Perhaps some could write about people they are fearful of, and how they may get acquainted.

Story Structure: The shortness of this story makes story structure analysis a possibility. The style is also worth using as a model.

COUNSELOR FOCUS

Moral Choice: When put to the test, Nat finds himself to be courageous and caring enough to make the right choice.

Conformity: Neither Nat nor his family accepted the community belief that Miss Maggie was crazy.

MAKING CONNECTIONS

Art: One teacher created an art project with leftovers to enhance the meaning of the story. Children discussed how Miss Maggie is a leftover. She is old and, in a sense, from another time. No one knows exactly what to do about her. They discovered examples of leftovers in the story. Miss Maggie gathered the leftover potatoes. The buttermilk Nat delivered was left over. Finally the gifts that symbolize the friendship are fittingly made of leftover tobacco tins and coffee cans. A threefold art project can emerge:

1. Children may collect treasures from the earth (as Nat did) for their tins.
2. Using all leftover materials, children may decorate the outside of discarded coffee cans or other tins. Materials may include old papers, lace, fabric scraps or ribbons, or construction paper or foil cut in geometric designs.
3. The activity may be extended to giving the tins as gifts to people who remind them of Miss Maggie.

Music: A song by Malvania Reynolds entitled "Magic Penny" has a line: "Love is something, if you give it away, you'll end up having more." It is on the tape *I've Got a Song* recorded by Carolyn and Sandy Paton on the Folk Legacy label (Box 1148, Sharon, CT 06069, Phone: 1-800-836-0901).

BOOKS FOR FOLLOW-UP LITERATURE STUDIES

Blos, Joan V. (1987). *Old Henry*. Illustrated by Stephen Gammell. Morrow.
    Henry's neighbors are embarrassed by his run-down house until they discover how much they miss him.
Schotter, Roni. (1990). *Captain Snap and the Children of Vinegar Lane*. Illustrated by Marcia Sewall. Orchard Books.
    The children of the village care for an eccentric old sailor when he is ill.

Cynthia Rylant,
The Relatives Came

• •

Publisher and Date: Bradbury, 1985
Illustrator: Stephen Gammell

Audience Level: Kindergarten through fourth grade
Main Theme: Extended Family
Other Possible Themes: Helping, Love, Intergenerational Family,
    Mountain Life, Rural Life, Rituals
Values to Target: Joy in Family

● ●

ABOUT THE AUTHOR

Cynthia Rylant is a prolific and versatile writer of picture books, novels, and poetry. She has published over 35 books, a number of which have won awards. Her characters and themes are drawn from her experiences growing up in West Virginia where she lived with her grandparents in a coal mining community.

Rylant was a good student with many friends. She participated in nearly every available activity in high school and held leadership positions. Like many of her girlfriends, her extracurricular interests included boys, the Beatles, and reading comic books.

She didn't consider writing books until she began working in the children's room of a public library. She read boxload after boxload of the children's books she was supposed to be shelving in the library. She penned her first book in one hour, mailed it off without revisions, and two months later *When I Was Young in the Mountains* was accepted for publication. Most of Rylant's other books have been written with similar speed and precision. She now lives in Ohio with her son and their pets. Every summer they visit her childhood home in West Virginia (*SATA* v. 13, p. 155, and personal communication with Alice Naylor).

ABOUT THE ILLUSTRATOR

Stephen Gammell won the Caldecott medal for *The Song and Dance Man* and a Caldecott honor award for *Where the Buffaloes Begin* by Olaf Baker. He is the illustrator of more than 45 books, four of which are his own. Gammell was born in Des Moines, Iowa, in 1943. The son of an art editor, Stephen started drawing in early elementary school but didn't start illustrating professionally until the early 1970s. After moving to New York City, he submitted some of his work to a publisher for an assessment; the editor was so impressed that he offered him a contract and Gammell has been working steadily ever since.

"As an illustrator, he has secured a place in children's literature by consistently producing work described by Anne Schwartz in *Horn Book* as 'down-to-earth, spontaneous, warm, energetic, seriously playful'" (*Contemporary Authors*, Volume 35, pp. 50-58).

ABOUT THE STORY

The narrator is one of the children living in the Appalachian mountains, waiting for the relatives to arrive from Virginia. The sense of a summer's visit is keenly experienced through words and pictures. The relatives arrive, hug for hours, and then hug some more. They laugh, eat, sleep with overlapping arms and legs, fix things, make music, and talk in twos and threes. After weeks and weeks, the relatives pack up and return home. Each misses the other and dreams of next summer. The rollicking pictures add a dimension all their own to the story as the conversation below will confirm.

The story structure is exquisite in form and predictability. The few details in the text are rich in suggestion about the long summer visit. Readers can easily read between the lines based on their own experiences with family. The pictures provide a whole new way of keeping track of all that goes on. They beg for exclamation and comment. The flying suitcases and spilling food create mood and feelings, not literal recording of fact. Most importantly, relatives mean belonging to someone and having someone belong to you.

DIALOGUE

Talk about What You Notice in the Story

• •

Eight mountain children, kindergarten through fourth grade, discuss the story. The children experience delight, surprise, projection, and prediction. With everyone paying attention, Lee Ann provides her own extended simile. The children's responses are a tribute to the liveliness of the illustrations and the richness of the text.

• •

TEACHER:	WHAT DID YOU NOTICE ABOUT THIS STORY?
Becky:	A lot of hugging!
Sarah:	The pictures are colorful.
Jennifer:	They lived in Virginia.
Michael:	Did the car break down?
Becky:	Look at that car, it's off the ground.
Christy:	They broke the mailbox.

Leslie:	*[Looking at full-page spread]* You think that's a different time of day?
Teacher:	SOMETIMES WHEN I LOOK UP AT THE SKY IT'S BLUE IN ONE DIRECTION AND GREY IN ANOTHER.
Leslie:	The hood is open.
Sarah:	They hugged a lot.
Jennifer:	Why did the people from Virginia have holes in their pants, and holes in their shirts and stuff?
Christy:	And big hats to cover up their heads? People from Virginia have holes in their pants.
Michael:	His head is flat on the top.
Lee Ann:	This man who came to visit us was giving me a hug, and he was squeezing me until I felt like a pancake.
Teacher:	WAS HE A RELATIVE?
Lee ann:	I don't know. I'm kin to somebody who is kin to him. I felt like a pancake. I had to blow myself back up. *[laughter]*
Leslie:	Look at the babies spilling the food.
Sarah:	Oh, gosh look at . . . look at the guy sitting on the stool; he's tipping over.
Lee Ann:	Wow! They got a messy house, no matter where you're going to put something it's going to fall.
Becky:	Cookies are falling everywhere.
Leslie:	The food is falling on the little boy's head.
Michael:	When he ate that sandwich the plate fell off.
Jennifer:	And the dog food scattered everywhere and the dog is eating the people's food instead of its.
Leslie:	It's eating a hot dog.
Becky:	You can see that one lady's slip.
Sarah:	Where?
Jennifer:	Look at the shoes. People don't have shoes like that.
Christy:	And the stool that the baby is on is about to tip over.
All:	Oh, oh!
Lee Ann:	It'll be funny.
Sarah:	The grandmother is sucking her thumb.
Becky:	Mostly everybody don't have a coat.
Teacher:	THEY DON'T HAVE A COAT?
Becky:	All of them don't have a cover to sleep under.
Teacher:	MUST HAVE BEEN WARM THAT NIGHT.
Jennifer:	Why do people have to throw their legs over each other?
Teacher:	DO YOU SUPPOSE IT'S BECAUSE THEY'RE FROM VIRGINIA?
Leslie:	No, it's because they're so tired from driving.

TEACHER:	AND BECAUSE THERE ARE SO MANY OF THEM, RIGHT?
All:	Uh huh!
Becky:	His hair is falling off.
TEACHER:	HE'S CUTTING IT, ISN'T HE?
Michael:	Maybe he just had a haircut.
TEACHER:	DID YOU NOTICE IF THEY EVER FIXED THE FENCE THAT THEY RAN IN TO?
All:	Yea!
Leslie:	They didn't fix the mailbox.
Christy:	That lady has a baby on one arm and watermelon on the other.
Leslie:	Here's two babies.
Christy:	One of her babies is a watermelon.
TEACHER:	THAT'S IT!
Sarah:	Look at the dog, look at her!
TEACHER:	OH, THERE'S SO MUCH TO SEE IN THESE PICTURES.
Jennifer:	It's got lots of details.
Lee Ann:	Their luggage is falling off the car.
Becky:	She looks like she's wearing her pajamas.

Talk about How the Story Makes You Feel

• •

The children are working at finding the right language to describe, comment, identify, and express wonderment.

• •

TEACHER:	STEPHEN GAMMELL MADE THE ILLUSTRATIONS FOR THE AUTHOR. WHY DO YOU SUPPOSE HE DREW THESE PICTURES LIKE THAT?
Michael:	He wanted people to laugh at it.
Lee Ann:	He wanted to make it a good book and funny, so children would like it.
TEACHER:	HOW DOES IT MAKE YOU FEEL WHEN ALL THESE FUNNY THINGS HAPPEN?
Leslie:	Maybe the people from Virginia live on one side of the world where it's dark when the relatives are on the other side where it is light. They could still go to bed when it's light.
Jennifer:	It makes us feel like through the pictures, we see all the funny stuff.
Becky:	Makes us wonder what's going on.
TEACHER:	WHAT DOES IT HAVE TO DO WITH RELATIVES VISITING? WHY DID HE MAKE IT SO FUNNY AND FULL OF DETAILS?
Sarah:	It's nice.

Lee Ann:	So children would like it and wouldn't be bored. I hate boring stories.
Teacher:	THIS WASN'T BORING.
All:	Nooooooo!

Talk about What the Story Reminds You of in Your Life

• •

The teacher attempts to have the children think about the illustrator and how he had to make a choice about the kind of pictures to paint. The children prefer to stay in the story and simply enjoy the experience.

• •

Teacher:	DOES IT REMIND YOU AT ALL OF WHEN YOU HAVE RELATIVES COME?
Becky:	I've never had relatives come.
Sarah:	I have. Our great aunt and uncle, but not to spend the night though.
Leslie:	My Mamaw stays all the time.
Sarah:	Not from Virginia.
Teacher:	THEN WHEN THEY CAME WAS THERE ANYTHING IN THE BOOK THAT WAS LIKE THAT?
Lee Ann:	When my whole family comes I get excited. And I get hyper.
Jennifer:	One day Mama had to drop us off at Diane's and she didn't have time to get back from Stony Creek, and Mama had to spend the night at my great aunts. One time my cousin Chris came from Nebraska and they live in Nebraska, and they stayed for a couple weeks. Diane is my second cousin and Chris is my third cousin, and they came from Nebraska and stayed with us and all.
Teacher:	WHAT WAS THAT LIKE?
Jennifer:	Well, they got to go places, and in the city, and I remember one time I went with them, and they all went shopping and they bought lots of stuff.
Teacher:	I WANT TO GO BACK TO LEE ANN. YOU SAID THAT WHEN THE RELATIVES COME YOU GET ALL HYPER.
Lee Ann:	Yea, because I'm not used to them coming. And I'm just used to one person at a time. I get hyper because she came once and stayed for two months.
Teacher:	LET'S LOOK AT THE PICTURES AGAIN. DO YOU SUPPOSE STEPHEN GAMMELL GETS ALL HYPER WHEN HIS RELATIVES COME AND THAT'S WHY HE PAINTED ALL THESE FUNNY THINGS? WAS HE SOMETHING LIKE YOU?

Lee Ann:	Maybe that's kinda true. Maybe all his relatives came and they made a big mess and he thought of that book.
Jennifer:	It's like I read in Dear Abby that one day the relatives came and they were real rude. And they said something about they fed their dog out of their dishes without even asking them.
TEACHER:	WERE THESE RELATIVES LIKE THAT? I THINK THEY WERE HELPFUL.
Lee Ann:	They weren't too helpful. They fixed things like the fence.
Leslie:	They didn't fix the mailbox.
Becky:	I had some friends sleep over, like three or four people, we were up in the living room while everyone else was sleeping.
TEACHER:	WHEN YOU'RE UP AND JUMPING AROUND LIKE THAT DOES IT FEEL LIKE THESE PICTURES?
Becky:	Let me see. *[trying it out]* Yes!

TEACHER FOCUS

Visual Literacy: The outrageously funny illustrations are intended to show feelings, mood, and nostalgia. The illustrations could be compared to those in *When I Was Young in the Mountains* which are realistic, or with other books by Stephen Gammell.

Setting: The sense of time and place are especially strong in this book as they relate to extended family. The text is particularly good at conveying the lasting connection between the members in spite of the physical separation.

Language: How does the choice of words influence the response readers have to the story? Children could think of synonyms and compare them with those that Rylant chose instead.

COUNSELOR FOCUS

Ritual: The story is a concrete example of how ritual binds together the members of a group. The ritual visit creates the memories that last over the year.

Unconditional Love: The family provides the model for loving relationships unencumbered by judgments and expectations. In groups the children recall and tell stories of their own "hugging," which in itself is affirming.

MAKING CONNECTIONS

Art: Teachers often spend time on the differences between real and unreal in books. The use of "unrealistic" images in illustration in order to convey mood and emotion is conceptual, but even with young children the expression of feelings can be demonstrated through color and pictures. Drawing experiences with relatives seems a natural after this experience.

Geography: The language of the text in this book is repeated by the children spontaneously. A map of the United States is needed for children to learn the relationship between Virginia and wherever they happen to live. *Questions to answer:* Where is it night when it is daytime in your state? What's different about mountains and flatlands? How far must we travel from here to there? Where do grapes grow?

Genealogy: Even in the group discussing this book, where relatives fill the neighborhood, some of the children have never had relatives stay overnight. Some children have no relatives. Perhaps building genealogical charts would bring children in touch with their families in a way that is possible.

BOOKS FOR FOLLOW-UP LITERATURE STUDIES

Caines, Jeannette. (1982). *Just Us Women.* Illustrated by Pat Cummings. Harper and Row.

> Aunt Martha and the hero of this story are driving together to North Carolina from, presumably, Virginia. "No boys and no men, just us women," says Aunt Martha. The same journey was taken by the two the year before, so they have established rituals: ways not to forget maps and lunch, flea marketing, shopping at farms, walking in the rain, and eating in restaurants. It's no wonder that when they arrive, they are asked, "What took you so long?" The family is African-American.

MacLachlan, Patricia. (1980). *Arthur, for the Very First Time.* Harper and Row.

> Arthur spends a summer with his relatives and finds out more about himself in the process. This title could be used with fourth through sixth grade.

Mathis, Sharon Bell. (1975). *The Hundred Penny Box.* Illustrated by Leo and Diane Dillon. Viking Press.

> Michael and his mother have differing reactions to Aunt Dew who is 100 years old and remembering her life through the pennies her husband gave her. All ages will enjoy this story, but it will take more than one session to read.

Rylant, Cynthia. (1972). *When I Was Young in the Mountains.* Illustrated by Diane Goode. Dutton.

> In similar format to *The Relatives Came,* the child in this story remembers her grandparents and other family rituals of childhood in the mountains.

Robert D. San Souci, *The Talking Eggs: A Folktale from the American South*

- -

Publisher and Date: Dell, 1987
Illustrator: Jerry Pinkney
Audience Level: Kindergarten and up
Main Theme: Obedience, Reward and Punishment
Other Possible Themes: Goodness, Meanness, Cleverness,
　　　Kindness, Patience, Magic, Temptation
Values to Target: Goodness, Kindness

- -

ABOUT THE AUTHOR

Robert D. San Souci was born in San Francisco in 1946. He has been a free-lance writer, theater critic, and educational consultant. He has written for adults as well as children. In his work for children he has focused primarily on adapting folktales. His brother is an illustrator and collaborated with him on his earlier books. San Souci says, "I use narrative to explore ideas and suggest answers to questions about why and how the world works" (*SATA*, v.40, pp. 200-01).

ABOUT THE ILLUSTRATOR

Jerry Pinkney is a prolific and versatile illustrator for children. He grew up in Philadelphia in a family that supported his interest in drawing. Pinkney doesn't remember being a terrific reader, or even associating drawing with stories. He simply drew anything and everything. He says that he was assigned every project in school which had anything to do with drawing. This made him feel special. As a adult, he worked as a designer/illustrator for various companies before opening his own studio. He worked for a greeting card company in Boston before he began illustrating for textbooks. By the early seventies publishers were seeking African-American artists to illustrate the work of black writers. When Pinkney was presented with opportunities, he researched his material extensively, and produced such high quality work that he became very much in demand. Over the years he has won many awards. Some of his more well-known works in children's literature are the cover for *Roll of Thunder, Hear My Cry*, and *The Patchwork Quilt* which has been produced for *Reading Rainbow*. Pinkney uses both photography and models for developing characters such as those that appear in *The Talking Eggs* . Children may notice how he tries to depict motion in his drawings.

Pinkney and his wife have four children, two of whom are artists. Other interesting projects Pinkney has completed include a cover for *National Geographic*, commercials for Kool Aid, art design for Sesame Street, dinner plate designs, and the commemorative stamps for the U.S. Postal Service "Black Heritage" series (*SATA* v. 41, pp. 164-70).

ABOUT THE STORY

This old Louisiana folktale, complete with delicious dialect and idiom, is a favorite of children of all ages. Blanche, the good daughter, is kind, obedient, and "sharp as forty crickets." Her sister Rose is cross and mean and doesn't "know beans from bird eggs." Their mother is spoiled and lazy, spending her time sitting on the porch with Rose dreaming about the days when the two of them can wear "trail train dresses" and live like ladies. Blanche does all the chores. One day on her way to the well to fetch water for her sister, she encounters an old woman and magical adventures begin. She meets all the tests for kindness and obedience, finally obeying the old woman's warning *not* to take the talking jeweled eggs which say "Take me! Take me." Then the story of the opposites takes place, as Rose and her mother conspire to take away Blanche's treasures. After all the magical events, it is Blanche, not Rose and their mother, who goes to the city to live as a lady.

This folktale is rich in archetypal patterns, so the possibilities for response are endless. We paired this story with *Mufaro's Beautiful Daughters* for comparison and contrast of authored folktale motifs.

DIALOGUE

Talk about What You Notice in the Story

• •

The first responses recorded from these kindergarten children during the reading of the text are interactive and predictive. The magical foods and the party with the dancing rabbits offer more opportunities to discover magic. The dance reflects the spirit of Cajun music. Children fully enjoy predicting Rose's disobedience and the ugly creatures the jeweled eggs contained. Their great pleasure is the satisfaction that it is *Blanche* who goes to live like a lady. Emily concludes, "Well, she *is* the lady!" Notice that Corey wishes he was in the brambles, after he found out what they were.

• •

Emily: Blanche is stringing the beans.

Corey: She's doing work.

Aubree: The mama and sister are being mean to her.

Teacher: BLANCHE HAS MET AN OLD WOMAN. DO YOU THINK SHE WILL GIVE HER A DRINK OF WATER?

Timmy: Yes, because she's good.

Meredith: Even when she brings the water.

Corey: What are brambles?

Aubree: Those sticker things in the woods that scratch your legs.

Corey: Oh, I know now. I wish I was in that story so the brambles would let me through.

Teacher: YOU NOTICED THE BRAMBLES OPENING UP. I WONDER HOW THAT CAN BE.

Aubree: The old woman is a magic lady.

Emily: She must have told the brambles to open up.

Aubree: Brambles keep people from getting to her house.

Teacher: I WONDER WHY THE WOMAN WORKS HER MAGIC FOR BLANCHE.

Corey: Because she got her a drink of water.

Teacher: I NOTICE THAT THE OLD WOMAN SAYS TO BLANCHE "DON'T LAUGH." DO YOU THINK BLANCHE WILL DO WHAT THE OLD WOMAN SAYS?

Chorus: Yeah.

Timmy: Because she's *good.*

Teacher: LET'S PLAY A GAME TO SEE HOW HARD IT IS FOR BLANCHE TO DO WHAT THE OLD WOMAN SAYS. BEFORE I READ THE NEXT PAGES, LET'S SAY I'M THE OLD WOMAN AND I SAY TO YOU, "DON'T LAUGH." YOU DO YOUR BEST. REMEMBER NOW, WHAT IS THE RULE OF OUR GAME?

Chorus: *[loud and admonishing]* Don't laugh!

• •

The children thoroughly enjoy trying to hold back laugher at the three horned cow, and collapse with giggles when the chickens sing like mockingbirds.

• •

Teacher: WE ARE LAUGHING! LET'S TRY AGAIN. NOW I'M GOING TO READ ANOTHER PAGE. DON'T LAUGH.

(more laughter and gasps as the woman removes her head)

Aubree: Oh my gosh! The old woman is taking her head off!

Timmy:	I would scream if I saw that!
Meredith:	You should have said "Don't Scream!"
Timmy:	How can she comb her hair if her eyes are on her head?
Aubree:	She's magic. It doesn't matter much.
TEACHER:	IS BLANCHE LAUGHING?
Chorus:	No!
Emily:	I bet she's smiling a little bit.
TEACHER:	NOW WE CAN LOOK FOR EVEN MORE MAGIC. THE TITLE OF THIS STORY IS ABOUT TALKING EGGS. I HAVEN'T SEEN ANY TALKING EGGS IN THIS STORY YET.
Emily:	*[laughing]* Eggs can't talk!
Corey:	Oh, yes they can!
TEACHER:	DO YOU THINK SHE WILL THROW THEM OVER HER LEFT SHOULDER?
Chorus:	*[delighted at their prediction]* "She's good." "She will do the right thing." "Look! Treasures." "Like Cinderella!"
Aubree:	Now it's Rose and the old woman.
TEACHER:	IT'S LIKE THE STORY IS HAPPENING OVER. DO YOU THINK IT WILL BE THE SAME FOR ROSE?
Timmy:	*[confident of his prediction]* No. She's mean.
Aubree:	I think it will be *just* the other way around.

Talk about How the Story Makes You Feel

• •

This conversation with a third and fourth grade remedial reading class became earnestly involved in the meaning of verbal "picking," which caused children enormous difficulty. The class conducted a literature study of the story over a three-week period.

• •

Tim:	I hated Rose. She was lazy!
Michael:	My mother wouldn't have liked Rose best!
Paris:	Mine would have liked Blanche best because she was good.
Tim:	She was honest. She worked hard.
Octeria:	Her mama was still mean.
TEACHER:	IT'S IMPORTANT HOW WE THINK ABOUT OUR MOTHERS.
Michael:	My mama is good. I get mad when anybody says anything about my mama. *[chorus of agreement]*
Paris:	Nobody better say anything to me about my mama!
TEACHER:	SO WE HATE ROSE. AND WE DON'T THINK BLANCHE WAS TREATED FAIRLY. HOW DO YOU FEEL ABOUT BLANCHE?

Shan:	Well, I want to be like Blanche, but I don't want to take all that picking.
TEACHER:	IT'S HARD TO BE KIND WHEN SOMEONE IS MEAN TO YOU.
Shan:	We get a mark on the board when we pick.
TEACHER:	IS THIS FAIR?
Paris:	Yes. If we don't pick, it's like getting treasures.
Octeria:	I'm going to be like Blanche when I get to be a grandma!

Talk about What the Story Reminds You of in Your Life

• •

These responses are from fifth and sixth graders in a regular classroom. Dustin's and Kevin's appreciation of the language of the text is in part due to the teacher's same appreciation. Kelly's remark about being half Rose and half Blanche is exactly what teachers want children to see in folktales.

• •

TEACHER:	ONE REASON I LIKE FOLKTALES IS THAT THEY TAKE US OUT OF OURSELVES INTO A MAGICAL WORLD. BUT SOME THINGS REMIND US OF OURSELVES. LET'S TALK ABOUT SOME OF THE METAPHORS IN THE STORY. THE PLAIN EGGS CONTAINED THE TREASURES, NOT THE JEWELED ONES.
Daniel:	Yep! You can't tell a book by its cover!
Kelly:	Some things that look good aren't good.
B.J.:	Sometimes the coolest looking stuff in the store is cheap and tears up.
Kevin:	I know! Maybe the jeweled eggs are temptation.
TEACHER:	CAN YOU SAY MORE, KEVIN?
Kevin:	It's like we just want to do something because we've been told *not* to do it.
Dustin:	Yeah! Like I was walking through the pasture with my B.B. gun and I found this old deserted shack with windows. They weren't broken. It was like they were talking, "Don't shoot me! Don't shoot me!" So I did!

• •

After the laughter subsided, many more had "stories" of temptation. Dirt clods said, "Don't throw me, Don't throw me!" Stephanie's sister's coke said, "Don't drink me! Don't drink me!"

• •

| TEACHER: | SO YOU FIND IT'S HARD TO OBEY LIKE BLANCHE ALL THE TIME. |
| Kelly: | Well, I think I'm just half and half! Half Rose and Half Blanche. |

Kevin: [philosophically] Life is full of lizards and treasures!

TEACHER FOCUS

Folktale Motifs: This story is much like other folktales but also very different. Comparisons will lead to better understanding of the construction of folktales.

Follow Directions: The predictive nature of this story like other folktales lends humor, but the moral is still the same—follow directions or get in trouble.

COUNSELOR FOCUS

Choices and Consequences: How does one decide which choice to make? What is the difference between Rose and Blanche that makes them choose differently?

MAKING CONNECTIONS

Talking Eggs Game: The teacher brought "jeweled eggs" and boiled eggs to the kindergarten group. A parent volunteer spontaneously invented a game that included different whispered instructions, such as "When I say take an egg, *don't* take one." Children added their own whispered ideas, such as "Tell only four people to take jeweled eggs, since that's all we've got." The final celebration was eating the boiled eggs!

Art: Dustin's story about the "talking window pane" stimulated other stories of temptation that were told and enjoyed through pictures in his sixth grade class.

Music: The rabbits' party inspires a closer look at Cajun music. There are two distinct sounds to Cajun music. The more traditional comes from the French influence in Louisiana. This music inspired a style of dancing called the cajun two-step. This sound was modified and became more energetic when African-American musicians joined the band. To catch the flavor of the Zydeco music for children, use a tape entitled *Cookin' with Queen Ida and the Zydeco Band* (Crescendo Records # 2197, available by mail from Note-ably Yours, 6865 Scarff Road, New Carlisle, OH, Phone: 1-800-828-0115). Cookin' means jammin'!

BOOKS FOR FOLLOW-UP LITERATURE STUDIES

Starred titles have full entries elsewhere in the book.

Aardema, Verna. (1975). *Why Mosquitoes Buzz in People's Ears*. Illustrated by Leo and Diane Dillon. Dial.

> In this cumulative West African tale each of the characters denies his responsibility for killing owlet. In one class that read this story, conversations between children and the teacher were built on earlier discussions of kindness and obedience, with added emphasis on responsibility and the ineffectiveness of "tattling." With the guidance of the teacher, the children were able, with some humor, to understand their classroom behavior, in the light of the mosquito's whining, as cumulative blaming.

dePaola, Tomie. (1975). *Strega Nona*. Prentice Hall.

> Big Anthony finds it hard to obey when Strega Nona leaves him alone with the magical pasta pot.

Hooks, William. (1990). *The Ballad of Belle Dorcas*. Illustrated by Brian Pinkney. Alfred A. Knopf.

> This conjure tale from tidewater Carolina contains a magical old woman whose powers are sought by a slave girl, Belle Dorcas.

*Steptoe, John. (1987). *Mufaro's Beautiful Daughters: An African Tale*. Lothrop, Lee and Shepard.

> Common motifs include the two sisters, the magical old woman, and the theme of goodness in return for meanness. See the full entry for this story for more references to Cinderella.

Other Books with Kindness as a Theme

McDonald, Megan. (1990). *The Potato Man*. Illustrated by Ted Lewin. Orchard Books.

> Neighborhood boys tease the potato man and steal his wares. The old man returns only kindness.

Tolstoy, Leo. (1986). *Shoemaker Martin*. Adapted by Brigitte Hanhart. Translated by Michael Hale. Illustrated by Bernadett Watts. North-South Books.

> A shoemaker gives food and shelter to many passersby, not recognizing the full meaning of what he has done.

Maurice Sendak, *Where the Wild Things Are*

• •

Publisher and Date: Harper and Row, 1963
Illustrator: Maurice Sendak

Audience Level: Kindergarten and up
Main Theme: Anger
Other Possible Themes: Misbehavior, Homesickness, Love, Fear, Powerlessness
Values to Target: Self-knowledge

● ●

ABOUT THE AUTHOR

There is much about Maurice Sendak that is fascinating. Both of his parents came from Poland before World War I. Maurice, born in 1928, was the youngest of three children. To him his childhood seemed like "one long series of illnesses." He had a reputation for being very frail. "I was miserable as a kid . . . I couldn't make friends. I couldn't play stoopball terrific. I couldn't skate great. I stayed home and drew pictures." He hated school. In order to get there, he said, "I had to talk myself out of a state of panic every day" (p. 182). He loved Mickey Mouse, monster films, and comic books. He had his first job as a cartoonist, drawing in the backgrounds for Mutt and Jeff, when he was still in high school.

His art style was influenced by cartoonists. He constructed some animated toys for F.A.O. Schwartz in New York, and by 1950 had his first chance to illustrate a children's book.

Where the Wild Things Are is his most popular book. He says that the Wild Things started out as wild horses, but he couldn't draw horses. He changed his idea to "things." He wanted them to be frightening. He writes that this book was written, "not to please everybody, only children." He once received a letter from a little boy: "How much does it cost to get to where the wild things are? If it is not expensive, my sister and I want to spend the summer there. Please answer soon."

In his acceptance speech for the 1964 Caldecott Medal, Sendak said "What is obvious is the fact that from their earliest years children live on familiar terms with disrupting emotions. And it is through fantasy that children achieve catharsis. It is the best means they have for taming Wild Things" (p. 286).

"Max," said Sendak, "is my truest and therefore my dearest creation. Like all children, he believes in a flexible world of fantasy and reality, a world where a child can skip from one to the other and back again in the sure belief that both really exist. Another quality that makes him especially lovable to me is the directness of his approach. Max doesn't shilly-shally around. He gets to the heart of the matter with the speed of a superjet. Max has appeared in my other books under different names: Kenny, Martin, and Rosie. They all have the same need to master the uncontrollable and frightening aspects of their lives . . ." (p. 188) (*SATA* v. 27, pp. 181-200).

ABOUT THE STORY

When Max makes mischief, his mother calls him a "wild thing" and banishes him to his bedroom with no supper. Max conjures up a fantasy world that he reaches by boat "in and out of weeks and almost over a year." It is a place where there are Wild Things who are both scary and lovable. Max is in control in the land of the Wild Things. He tames them by staring into their yellow eyes. When he remembers a place where "someone loves him best of all," he says goodbye and returns to his very own room where a supper has been put out for him—and it's still hot!

We believe that Maurice Sendak was right about fantasy and catharsis. It is our experience that while young children may not be able to verbalize all they feel during a reading of this story, the catharsis is readily achieved through interaction. Tapes of our sessions with this story are full of chuckles, squeals, roars, belly laughs, and wistful sighs.

DIALOGUE

Talk about What You Notice in the Story

• •

Christopher answers his own question about the meaning of the word mischief with the help of contextual clues from the other children. These elementary age children work together on the meaning of rumpus. The teacher promotes dramatic speech in reciting the words of the story. You can easily tell why this story is dramatized in many schools.

• •

Paula:	His wolf suit has whiskers!
Christopher:	What's mischief?
Brandon:	Mischief is playing around maybe.
Paula:	But he's playing too rough with the dog.
Kristy:	And his poor little teddy bear's just hanging there.
TEACHER:	NOW DO WE KNOW WHAT MISCHIEF IS?
Christopher:	He may be playing, but he's being mean.
TEACHER:	YOU GOT IT! THAT'S MISCHIEF!
Brandon:	Oh! He talked back to his mother!
TEACHER:	CAN YOU SAY IT LIKE MAX SAID IT?
Brandon:	*[fuming]* I'll eat you up!

Kevin:	*[with a sing-song voice]* He's in trou-ble! *[gales of laughter]* (From the text: ". . . a forest grew.")
Megan:	I know what he's thinking. "Ha! Mama can't get me now."
Paula:	He's giggling!
TEACHER:	LET'S ALL TRY OUT HIS GIGGLE. *[a chorus of snickers behind hands.]*
Ricky:	I'd love to have a forest grow in my room.
Tara:	*[authoritatively]* This is a make-believe story. I can *tell.*
Brad:	*[with conviction]* Right! And a river can't be in your room either.
Christopher:	*[joking]* Well, you could always open the door when it is raining!
Brandon:	Un oh! No way! *[as Max travels in his boat]*
Paula:	*[dreamily, in the mood of the text]* I think he is having a nice dream now. *[as the Wild Things are introduced in the illustrations]*
Ricky:	Wow! That lady has chicken feet.
Paula:	That girl monster is going to step on everybody's tail.
TEACHER:	NOW THIS IS A RUMPUS. WHAT DO YOU THINK ABOUT IT?
Chorus:	"It's a dance." "I think it's a march." "It might be ballet." "I just think it's a wild party." *[As Max stares into the eyes of the monsters]*
TEACHER:	NOW I'D LIKE TO PRACTICE A MAGIC TRICK. WHEN I SAY "BE STILL!" YOU FREEZE. I'LL STARE WITHOUT BLINKING, LIKE MAX. *[A short spontaneous role play with Max's taming trick]*
Paula:	Max is the boss. He's king. *[As Max's thoughts turn toward home]*
Christopher:	I think he's thirsty and hungry and he wants to go home.
Paula:	I think he's missing his bed.
Christopher:	He's homesick. *[Sighs and smiles as Max's boat returns home to the place where "someone loves him best of all"]*

Talk about How the Story Makes You Feel

• •

The teacher asks, "How do you feel when you have on your wolf suit?" The children accept the metaphorical question with understanding. Stories about the pain of physical separation are related by

the children in concrete terms, but they eventually build an understanding of the separation that results from anger as well.

● ●

TEACHER: I NOTICED THAT BRANDON COULD TALK JUST LIKE MAX WHEN HE WAS
ANGRY. LET'S FIND OUR ANGRY VOICES. READY. READ TOGETHER!

All: "I'll eat you up!"

TEACHER: NOW WE KNOW HOW IT FEELS TO BE ANGRY. MAX DID MISCHIEF AND
TALKED BACK TO HIS MOTHER. HOW DO YOU FEEL WHEN YOU HAVE ON
YOUR WOLF SUIT?

Brandon: I get scared I'll get in trouble.

Ricky: I got sent to my room before.

Jonathan: I talk back and I don't mean to.

Chorus: "Me, too." "It feels bad."

TEACHER: SOME THINGS HAPPENED TO MAX IN THE KINGDOM OF THE WILD
THINGS.

Brandon: He wanted to change the Wild Things.

Christopher: He made them nicer.

TEACHER: WOULD YOU BE SCARED OF THOSE WILD THINGS?

Tara: Not if I was Max! He was the king.

TEACHER: MAX WAS IN CHARGE. BUT HE DIDN'T WANT TO STAY FOREVER. "OH
PLEASE DON'T GO. WE'LL EAT YOU UP. WE LOVE YOU SO."
[Gales of laughter and requests to repeat the phrase]

Paula: He got homesick and thirsty and hungry and wanted to
come home to supper. I felt homesick when I spent the night
with my aunt and Mommy and Daddy were at home.

Kristen: Me, too. I feel it all the time in my tummy. Like the time
Mama and I went off and Daddy was still at home because
he was working. I got homesick for Daddy.

Talk about What the Story Reminds You of in Your Life

● ●

The teacher does grand questioning to follow up on the metaphor.
Then she draws them out of the story to an evaluative stance, "I
wonder why . . ." people have read the book for 25 years. The
answers demonstrate appreciation for literary language and story
structure.

● ●

J.D.: It reminds me of the time I thought there was a monster
outside my bedroom window. And it was just a raccoon!

Megan: My cat Tiger is a Wild Thing when he yowls at me.

TEACHER:	LET'S TALK ABOUT TAMING WILD THINGS. CAN YOU DO IT?
Shawn:	I give my brother a pickle and it tames him.
Linda:	I tickle my little sister and it tames her.
TEACHER:	WHAT ABOUT YOUR OWN FEELINGS, THE WILD THINGS INSIDE YOU? CAN YOU TELL THEM TO "BE STILL."
Josh:	I don't know. If a bully gets after me, I go wild. I am a Wild Thing.
TEACHER:	CAN YOU TELL YOURSELF, "BE STILL"?
Josh:	Well, if I can remember to breathe deep, I won't get in trouble.
TEACHER:	WHEN YOU BREATHE DEEP, YOU ARE LIKE MAX.
Josh:	*[a light going on]* Yeah! If I've been making mischief, *[with dramatic flair]* I can say, "Be still."
TEACHER:	GREAT! DO IT AGAIN FOR US. I'LL BE A WILD THING AND YOU STARE ME DOWN AND DO ALL YOUR MAGIC.
	[Several improvisations and versions of taming Wild Things]
TEACHER:	THIS BOOK HAS BEEN AROUND FOR MORE THAN 25 YEARS AND PEOPLE STILL LOVE IT. I WONDER WHY.
Megan:	I like saying, "I'm going to eat you up" like Max. I wouldn't say that to my mama in real life though.
Brad:	I think it's because it has the happy ending. His supper was still hot.

TEACHER FOCUS

Cooperative Learning Through Conversation: Children enjoy working out the meaning of a story together. They learn to speak one at a time and listen to each other to help themselves learn.

Metaphor: The wild things become part of the children's vocabulary and can be referred to as a model for other expressions to describe behaviors, concepts, and feelings.

Author Study: Even kindergarten children are not too young to study more of Maurice Sendak's work. For older children, there are videotapes of interviews with Mr. Sendak available from Weston Woods.

Writing: This book serves as a model for choice of words, rhythm of language, and development of fantasy. Analyzing the language could lead to the writing of poetry or the children's own fantasy stories.

COUNSELOR FOCUS

Anger: How do we handle anger? The counselor can be supportive of children's fantasies in dealing with problems in the children's lives that cause anger.

Mothers: Max's mother is scolding, angry, punishing, and loving, allowing for many connections to be made with the real experiences of children.

Managing Negative Feelings: The taming of the Wild Things is Max's greatest achievement. Managing feelings is an ongoing developmental task for children. *Where the Wild Things Are* demonstrates one way that it can be done, which is why children will ask for this story over and over.

MAKING CONNECTIONS

Art: One cooperative learning group used papier-mâché to construct a Wild Thing. Each child made a body part, learning proportion together as other body parts were constructed. All enjoyed painting the creation.

Music: A fourth grade class produced an original musical version of this story, composing an original song entitled "King of the Wild Things." They created the instrumentation using rythmn and percussion instruments. Masks were made in art class for the Wild Things.

BOOKS FOR FOLLOW-UP LITERATURE STUDIES

Lionni, Leo. (1963). *Swimmy*. Alfred A. Knopf.
> A small fish is frightened and lonely when all his brothers and sisters are eaten by a large fish. He finds a creative way to swim in safety, overcoming his fears and the dangers of the deep.

Mayer, Mercer. (1968). *There's a Nightmare in My Closet*. Dial Press.
> A little boy encounters and conquers his nightmares.

Susan Shreve, "Cheating" from Family Secrets: Five Very Important Stories

• •

Publisher and Date: Alfred A. Knopf, 1979
Illustrator: Richard Cuffari
Audience: Grades four and up
Main Theme: Cheating

Other Possible Themes: Choices, Forgiveness, Rules
Values to Target: Honesty, Responsibility for Choices, Moral
    Reasoning

● ●

ABOUT THE AUTHOR

Susan Shreve writes that she "grew up in a house full of stories." Her father was a reporter and not only told stories but "made our lives into stories." Susan was ill as a child with rheumatic fever and was in bed for months during which time she played "pretend" and made up stories. She graduated from college, and has taught English in England, Pennsylvania, and rural Virginia. She is married to a family therapist and is the mother of four children. She wrote first for adults but as her children grew, she began to write for them (*SATA* v. 46, pp. 197-99).

ABOUT THE BOOK

All five stories in this collection affirm the wisdom, strength, and love within Sammy's family. Issues such as the death of a pet, the suicide of a friend, cheating in math class, divorce, and aging are presented in the five episodic chapters. Shreve creates a believable character, Sammy, through a well-sustained first-person point of view. In the story "Cheating" (Chapter 5), Sammy is convinced that he has become a criminal because he cheated on a math test. After wrestling with his conscience, he eventually chooses to obey the family rule of telling the truth.

Upper elementary children are eager to discuss cheating, lying, fairness, and rules. In our many experiences with this story, we have found it helpful to keep in mind the levels and stages of moral reasoning as described by Kohlberg. Here we briefly outline the theory up to stage 5, categorize some typical responses, and suggest some questions that the teacher may use to attract children to higher level thinking:

Stage One: Right is avoidance of punishment.

Key Words: "You shouldn't cheat or you'll get in trouble." "You might get caught and get a zero." "If you don't stop cheating now, it will catch up with you." "You may end up in jail."

Question to elicit next level of response: "What are some other reasons you might decide not to cheat (or lie) even when you think you might get by with it?"

Stage Two: Right is obedience in order to get a reward.

Key Words: "Your friends don't like it when you copy their paper." "You might not get the answer right anyway if you copy a paper and theirs is wrong."

Question to elicit next level of response: "How do you feel if you cheat (or lie)?" "What if you did get a good grade and only you knew you cheated, does that make it right?"

Stage Three: Right is being good, or being approved of by others.

Key Words: "If I cheat, I feel terrible." "It's almost easier if you get spanked when you're bad. I don't like to let my mama down."

Question to elicit next level of response: "Who really gets hurt by cheating or lying?" "Why do you think we have laws and rules against cheating?"

Stage Four: We need to have rules and to do our duty.

Key Words: "You hurt yourself because you might not learn anything. Besides it's a bad habit." "If everybody cheated, we would have a terrible school." "If adults cheat, I feel like the whole world can fall apart." "If everybody could just steal everything, nobody would have anything."

Question to elicit next level of response: Can you think of any situation where the usual rules about cheating, lying, or stealing might need to be changed?

Stage Five (rarely attainable in elementary children): Laws are changeable to meet human needs.

Rules and laws are seen in terms of individual human rights.

BEFORE THE READING

Before beginning to read, it helps to introduce the characters: Sammy, Nicho (his little brother), Carlotta (his baby sister), his mother and father, and Mr. Burke (his teacher), who appear in previous chapters.

DIALOGUE

Talk about What You Notice in the Story

• •

These fifth graders are beyond being affected by punishment for a "crime." They support the harder choice of having to rectify the "crime" of cheating. Beth says Sammy will just forget a spanking. Daniel takes the thought one step farther. Holly insightfully distinguishes "bad" from disobeying a rule. The whole subject of rules leads to definitions of rules emanating from family.

• •

TEACHER: SOMETIMES WE CAN START BY NOTICING HOW MANY CHOICES A CHARACTER MAKES IN A STORY. I NOTICE THAT SAMMY MADE MANY CHOICES.
(The children came up with the following and recorded it on newsprint.)

Sammy chose:
- not to do his homework
- to lie about it
- to cheat on the math test
- to tell his father the truth
- to do what his father asked as "punishment" or "consequences"

Sammy's father chose:
- to insist that Sammy remember the one important family rule (tell the truth)
- to listen without blaming Sammy
- to make him call his teacher
- to kiss him goodnight that night—to forgive him

TEACHER: NOW THAT WE HAVE OUR OUTLINE OF CHOICES IN FRONT OF US WE CAN FIND LOTS MORE TO TALK ABOUT. WHAT HAPPENED AS A RESULT OF SAMMY'S CHEATING ON THE TEST?

Regina: Sammy got in trouble.

Haley: His father could have spanked him.

Chris: I think calling the teacher was a better idea, because that's hard.

Beth: I think it's almost harder, and it makes more sense. Sammy won't ever forget that day. He might forget it if he just got a spanking.

Daniel:	He felt better after the phone call. After a spanking, you usually feel worse.
Shanna:	Sammy had a good father.
TEACHER:	REMEMBER HOW SAMMY SAID HE WONDERED IF HE "WAS JUST PLAIN BAD TO THE CORE?"
Jessica:	Yes, he mostly wished he was dead!
Chris:	(smiling) He thought he was going to turn into a criminal.
Holly:	He won't. He cares too much. People who are really bad don't care.
TEACHER:	WHY DO YOU SUPPOSE HE CARES?
Angela:	His family helped him by caring about him.
TEACHER:	HERE ARE IMPORTANT SENTENCES FROM THE STORY. "NOT MUCH IS IMPORTANT IN OUR FAMILY. MY PARENTS DON'T BOTHER MAKING UP A LOT OF RULES. BUT WE DO HAVE TO TELL THE TRUTH, EVEN IF IT'S BAD, WHICH IT USUALLY IS."
Shanna:	Telling the truth *is* important.
Charles:	That's a pretty good rule. We have that in our family.
TEACHER:	SAMMY'S FRIENDS HAVE MORE RULES THAN HE DOES.
Allie:	We need rules. Sometimes people make up too many though.
TEACHER:	THEN WHAT ARE THE MOST IMPORTANT RULES?
Rob:	The ones that keep people from getting hurt.
Jerome:	Ones like not stealing or fighting.
Jennifer:	Our class needs rules so we know what to do. We couldn't get work done if were all did just what we want to do all the time.
Shanna:	What about the Golden Rule?
	(Not many were really sure of the exact wording of the golden rule. The group's collective memory recalled pieces of the Ten Commandments and the Bill of Rights. Consensus was that the Golden Rule stood the test of the best rule if we could have only one.)

Talk about How the Story Makes You Feel

• •

The teacher informs the children about writing in the first person. The discussion centers on Sammy's voice, and why the author chose not to use an "outside" voice or third person point of view. The children appreciate being close to Sammy's "real feelings."

• •

TEACHER:	I NOTICED HOW ATTENTIVE YOU WERE DURING THE STORY. THAT TELLS ME THAT MANY OF YOU HAVE FELT LIKE SAMMY.
Jessie:	I feel like Sammy lots of times when I get in trouble. Like being too sick to eat lunch.
Regina:	The author wrote it so we really knew about Sammy's feelings all the way through.
TEACHER:	WHAT WERE THE FEELINGS YOU NOTICED? *(Children compiled more evidence of Sammy's feelings of guilt and apprehension about facing the consequences. "He couldn't eat." "He was sure he would turn into a criminal.")*

Talk about What the Story Reminds You of in Your Life

● ●

The teacher praises the children for their honesty in discussing their own experiences with cheating. Jessie and Alan attempt to put the topic into a philosophical perspective.

● ●

TEACHER:	THE TITLE OF THIS STORY IS "CHEATING." THERE IS PLENTY OF CHEATING IN OUR WORLD TODAY. WHY ARE THERE LAWS AND RULES AGAINST CHEATING?
Chad:	Well, everybody cheats some time in their life.
Jennifer:	In school it's like stealing somebody's work. It's not yours. So it's not right.
Chris:	The teacher doesn't know whether you know anything or not if you copy a paper.
TEACHER:	WHAT ABOUT YOU? DO YOU CARE TO KNOW?
Holly:	You should care. You might not be sure what you do know and what you don't. Then you'd get promoted and you wouldn't know anything in the sixth grade.
TEACHER:	WHO GETS HURT WHEN A PERSON CHEATS?
Valerie:	The one who does it might feel bad.
Casey:	If you get by with it, you might get in a bad habit and cheat all your life. You'd get caught sometime and maybe get in jail.
Melissa:	It's not fair to the one whose paper you copy, because maybe she has studied and you haven't.
TEACHER:	WHAT IF EVERYBODY CHEATED?
Jennifer:	We would *not* have a good world.
TEACHER:	SAMMY SAID IT WAS NO ACCIDENT THAT HE CHEATED. HE DID IT IN "COLD BLOOD." IS IT EVER AN ACCIDENT WHEN YOU CHEAT?

Chris:	Well, maybe. You might realize at the last minute that you forgot some of your times tables and you just accidentally look at somebody's paper. (sheepishly) Or maybe they had it too close to you so you could see it without trying. *(Laughter)*
Alan:	Now, really, do you accidentally look at somebody's paper?
Casey:	Accidentally, on purpose! *(laughter)*
TEACHER:	I REALLY LIKE HOW HONEST YOUR DISCUSSION IS! NOW, WHICH IS EASIER—TO SAY CHEATING IS WRONG OR TO KEEP YOURSELF FROM DOING IT?
Regina:	Easier to say it!
Casey:	I think lots of people cheat who know it's wrong.
Alan:	And they do it anyway.
Jessie:	But people who are mostly good don't do it all the time.
Alan:	Yeah, not like a habit or anything.
TEACHER:	IS THAT WHEN IT'S BAD, WHEN IT'S A HABIT?
Alan:	Well, I guess it's worse then, but you can't say it's good or right any time.

TEACHER FOCUS

Literature Study: This story is good for analyzing the elements of story. How does the author inform us that the father is a "good father" as Shanna said? The use of cliches in unexpected places is effective. When do cliches work, and when not?

Government: The story is a good place to begin with a study of law in society. How far can we go with a "little cheating?" The term "skeletons in the closet" could be introduced with older classes. The relationship between secrets and candidates for public office is another connection.

COUNSELOR FOCUS

Cheating: Cheating is a big issue in schools, and the feelings associated with it are presented in this story.

Secrets: The topic of secrets in group discussions is pleasing to children simply because they feel better knowing that everyone has secrets. This book can be used to introduce the role of the counselor who listens to "secrets" and can be trusted to be confidential.

MAKING CONNECTIONS

Music: This is a good opportunity to talk about rules and to use John McCutcheon's song "Kindergarten Wall" on the tape *Water from Another Time* (Appalseed Productions, 1025 Locust Ave. Charlottesville, VA 22901. Telephone: 804-977-6321). This song is based on the well-known selection from the book, *All I Ever Wanted to Know I Learned in Kindergarten* by Robert Fulghum.

The rules stated in McCutcheon's song are:

1. Don't hurt each other.
2. Clean up your mess.
3. Take a nap every day.
4. Wash before you eat.
5. Hold hands. Stick together. Look before you cross the street.

Students may compare codes of law such as the Ten Commandments, the Golden Rule, and the Bill of Rights with the "Kindergarten Wall" rules.

BOOKS FOR FOLLOW-UP LITERATURE STUDIES

Bauer, Marion Dane. (1986). *On My Honor.* Clarion Books.
> Joel promised never to go swimming in the river that flowed near his home. He does, and his best friend drowns.

Fox, Paula. (1984). *The One-Eyed Cat.* Bradbury Press.
> An eleven year old is told never to shoot the air rifle he has received as a present. He cannot resist. When he sees a stray cat with a bullet wound, he assumes that he must be guilty. He struggles with his conscience.

Hurwitz, Johanna. (1978). *The Law of Gravity.* Morrow Books.
> The family secrets in this story include an obese mother who won't leave the apartment. The girl protagonist tries on her own to resolve the problems.

Shel Silverstein, *The Giving Tree*

● ●

Publisher and Date: Harper and Row Publishers, 1964
Illustrator: Shel Silverstein
Audience Level: Grades four and up
Main Theme: Giving

Other Possible Themes: Happiness, the Environment, Gender, Taking
Values to Target: Giving and Taking

● ●

ABOUT THE AUTHOR

Shel Silverstein, who also writes under the name "Uncle Shelby," was born in Chicago in 1932. As a kid, he remembers feeling that he was no good at playing ball and dancing; therefore, he started to draw and write. In the 1950s he became a cartoonist for a military newspaper while serving in the army in Japan. He was introduced to children's books by Tomi Ungerer who illustrated some of Silverstein's early verses. He now illustrates all his own work, including the well-known poetry collections, *Light in the Attic* and *Where the Sidewalk Ends*. A *New York Times* reviewer wrote: "Uncle Shelby has a theory that children and elderly parents like to be treated as anyone else, not as children and elderly parents."

Silverstein is not only an artist and writer, but a composer, singer, and guitarist. He wrote the hit song, "A Boy Named Sue," made popular by Johnny Cash. He currently divides his time between New York, Chicago, Key West, and Sausalito (*SATA* v. 27, pp. 210-13).

ABOUT THE BOOK

The Giving Tree has been one of the most widely read books for children during the past 25 years. On the surface it is a simple story. A tree (she!) loves a boy. The boy loves the tree. He eats its fruit and swings on its branches. As the boy grows older, he has less and less time for the tree. He does return to the tree as a youth, a young man, a middle aged man, and, finally, as a dejected old man. The tree continues to refer to him as "boy" and to give him all she can give, apples, branches, even her trunk. The tree is happy, but "not really" says the narrator. The boy is happy only as a child. The black-and-white ink drawings are essential to the story and provide clues to interpretation.

A reviewer has described the book as "enigmatic," adding, "One wonders what Silverstein was trying to say." Adult responses may vary from anger that the tree is depicted as a "she" to praise for the work as an allegory about sacrifice. Nothing works quite as well as this book for getting widely diverse responses. The illustrations are an important source of information about the character of the tree and the boy. Note that the tree is never "whole" throughout the book. No one feels quite the same about giving and receiving after participating in a discussion of this book.

DIALOGUE

Talk about What You Notice in the Story

● ●

The children in this neighborhood group range in age from grades three to six. Jennifer and Michael see the relationship of the boy and the tree as satisfactory and reciprocal. Judy, on the other hand, questions whether that was so. Paula feels the tree acts out of love. All of these responses are conceptual in contrast to Jane's concrete responses. With a less mixed group of age levels, the teacher may have followed up on the question, "Who is calling the boy a boy when he is an old man?" That question would move the children out of the story into the author's craft.

● ●

Leslie:	Why did they call him boy when he was an old man?
TEACHER:	WHO IS CALLING HIM "BOY?"
Phoebe:	The tree. She wanted to go back to old times.
Jane:	You think about trees, and apples. We couldn't live without trees. They give us apples for food, wood for homes. We should take care of trees.
Courtney:	He was mean.
Leslie:	Yeah!
Jennifer:	It was good because it had the boy and the tree getting bigger together. The boy wanted to do stuff and the tree wanted him to do it. They both got older. The boy wanted all the things that the tree wanted to give him.
Michael:	The boy had everything he wanted. The tree risked her life for that boy. He got what he needed and wanted.
Judy:	It seems like he was spoiled.
Paula:	He would need more than one tree to make a house.
TEACHER:	WHAT IF THERE HAD BEEN ANOTHER TREE? WOULD THAT TREE HAVE GIVEN HIM WHAT HE WANTED?
Paula:	I don't think so because this tree really liked him.

Talk about How the Story Makes You Feel

• •

Michael's experience on a farm growing fruit trees overwhelms his willingness to suspend disbelief about the tree.

• •

Michael: I don't think so either. She risked her life for someone. Humans would do that but not trees.

TEACHER: IS THAT WHAT YOU WOULD DO IF YOU WERE THE TREE?

Michael: I would take care of the tree. I wouldn't take all that stuff from the tree. Maybe a little bit. So she can grow more apples. If you trim a tree it can still grow more.

Talk about What the Story Reminds You of in Your Life

• •

Jennifer goes on at some length to clarify her own philosophy about giving, a topic to which she has already given thought.

• •

Michael: I try to help my sister. Sometimes she's "growly."

Jennifer: There is this girl in my class. She wanted some of my stuff, money, pencils, and this and that.

TEACHER: HOW DID THAT MAKE YOU FEEL?

Jennifer: When I was little I gave her what she wanted. Now that I'm big its different. I was going to give her lunch, money, and stuff. She understood that I needed it for my lunch. If I get sherbet or something I don't just give it to her. I don't care about money. I just care about life.

TEACHER FOCUS

Metaphor: This story, more than many others, is useful for teaching metaphor since the author tells and illustrates the story in a stark, simplified fashion.

Sex Roles: The author has chosen to make the tree a "she" and the "boy" a boy regardless of age, so that the relationship between the two is the subject of response. The response to the relationship depends on the developmental stage of the children. However, first graders often respond to the relationship by saying, "Its not fair."

Environment: Many children feel sorry for the tree as a tree, and respond with protective suggestions.

COUNSELOR FOCUS

Rewards: The boy continually expected to be given what he needed. The results show that no matter what he got it was never enough to make him happy. Our culture conditions children to expect rewards for behavior that should be a reward in itself, such as giving.

Reciprocal Giving: The book is a stimulus to moral reasoning about reciprocation, Kohlberg's stage 2 (see the Susan Shreve entry, What's in it for me?) Most primary children are there and can be challenged to think about the importance of putting limitations on giving, such as Jennifer discovered in the conversation above.

MAKING CONNECTIONS

Writing: We asked fifth grade children to write what the book is about. Jeff's writing is a concrete interpretation of the story. Anthony thinks similarly, but expresses more feeling. Dwayne is ready to understand metaphor, but seems to need more experience with literature. Malinda, Raymond, Sarah, and Sherron were able to think about the story more in terms of metaphor and thematic purpose. Sherron expressed evaluative comments as well as a strong response. The responses given below indicate the extent of developmental differences among a group of children in the same class:

Jeff: The tree could give me leaves and I could make a collection of them; and branches, bark, and parts to make stuff like decoration boats and toys, and wooden airplanes and planks to decorate up to have and all sorts of things.

Anthony: The story to me meant that we depend on trees. We get pleasure from them by playing in their shade. We get money and food by selling and eating their fruit. We get homes from their wood. We get pleasure in our younger years by playing in their limbs and shade. We should give more thought and care to trees.

Dwayne: The book taught me that you should not expect everything and that the tree can make you happy but it cannot give you money and a house. It can give you leaves, vines, apples. You should not expect to be happy all of the time because it would not be like an average life. You should not expect a tree to give you money because a person should know that a tree cannot give you that. A person should know that a tree cannot give you a house.

Malinda: It meant the boy loved the tree. The tree loved the boy and as the boy grew older the tree wanted him to be happy and he wanted the tree to be happy. The tree was useful in many ways. For example, he had apples to give the boy to get money. He has wood for a fire, to build a house, make a boat or something like that.

Raymond: This book tells about love and about giving. The tree gave the boy all she had, because she loved him, and it teached me a lesson to give things to those you love, and they will love you back.

Sarah: (after relating the events of the story) He (the Boy) kept coming back to get more and the tree gave it to him but at the end he was still not happy.

Sherron: This is a good book and a sad book. This tree is a giving tree because it gave things that it could give. It gave its branches to the boy to build a house and that was stupid, you know it. It really was; but I guess the tree liked him so she gave them to him. And that's how I feel about the story. The end.

Gifts with Words: The following activity encourages reciprocal giving. Give children different sizes of paper and markers, ribbon, glue, and crayons. Ask them to consider "kind words" as a gift that does not cost money, but indeed is a gift. Children may make several gifts for classmates. Children may draw ribbons or glue ribbon or other art materials on their "packages." Kind words are written on the back. If each child makes several gifts, and the teacher includes him or herself as a gift maker in the activity, it is unlikely that any child in the room will be left out as a receiver.

Art: Silverstein never presents the whole tree anywhere in the book. Child artists may want to draw the entire tree as they see it.

Dramatics: Another way of examining feelings about the tree would be to have children mime her life story as they see it. Have two participants play the parts of the boy and the tree, and have them talk with each other at specified periods in their relationship.

BOOKS FOR FOLLOW-UP LITERATURE STUDIES

Starred titles have full entries elsewhere in the book.

Byars, Betsy. (1975). *The Lace Snail*. Viking Press.
> The snail makes lace, so all the other animals beg for some. She responds to each individually until it's time to think of herself.

* Fox, Mem. *Wilfrid Gordon McDonald Partridge*. Illustrated by Julie Vivas. Kane Miller, 1985.
> A small boy learns about giving, and becomes an important part in the life of an elderly lady.

* Griffith, Helen. (1987, 1985). *Grandaddy's Place* and *Georgia Music*. Illustrated by James Stevenson. Greenwillow.
> In the first of these titles, it is the grandfather who does the "giving." The relationship becomes reciprocal as Jannetta grows a year or two older, and her grandfather needs her.

* Williams, Vera. (1982). *A Chair for My Mother*. Greenwillow.
> Children may examine all the ways in which giving takes place in this story of a family encountering hard times.

Zolotow, Charlotte. (1978). *Do You Know What I'll Do?* Illustrated by Garth Williams. Harper.

> A big sister tells her baby brother about all the things she would like to do for him. Although the book is for the very young, it has been used succcessfully as a writing model for older children with varying titles such as "Do You Know What I'll Say?"

Isaac Bashevis Singer, *The Power of Light: Eight Stories for Hanukkah*

• •

Publisher and Date: Farrar, Straus and Giroux, 1980
Illustrator: Irene Lieblich
Audience Level: Grades four and up
Main Theme: Courage
Other Possible Themes: Suffering, Survival, Trust, Family and
    Tradition, War
Values to Target: Empathy

• •

ABOUT THE AUTHOR

Isaac Bashevis Singer, the son of a rabbi, was born in Poland in 1904. "Our house was a poor house. We were a rabbi's house. We had very little furniture, but many books" (p.205).

He remembers always asking questions such as: "Where is the end of the world?" "Why do birds fly and worms crawl?"

His father always had an answer: "That is how the Lord made it."

"Then where is He?" Isaac would ask.

"In Heaven," was the reply.

"Show me!" insisted Isaac.

Although his family immigrated to the United States in 1935, his "spiritual address" is clearly still in Poland. Singer's stories have emerged from events in the little towns and villages where he grew up. He writes,"I describe Jewish children, Jewish sages, Jewish fools, Jewish bridegrooms and Jewish brides." He particularly enjoys writing for children because he sees children as the ultimate literary critics. They like real stories, rooted in folklore. They like stories to be told in the way they have been told for thousands of years.

Singer is a winner of the Nobel Prize for Literature. His story, *Zlateh, the Goat,* was a 1966 Newbery Honor Book (*SATA* v. 27 pp. 202-15).

ABOUT THE STORY

The story takes place in the Warsaw Ghetto during World War II. David and Rebecca, 14 and 13 years old, have not left their hiding place in a cold, dark cellar for months. Both have lost their families to the Nazis. David, who goes in search of food each day, returns with some meager portions, as well as a candle and matches. On the first day of Hanukkah, they light up their dark space briefly and pronounce the benediction over the candle. They feel renewed courage there by the light of the candle. David suggests that they try to escape through the sewer. Eight years later David and Rebecca celebrate Hanukkah in Israel with their young son who someday would understand the miracle of how they were saved and the courage that was given to them by the power of light.

Sometimes we ponder how our children must be overwhelmed with the suffering and evil they see daily in the world. Our task is surely to educate them for caring citizenship and to empower them to do justice. Through stories like this we can seek to foster in ourselves and the children caring for more that our own comfort.

DIALOGUE

Talk about What You Notice in the Story

• •

The teacher asks this 6th grade group to focus on the story structure. The children take on the perspective of David and Rebecca by sharing how hard it is to imagine. Jennifer recognizes the metaphor of light that connects to the title.

• •

TEACHER: LET'S BEGIN BY WRITING THE MAIN EVENTS OF THIS STORY ON THE NEWSPRINT.
Collaboration produced the following list.

- David and Rebecca hide in the cellar
- Rebecca waits for David's return
- David returns with food and candle
- They eat the food
- They light the candle for Hanukkah

- They plan the escape
- They decide it is "now"
- They trek through the sewer
- They search for and join the Partisans
- They travel by land and boat
- They find relatives in Israel
- Eight years later they tell the story

TEACHER:	I NOTICED THAT YOU LISTENED TO THE STORY INTENTLY. WHAT STANDS OUT IN YOUR MIND NOW?
Malinda:	*[with a shudder]* The frozen sewer, and rats.
Jennifer:	It's hard to imagine!
Nathan:	I noticed the feeling of darkness. They didn't know if it was night or day. Or even what season it was.
Brooke:	I noticed the suspense of the escape.
Malinda:	It was like one thing after another. There was such a long way to go even after they got out of the sewer. They had to cross three countries.
Nathan:	I wonder how long it really took.
Malinda:	Well it was spring when they finally got all the way to Israel.
Jennifer:	Now exactly when is Hanukkah?
Nathan:	November or December. Before Christmas.
Malinda:	So, it was maybe five months.
TEACHER:	YOU NOTICED THE SUSPENSE. LET'S LOOK BACK FOR A MINUTE AT THE EVENTS OF THE STORY. WHERE WAS THE TURNING POINT IN THE PLOT?
Brooke:	It is when they decide it is now that they must do it.
Nathan:	I think it goes back to the lighting of the candle. There were some words in the story about being renewed by the light. (The group located the exact words. "Rebecca suddenly felt renewed courage.")
Jennifer:	I think the light made them decide they could make it.
TEACHER:	GOOD THINKING, JENNIFER. NOW YOU SEE THE CONNECTION WITH THE TITLE.

Talk about How the Story Makes You Feel

• •

The children are quiet and reflective during this discussion. The relativity of suffering is addressed by Malinda and Nathan.

• •

Jennifer:	It makes me all of a sudden realize how I shouldn't complain about anything in my life.

Malinda:	Yeah. They were glad to get a dried mushroom to eat. And we might complain about the food in the cafeteria!
Nathan:	They are trying to survive. We worry about what we are going to buy or what we will wear and if will it be "cool."
Jennifer:	It makes us seem sort of self-centered in a way.
TEACHER:	SO THE STORY MAKES US FEEL THANKFUL JUST FOR OUR SAFETY.
Jennifer:	Really!
Nathan:	But I guess some people in Russia are without food.
Jennifer:	We should send them more!
Malinda:	And those people came from Haiti on the boats. We turn off the TV and forget about it.
Brooke:	Every day we see all that suffering somewhere, like Africa.

Talk about What the Story Reminds You of in Your Life

• •

The story has a spiritual dimension that is evident in this conversation. Nathan makes an interesting metaphor for the psychological pain of daily life.

• •

TEACHER:	SINCE YOU HAVE NEVER FACED SUCH DANGER, IS IT HARD TO IDENTIFY WITH IT?
Nathan:	Well, we don't have to be afraid of Nazis like those children in the story but we do have to survive.
Brooke:	Well, there are plenty of other things to be afraid of.
TEACHER:	NOW YOU MAY BE GETTING TO WHAT YOU THINK THE STORY IS REALLY ABOUT. MALINDA, WHAT DO YOU THINK?
Malinda:	Well, you might say, this is about hope.
Nathan:	And determination and courage.
TEACHER:	SO DO WE NEED HOPE, DETERMINATION, AND COURAGE TO SURVIVE IN OUR WORLD?
Nathan:	Sure. We may not be in a sewer, but it's like we go down our own trails of bad times.
Jennifer:	The story has to do with feelings.
Brooke:	And pressure. Stress.
TEACHER:	NATHAN NAMED OUR SMALLER STRUGGLES "TRAILS OF BAD TIMES." HE HAS MADE A METAPHOR. HOW DO YOU GET THROUGH YOUR "TRAILS"? WHAT IS THE POWER OF LIGHT FOR YOU?
Chorus:	"Friends." "God." "Family." "Nature." "Education."
TEACHER:	LET'S LOOK AT THE METAPHOR OF *THE POWER OF LIGHT* AS WE MAKE SOME OTHER APPLICATIONS TO OUR OWN LIVES.

The group brainstormed and recorded on the newsprint associations with light. The following comments were transcribed as the children used the newsprint chart for reference.

Malinda: Hope was the first thing we thought of. I think Rebecca saw a spark of hope with the light and then said, "Let's leave."

Jennifer: Remember when the match was lit, Rebecca saw David for the first time in a long time. It was like she could hardly remember what he looked like.

Nathan: Yeah, I always notice how things look different in the dark. Like in my room at night. Dark can make me a little scared.

Brooke: Did you ever wake up in the middle of the night, like at a friend's house when you're spending the night, and not know where you are?
[chorus of agreement]

Malinda: Well, we said that nothing can live without light. Plants die. They could have died there in the dark.

Jennifer: We said warmth. Fire is warm. I noticed that after they let the Hanukkah candle go out, but they took their matches.

Brooke: Actually the dark protected them at one point after they got out of the sewer. So light and dark can mean safety in opposite kinds of ways.

TEACHER: ANY OTHER ASSOCIATIONS WITH LIGHT?

Jennifer: I always think about light at the end of the tunnel.

Nathan: Well, we light candles in church. The Menorah reminds me of our Advent wreath in church.

Jennifer: The candles are the spirit of God.

Malinda: Or the light of Christ.

TEACHER: RIGHT—FOR CHRISTIANS.

Malinda: Oh, right, I forgot for a minute about the differences in Jews and Christians.

Nathan: There are gospel songs—"I Saw the Light."

Jennifer: There are really lots of songs about light. Popular songs, country songs, and religious songs.

TEACHER: WHAT QUESTION WOULD YOU LIKE TO ASK THE AUTHOR IF HE WERE HERE?

Nathan: Is the story true?

Jennifer: Maybe it doesn't matter if every little detail is true. It seems true to me.

TEACHER FOCUS

War: The story invites empathy for the suffering of the Jewish people, and therefore presents a good starting point for research.

Jewish History: Non-Jewish children often have much misinformation about the history, religion, and culture of the Jewish people. Identification with the characters in this story provides motivation to set learning goals.

COUNSELOR FOCUS

Suffering: The story invites a new dimension of empathy as children take the perspective of the children in the ghetto.

Courage: Identifying with children near their own age who act with courage in the face of danger and death may inspire children to look within themselves for strength.

MAKING CONNECTIONS

Music: The words to "Don't Let the Light Go Out" as sung by Peter, Paul, and Mary are instructive about the liberation of the Maccabees as well as being a wonderful piece of music. Peter Yarrow wrote the song for a Christmas concert his group was asked to do in Carnegie Hall. He wrote the song to celebrate Hanukkah and as a gentle but powerful reminder of the suffering of his people. The tape, *No Easy Walk to Freedom*, is available at record stores.

BOOKS FOR FOLLOW-UP LITERATURE STUDIES

Knight, Margy Burns. (1992). *Talking Walls*. Illustrated by Sibley O'Brien. Tilbury House.

> This picture book depicts the famous walls of the world, the stories they tell, the impact they have on people, and how some children live with adversity and lack of freedom.

Singer, Isaac Bashevis. (1984). *Stories for Children*. Farrar, Straus, & Giroux.

> This collection, which includes "The Power of Light," contains a wealth of rich stories for further reading. Some are funny, some sad. Included is *Zlateh the Goat*.

David Small,
Imogene's Antlers

● ●

Publisher and Date: Farrar Straus & Giroux, 1985
Illustrator: David Small
Audience Level: Kindergarten and up
Main Theme: Being Different
Other Possible Themes: Acceptance, Individuality, Humor
Values to Target: Acceptance of Difference

● ●

ABOUT THE AUTHOR

David Small grew up in the Midwest in the 1940s and 1950s. His family lived in Detroit, but he spent summers in rural Indiana. He loves animals. His mother introduced him to art museums and art lessons, which taught him about the power of visual images and determined his life's work. He was a sickly, shy child and admits to feeling "different" and like an outsider. Although these feelings are inherent in the themes of his books, he tells his stories with marvelous originality and good humor. He hopes that his books will reach those children who felt as he did. Small also illustrates for other writers. He still lives in Michigan, and he has five children of his own (*SATA* v. 50, pp. 203-06).

ABOUT THE STORY

Imogene wakes up on Thursday morning with antlers. Her facial expressions inform us that she is enjoying every minute of it, but that is not the case for her mother. After consulting the doctor and the principal, she brings in a milliner to cover the damage. Her precocious brother determines she is part miniature elk. The next morning the antlers are gone, but the story isn't over there.

The illustrations and text work together beautifully in this story. The affluent home complete with servants gives Small numerous characters to be foils for Imogene's challenge to conformity. However, there is pathos in the story as much as principle. The children will begin comments with the very first page because so much is going on in the pictures.

DIALOGUE

Talk about What You Notice in the Story

• •

As soon as the story ends Lily has a prediction. The teacher takes these fourth grade children "out of the story" so they can talk about why the author chose antlers. The children seem to want more time to "stay in" to retell and adapt the story. However, the question remains for future consideration.

• •

Lily:	The mother probably fainted again.
Jay:	Every time she fainted.
Chad:	After the peacock disappeared maybe she's an elephant.
Jennifer:	When she went to bed, she'd have to think of what animal she'd be the next day, and that could be her science project.
TEACHER:	WHY DO YOU SUPPOSE THE AUTHOR CHOSE ANTLERS?
Sarah:	Well, antlers are funny and make children laugh.
Jay:	Maybe deer must be his favorite animals.
Chad:	Antlers are easy to see in the book even though you're sitting a long way from the teacher.

Talk about How the Story Makes You Feel

• •

The comment about David Small is a good one. Chad asks later whether Small created the illustrations. After exploring alternative possibilities in an interesting fashion, the children revert to "what they noticed" in the story.

• •

TEACHER:	WHAT IF I TOLD YOU THAT DAVID SMALL LOOKS SOMETHING LIKE IMOGENE, AND THAT HE SAYS HE ALWAYS FELT ODD AND DIFFERENT WHEN HE WAS GROWING UP. HOW DOES THAT MAKE YOU FEEL ABOUT THE STORY. WHAT WOULD YOU THINK?
Lily:	You could be Imogene.
TEACHER:	DO YOU MEAN ANY ONE OF US?
Lily:	Yes.
Chad:	He could be worried about how people might have reacted.
Jay:	His mother fainted when she saw him.
Jennifer:	It's sort of how it was like. It's like a small diary.
Chad:	Maybe everybody called him a girl.

Lily:	How did he feel about his life if that's the way it was? It's very sad.
Jay:	He was feeling like he was nothing compared to a lot of people because people might say that he was weird.
Lily:	I think that if he was small or different, it is sort of writing about his life.
Jennifer:	Sort of writing about another person.
Jay:	He could have had a strange haircut and it came out looking like antlers.
Chad:	He might have been thinking about himself because he was different than anybody else.
TEACHER:	IS THERE ANYTHING IN THE BOOK THAT MAKES YOU THINK THAT?
Lily:	Yeah, because it might be that it would be better to be different than to be the same. Then you would be doing everything the same. Then you'd think and do everything the same.
Jennifer:	Life is pretty much the same.
Lily:	Everybody was doing stuff to hide the antlers, and her mother fainted. It's like other people didn't like the effect.
TEACHER:	HOW DO YOU FEEL ABOUT THAT?
Lily:	It's hard to explain.
TEACHER:	YES, BUT THAT'S A GOOD OBSERVATION.
Chad:	Did David Small do the illustrations? He must like cats because there are cats in all the pictures.
Jennifer:	Either a cat or a dog. He must have liked animals.
Lily:	He must have really liked animals—peacocks, antlers, cats, dogs.
Jay:	He didn't say why the principal looks so mad at them.
Lily:	Probably because he was, well, he was amazed or puzzled because you don't see a girl walking in with antlers every day.
Chad:	Maybe he thought it was an excuse to get out of school.
Jay:	He may think that they are just fake, like plaster of Paris.
Jennifer:	I'd like to write a sequel to this story. Most good stories have a part two.

Talk about What the Story Reminds You of in Your Life

• •

Many of the children bring up examples of classmates who have "differences." However, our favorite response is from Elizabeth. Elizabeth, a quiet, beautiful second grader, looks forward to finding her favorite book, *Imogene's Antlers,* on the shelf in the guidance office. Elizabeth loves how Imogene woke up with unexpected changes each morning. Elizabeth often plays a game, "This is what I'll be today." She draws Imogene as herself, and sometimes a peacock, sometimes a unicorn. Pensive and quiet in class, Elizabeth seems especially energized by Imogene. She is the audience that David Small has in mind, the unique and different children who need encouragement to hold on.

• •

TEACHER FOCUS

Prediction: The book is especially good for prediction because there are many clues in the pictures. Notice the shadow of a peacock in the doorway before Imogene appears in full regalia.

Critical Analysis: Putting the children in the mind of the author having to plot the details of the story will stimulate critical thinking. The antlers, for example, cannot get through the doorway which allows Small to provide Imogene with interesting maneuvers.

Setting: The setting of the story contributes to a deeper understanding of the theme. The affluent, proper environment reinforces the idea that everyone is expected to conform. Audrey and Don Wood used a similar setting in juxtaposition in *Elbert's Bad Word.*

COUNSELOR FOCUS

Self-Acceptance: The story helps children manage the dilemma of their concurrent desires to be themselves and to fit in with others.

Feelings of Power: Imogene counters the expectations of others by feeling powerful within herself (and her imagination, perhaps.)

BOOKS FOR FOLLOW-UP LITERATURE STUDIES

Blos, Joan. (1987). *Old Henry.* Morrow, 1987.
> Old Henry prefers the wild weeds and flowers in his yard. His neighbors run him out only to discover that conformity isn't as virtuous as they thought. They found that they missed Old Henry.

Small, David. (1987). *Paper John.* Farrar, Straus & Giroux.
> Paper John makes just about anything out of paper including his home, birds, and flowers. When a demon attacks the town, his talent saves the day.

Thompson, Peggy. (1988). *The King Has Horse's Ears.* Illustrated by David Small. Simon & Schuster.
> The King keeps his ears a secret until his wedding day, when to his horror the secret is exposed.

William Steig,
Spinky Sulks

● ●

Publisher and Date: Farrar Straus and Giroux, 1988
Illustrator: William Steig
Audience Level: Kindergarten and up
Main Theme: Pouting
Other Possible Themes: Family
Values to Target: Nobody's Perfect

● ●

ABOUT THE AUTHOR

William Steig, born in New York, grew up in a family where every member was engaged in some area of the arts. In the thirties he was known primarily for his work as a cartoonist. His work regularly appeared in *The New Yorker*. He was in his sixties before he started writing for children. He has enjoyed his second profession, noting how his life changed as he began to be asked to go places, autograph books, and interact with children. He writes, "It feels darn good, like being dubbed into knighthood" (p. 276). Steig reports that the book about Sylvester began when he had a thought about doing a book with magic in it (SATA v. 18, pp. 275-77).

ABOUT THE STORY

Spinky has a long seige of pouting, a whole day in which he divorces himself from his family. The family on the other hand does everything imaginable to bring him back into the fold. They tell him they were wrong (Philadelphia *is* the capital of Peru) and they offer all of Spinky's favorite things as bribes to cheer him up. Neither brother, sister, mother, father, grandmother, nor friends can win him over. At long last he takes his problem into his own hands, and he and the family have a rousing good time.

As usual, Steig's sense of humor hits home. Who hasn't pouted and blamed everybody but themselves when they've done something stupid. Spinky epitomizes this human foible, and Steig has us recognizing ourselves on every page. The language is also the finest for savoring. There's no reason to pout if someone isn't there to notice, because the whole purpose is to find someone to tell you that you're okay in spite of your imperfections. Well, Spinky has a crowd, and they all go out of their way for him. The beauty of the story is that Spinky saves his pride by doing something for the family in return.

DIALOGUE

Talk about What You Notice in the Story

• •

This "grand conversation" between a teacher and a small group of her fourth graders is exceptional in at least two ways. The teacher maintains the supportive role throughout and manages to draw out the best in the students. This conversation was taped near the end of school after a year of literature studies in the classroom. The students have managed to talk their way through this book from initial responses to attempts to understand themselves. This verbatim transcription includes all the reinforcing messages the teacher communicates.

The teacher continually encourages the students to talk about what they notice. The children are working hard, rereading and relooking at the book, to understand who Spinky is and why he behaved as he did. Follow the comments of one child and it will show how the conversation is helping each to find meaning in the text. This conversation continued unabated for an hour, with no restlessness evident.

• •

John:	He got better when they started being nice to him.
TEACHER:	OKAY.
Zachary:	He got his pride and he didn't want to . . . and he had to do it in a way not to lose his pride or respect.
TEACHER:	WHAT DID YOU NOTICE ABOUT THAT?
Hilary:	I think that he's a little bit spoiled.
TEACHER:	HE'S A LITTLE BIT SPOILED. ANYTHING ELSE?
Hilary:	Also, when they tried to be nice to him and do things to cheer him up he didn't want to listen to them or nothing. He just sat there and wouldn't answer them.
TEACHER:	DID ANYBODY ELSE NOTICE ANYTHING?
John:	His father was really nice to him when he was in that mood.
TEACHER:	WHAT MOOD?
John:	That sulky mood. He was probably just trying to act spoiled.
TEACHER:	DID YOU NOTICE ANYTHING ELSE?

Crystal:	He didn't really care.
Teacher:	Didn't care about what?
Crystal:	About his family.
TEACHER:	HE DIDN'T CARE ABOUT HIS FAMILY.
Crystal:	He didn't really care. I don't think he cared about other people.
TEACHER:	OKAY. DID YOU NOTICE ANYTHING ELSE IN THE STORY?
Danette:	They tried to cheer him up in different ways so that he would get well.
TEACHER:	OKAY.
Hilary:	He stayed outside the whole time. Instead of that he could have come in the house 'cause they cared for him.
TEACHER:	OKAY.
Zachary:	His brother and sister had to beg him to forgive them.
TEACHER:	OKAY. WHAT DID YOU NOTICE ABOUT THAT?
Zachary:	His brother went to him, and they always went and tried to pry words out of him.
TEACHER:	OKAY, ROBERT?
Robert:	Even when his family tried to love and care for him, he wouldn't listen, he was just being a little brat.

Talk about How the Story Makes You Feel

TEACHER:	YOU THINK HE WAS JUST BEING A LITTLE BRAT. ALL RIGHT. SOUNDS GOOD TO ME. WHAT DID YOU THINK OR FEEL AS YOU WERE LISTENING TO THE STORY? I NOTICED A LOT OF EXPRESSION ON YOUR FACES WHILE I WAS READING THE STORY. SOME OF YOU WERE SURPRISED OR EVEN SHOCKED. YOU HAD THOUGHTS. WHAT WERE SOME OF THOSE THOUGHTS YOU HAD?
Sabrina:	I don't think they should have tried to be nice to him. Not tried to be nice, but tried to explain and just be normal and at least get him to come in the house.
TEACHER:	OKAY, GOOD.
John:	I couldn't believe what they would do, invite the clown, do everything, invite the grandmother, and they were doing all this stuff. I couldn't believe that he kept turning it down.
TEACHER:	HOW COME?
John:	Because they were actually being nice to him to get his forgiveness and he was just being a real brat.
TEACHER:	OKAY. WHAT ELSE DID YOU THINK OR FEEL ABOUT THIS?
Robert:	Can I ask a question?
TEACHER:	SURE.

Robert:	Why was he sulking is the question?
TEACHER:	WHY DO YOU THINK HE WAS SULKING? WHAT DO YOU THINK HAPPENED BEFORE THE STORY BEGAN? THAT'S A GOOD THING TO THINK ABOUT, ROBERT. WHAT WERE YOU THINKING OR FEELING WHEN YOU HEARD THE STORY? WHAT WERE SOME OF YOUR THOUGHTS?
John:	I don't think he was being a brat. I think he was just being himself.
TEACHER:	OKAY. YOU DON'T THINK HE WAS TRYING TO BE A BRAT. WHY WAS HE ACTING LIKE THIS?
John:	Because no one would talk to him. Everyone was being mean to him.
Claire:	Especially when you're the youngest you usually get petted and stuff and I guess his family disagreed with everything he said to them and they didn't agree with him and he didn't agree with them and they started to have arguments.
TEACHER:	GOOD. YES?
Hilary:	I think that John was right that he was being himself and he probably feels that he has to be that way in order to get some attention and he thinks nobody will listen to me and they will probably just boss him around like he was nothing.
TEACHER:	OKAY, ANNETTE.
Annette:	I don't think he was being so much more bratty than he was immature.
TEACHER:	OKAY. SO YOU THINK THAT WHEN HE WAS BEING BRATTY HE WAS JUST BEING A BABY, BEING IMMATURE. YES?
Crystal:	I think that they probably got into an argument over chores or something because now they're doing all the work for him and he is still saying that they don't love him but they really do because look what all they do for him.
John:	Also his brother said something about some place being the capital of Peru and that I think he was right.
TEACHER:	WAS HE RIGHT? NO. BUT HE KEPT SAYING HE WAS RIGHT EVEN THOUGH HE WASN'T RIGHT. LOOK HERE.
Claire:	They're also trying to buy his love.
TEACHER:	THAT'S A GOOD POINT. THANK YOU.
Hilary:	I feel . . . I forgot what I was going to say.
TEACHER:	WHEN YOU THINK OF IT, COME RIGHT ON BACK. WHY DO YOU THINK HE ACTED LIKE THIS HERE *[SHOWING PICTURE]*
Robert:	Because he hated them talking about him sulking. Why didn't they try to talk like normal parents would? Just like a family meeting.

Teacher:	Okay.
Hilary:	I agree with Robert, because I think we should talk through it. Why, if someone is so mad at us and then asks questions and then maybe get through it and have a family discussion.
Teacher:	Good point.
Zachary:	He must be real conceited. Every time his parents tried to do something for him, he would turn it down and that's sort of conceited and he thinks he's too good to have that stuff and he thinks he's too good to go kissing to make up.
John:	I think that Spinky's brother is a good brother because he went way out of the way to make Spinky feel better.
Teacher:	Yes, Robert.
Robert:	He took it out on his friends for no reason. I don't know why he did that. That's wrong.
Teacher:	You're saying that you can understand why he's mad at his family but not why he's mad at his friends.
Robert:	I understand why he did that to his family but I don't know why he did that to his friends. It's sort of dumb because if he gets mad at his friends his friends won't like him.
Teacher:	You mean his family would love him anyway, but his friends might not?
Robert:	His family might get sick and tired of him and start ignoring him; his family will love him still. But his friends might start calling him names.
Sabrina:	I don't agree.
Teacher:	You don't agree?
Sabrina:	No, I don't agree. If somebody was a real friend they wouldn't turn him down for anything.
Teacher:	That's a good point. You all are making good points.
Robert:	I'd like to ask a question.
Teacher:	Okay.
Robert:	I don't understand why through half the story he's just ignoring the whole family and then all of a sudden he comes in and makes them laugh.
Teacher:	Okay, you're saying that you don't understand why there was a change in his behavior. What caused that change? Zach?
Zachary:	He started to give in. He had dinner and his mother gave him a tarp and they even hired a clown, and all this stuff and, if you were real mad, I guess I would sort of get tired of being mad.
Teacher:	Okay, Claire.

Claire:	I think he got tired of being mad.
TEACHER:	HE JUST GOT TIRED OF BEING MAD. IT WORE HIM OUT.
Robert:	What I don't understand is how the day before he despised his family, and then so sudden the next morning he has a big breakfast for them. It's so sudden.

Talk about What the Story Reminds You of in Your Life

• •

The explanations of John, Robert, and Zachary are all different and correspond to different levels of reasoning. Notice that Zachary has projected himself totally into the character and refers to "me" instead of "him."

• •

TEACHER:	RIGHT. WHAT DOES THIS HAVE TO DO WITH YOUR LIFE? I THOUGHT WE'D GET MORE HANDS ON THIS. ZACH.
Zach:	Even though my brother isn't like that sometimes he does act like that. He tries to be real perfect, sometimes he cries and sometimes he tries to help me and I start to get real fed up. Sometimes I take away his hook when he has a fishing pole with a lure on it and he could give it to his sister.
TEACHER:	THAT'S RIGHT. SOMETIMES THERE'S REASONS TO CORRECT CHILDREN. ROBERT.
Robert:	We've all acted this way and we know what it feels like. And right now we're thinking about how we've acted and we look back and think how stupid we were to do it.
TEACHER:	OKAY.
Vanette:	When I acted like that my mom used to say it was a pity party.
TEACHER:	A PITY PARTY. THAT'S INTERESTING. INSTEAD OF SPINKY SULKS YOU HAD A PITY PARTY.
Vanette:	And she'd say that she never wanted to come to my pity party because it was always so sad.
	[Laughter here]
John:	If someone corrects me and I don't like it or if I have to do a chore I'll run out of the house and go read or something in a place where I always go.
TEACHER:	HOW IS HE FEELING RIGHT NOW WHEN HE'S SULKING?
Crystal:	I think he got out all different feelings and his being around his family, mad, sad, and lots of different things going on in his head.
TEACHER:	OKAY. GOOD POINT.

Hilary:	He's kind of mad at everybody and he's more mad at himself than at his family.
TEACHER:	RIGHT, VERY GOOD. MORE MAD AT HIMSELF THAN HE IS AT HIS FAMILY. GOOD POINT.
John:	I think he feels hatred, but he really doesn't hate his family as much as he thinks he does. He really loves them and is trying to say that he loves them and that he was wrong.
Zachary:	He expresses hatred. He's putting on this big hatred act.
TEACHER:	HAVE YOU EVER FELT THAT WAY?
Chorus:	"Yes." "Sure!"
TEACHER:	HOW MANY OF YOU HAVE FELT THAT WAY? EVERYBODY? ME TOO. OKAY. YES?
John:	I agree with Hilary that he's more mad at himself, and sometimes I'm that way. I think I don't know anything and I'll blame it on somebody else.
TEACHER:	REAL GOOD POINT.
Robert:	I say I hate someone and then I'll think of all the things they've done for me.
TEACHER:	ALL RIGHT. VERY GOOD POINT.
Zachary:	They are trying to buy him out ... at least they're trying to do something. He's thinking that they're doing all this stuff to show that they care about me (sic) and I'm thinking that they're doing all this stuff to make me realize that. And I'm thinking that they don't. Then why are they doing it? I think that they want to get something out of me, but they really did love me, I guess.

TEACHER FOCUS

Comprehension: The literal story is what prompted the children above to work so hard at finding out what is really going on. The book will be a good tool for measuring comprehension.

Critical Thinking: Some parents have questioned the effect of this book on children, assuming that they can't see beyond the behavior to the reasons why Spinky is feeling bad. Obviously the children not only understood but they also laughed at themselves for similar behavior.

COUNSELOR FOCUS

Pouting: The children delighted in telling their own stories about when they pout. Discussion allows for recognition that others pout as well, and how we might respond to that. Some of the children seem to understand that pouting is a painful state to be in and it is perfectly all right for the family to cater to Spinky during that time. Others thought he was just being bratty, but apparently his family did not.

Imperfections: This story is better than most in getting children to laugh at themselves and recognize that they aren't always behaving perfectly.

MAKING CONNECTIONS

Body Language: A study of body language fits into social studies as well as personal development. Start with sulking. Then try charades displaying the mannerisms that go with certain moods.

BOOKS FOR FOLLOW-UP LITERATURE STUDIES

Coleridge, Ann. (1987). *The Friends of Emily Culpepper*. Putnam.
> Emily pouts at first when she can't have her friends bottled up to play with when she chooses. But when she has her way, it is just as bad as pouting. A picture book for all ages.

Hurwitz, Joanna. (1987). *Class Clown*. Morrow.
> Lucas isn't a pouter but he does always have to be in the limelight. He, too, tries to change his ways. For middle grades.

Spinelli, Jerry. (1990). *Maniac Magee*. Little, Brown.
> Legendary Jeffrey Lionel Magee remains even tempered throughout, though a little sad. The people he meets, however, display all sorts of moods and tempers. Grades four and up will enjoy this Newbery winner.

William Steig,
Sylvester and the Magic Pebble

• •

Publisher and Date: Simon and Schuster, 1969
Illustrator: William Steig
Audience Level: Kindergarten and up
Main Theme: Wishes
Other Possible Themes: Loyalty, Familial Love, Hope
Values to Target: Unconditional Love

• •

ABOUT THE AUTHOR

William Steig was born in New York and grew up in a family with every member engaged in some area of the arts. In the 1930s he was known primarily for his work as a cartoonist. His work regularly appeared in *The New Yorker*. He was in his sixties before he started writing for children. He has enjoyed his second profession, noting how his life changed as he began to be asked to go places, autograph books and interact with children. He writes, "It feels darn good, like being dubbed into knighthood" (p. 276). Steig reports that the book about Sylvester began when he had a thought about doing a book with magic in it (*SATA* v. 18, pp. 275-77).

ABOUT THE STORY

Sylvester the donkey is a collector of pebbles. One rainy day as he holds one in his hoof, he wishes the rain would stop. It does. Other tests prove the pebble is magic! He encounters a lion on the way home and in panic wishes to be a rock. His mother and father are grief-stricken when they cannot find Sylvester, who is now a rock on the hillside. Sylvester's father picks up the magic pebble which reminds them of their son who loved pebbles. He lays it on the rock. "I wish I were my real self again," thinks Sylvester. And in an instant, he is. The reunion is joyful. The magic pebble is placed in an iron safe by the happy family who agree that they have no need for more wishes.

Everything about this story is superb and brimming with emotion. The language is worth savoring slowly. The pictures are rich in detail and perfectly placed with text. The emotional content begins with fear and wishes, moves to the sadness of separation and loneliness, and then blossoms into hope, love, and the comforts of family. The story structure comprises an elaborate beginning, middle, and end, which are comparable to three chapters. Possible interpretations are endless because of the archetypal nature of the plot. Every choice Steig made along the story line is impressive.

During the reading the teacher allowed for the children's interest in the illustrations, such as the humorous portraits of the policemen, the ever-present red pebble in the Strawberry Hill sequence of pictures, the anticipation of the change of seasons, and the pure celebration of the picnic scene. At the joyful emerging of Sylvester from the rock, Charmella exclaimed, "Why he's born again!" Tyree picked up the refrain and soon the group was singing and clapping their version of Charmella's gospel song.

DIALOGUE

Talk about What You Notice in the Story

• •

Trent compares the illustrations of the ceasing rain to a pause button on a video player, an insightful comparison and evidence of critical viewing skill. These first and second grade children try to help Sylvester by inventing solutions to his problem. The teacher prompts appreciation of language and story form.

• •

TEACHER:	*[PAUSING AFTER SYLVESTER DISCOVERS THE MAGIC]* I NOTICE YOU ARE EXCITED ABOUT THE STORY. WHAT STANDS OUT IN YOUR MIND ABOUT THE STORY SO FAR?
Trent:	The rain ceased! I know what that means. It's like every-thing went *pause* on the video.
TEACHER:	YES! THE DROPS VANISHED ON THE WAY DOWN!
Chorus:	Cool!
Heather:	What's a wart?
Trent:	I have one.
Heather	Let's wish it off!

• •

The group played a game of wishing Trent's wart off his hand and inquired about the meaning of fetlock on the donkey's anatomy.

• •

Ricky:	I don't think the magic will work for Sylvester at home. It will work better if he's out somewhere alone where it can be a secret.
Jessica:	If I told my mama I found a magic pebble, she'd say, "you're just joking."
Trent:	Well, sometimes when I want to believe something real bad, my parents can tell. Then they'll go along with it.
Jessica:	Right. They pretend like they believe when they don't. Mine did that once before too.
TEACHER:	*[PAUSING DURING READING ABOUT SYLVESTER BECOMING A ROCK]* WELL, SYLVESTER IS SAFE FROM THE LION NOW.
Trent:	That lion is sniffing around. I guess he says, "Whoa, what happened to that donkey?"
Jonathan:	Sylvester fooled him!
Heather:	Yes, but now he's not a donkey anymore.
Ricky:	Sylvester can't change back to himself because he can't hold the pebble any more. He doesn't have hands and stuff.

Nick:	*[enjoying his idea]* Well, he could have wished he was a rock with hands!
Jessica:	He could have wished himself invisible and still with hands so he could hold the pebble.
TEACHER:	THE SEASONS CHANGED THROUGHOUT THE STORY. *[Children enjoy looking for the pebble through fall and winter.]*
Jessica:	Oh no, it must be covered up with snow.
Trent:	*[proud of his prediction]* But snow melts.
Chorus of Celebration: There it is!	
TEACHER:	SYLVESTER NEVER SEEMED TO GIVE UP HOPE. HE WAS HELPLESS BUT NOT HOPELESS.
Chorus:	*[enjoying the sound of the words]* Helpless, not hopeless.

Talk about How the Story Makes You Feel

• •

The children's excitement grows as Mr. and Mrs. Duncan plan the picnic and choose Strawberry Hill. Ricky picks up on an archetypal "chicken and egg" reference that is very interesting. The chorus of "It hatches" is truly an accurate prediction for the story!

• •

Heather:	*[gales of laughter]* His mama is sitting right on him.
Nick:	She can't hear him talking.
Trent:	I'd sure feel weird if my mama was sitting on me.
Ricky:	It's like a chicken and an egg. *[Laughter]*
TEACHER:	AND, WHAT HAPPENS WHEN A CHICKEN SITS ON AN EGG?
Chorus:	*[delighted]* It hatches!
TEACHER:	BUT SYLVESTER WAS STILL STONE DUMB.
Trent:	*[echoing the words]* He was stone dumb! *[pausing to think]* What's stone dumb?
TEACHER:	IT'S LIKE THIS. *[MOUTHING THE WORDS FROM THE TEXT WITH INTENSITY BUT NO SOUND]* "MOTHER, FATHER, IT'S ME, SYLVESTER. I'M RIGHT HERE."
Ricky:	Is that how loud you talk when you're stone dumb? I want to pretend to be stone dumb! *[The game continues briefly.]*
TEACHER:	WE ARE IN SUSPENSE. I WONDER WHAT'S GOING TO HAPPEN NEXT.
Heather:	In just a minute all that picnic food is going to fall off all over the ground.

[A celebrative chorus, greets the joyful scene of "loving looks and fond exclamations!"]

Talk about What the Story Reminds You of in Your Life

• •

This discussion is a mixture of identification with the pain of separation and the joyful wishing for the best things one can imagine. The children's comments inform us about the reasons for the unending appeal of this book. Among them are the engaging animal community, almost unendurable suspense, unending familial love, humor, and the opportunity to make wishes that could come true.

• •

TEACHER:	I'M WONDERING IF YOU WERE A ROCK, WHAT WOULD YOU MISS MOST?
Jessica:	I would miss my mama and my daddy hugging on me.
Trent:	I'd be really scared and lonely and I'd wish I could be home again.
TEACHER:	IT'S PRETTY LONELY WHEN YOU WANT TO BE HOME.
Trent:	One time I went out to take the trash and I wanted to stay outside. I went off to find this big run-down barn down the road a piece. I was playing around and it got dark and my mama and daddy were looking all over for me. I was scared!
TEACHER:	AND WHEN THEY FOUND YOU?
Trent:	Oh, what a relief!
Heather:	My family has missed me lots of times and worried about me too.
Ricky:	Sometimes our mama cows lose their babies down in the woods. They look worried. I go help find them sometimes.
Jessica:	Did the baby cow turn into a rock?
	[Laughter]
TEACHER:	I WONDER WHY WILLIAM STEIG PICKED A ROCK FOR SYLVESTER'S WISH. WHY DID THE AUTHOR NOT HAVE HIM WISH TO BE A TREE, OR A FLOWER.
Janey:	Well, for one thing, a tree or a flower wouldn't hold a picnic.
	[Much laughter]
TEACHER:	WHAT IF SYLVESTER HAD A BROTHER OR SISTER?
Nick:	Well, *that* would be different.
Heather:	She might be jealous.
Jessica:	She would think Sylvester got all the attention.
Nick:	*[cautiously]* Well if it was a brother, he might have missed him some.

Teacher:	If you had a wish for your family, what would it be?
Jessica:	I'd wish for all the money in the world.
Heather:	I'd just wish my family was back together.
Jessica:	Well, maybe mine doesn't need all the money. Just enough to pay the bills.
Teacher:	I noticed in the story that the family put the pebble in an iron safe.
Janey:	I think they put it there because it is *dangerous*.
Teacher:	I like that. Wishes can be dangerous.
Heather:	Sylvester was all that they wanted!

TEACHER FOCUS

Vocabulary: The words and phrases used in this story are pleasant to the tongue, as a child said. Children could store their favorites in notebooks or word banks.

Story Structure: For third graders beginning to read chapter books, this story could be used as a project for creating chapters and recognition of the plot sequence.

Archetypes: This story has all the characteristics of traditional folktales such as the separation from family, taking a journey, transformation, seasonal changes, performing a task. Those patterns may be examined in other stories as well as this one.

Problem Solving: The children enjoy trying to solve Sylvester's problem for him. What are some of the ways in which he can solve each problem as the story progresses?

COUNSELOR'S FOCUS

Familial Love: Every person must have the kind of attachment depicted in the Duncan family. Each person finds it in the best way they can. This book is an all time favorite because it defines for children the concept that makes it possible for them to have hope and to love others.

MAKING CONNECTIONS

Story Structure: This story works well for teaching story structure to older children A group of sixth graders were asked to look at this story as a three-part "mini-series." The results of their collaborative thinking were recorded on newsprint, enabling them to focus on the structure of the story. This group then used this as a base for a discussion of feelings and applications. They moved out of the story more quickly than younger children, but were able to thoroughly enjoy identifying feelings of alienation and returning "home" in their own lives.

Part I

- Sylvester finds the pebble.
- He wishes the rain to stop.
- He tests it several times.
- The lion appears.
- Sylvester panics.
- He wishes he were a rock.
- He stays a rock.

Part II

- Worried parents start search.
- Neighbors join search.
- Fall, winter, spring come and go.
- Parents decide to try to be happy.
- They plan a picnic.
- They go to Strawberry Hill.
- Dad finds rock that reminds him of Sylvester.
- Dad lays pebble on rock.

Part III

- Sylvester wishes he were himself.
- He is!
- They celebrate.
- They have all they want now.

Role Play: A group of first grade students enjoyed role playing the story. Using only a red pebble as a prop, the teacher led the children by first setting up two scenes: home and Strawberry Hill. Acting as narrator and speaking in the present tense, the teacher coached the children to mime the feelings and postures of Sylvester and his parents. Children particularly enjoyed Sylvester's being "stone dumb" as the rock, and jubilantly emerging from his frozen state.

Music: "Ting-a-Lay-O" from *The Book of Kids' Songs* by Nancy Cassidy has a reggae beat and is about a donkey who walks, talks, and eats with a knife and fork (Klutz Press, Palo Alto, CA 94306). Using the song gives a class another chance to name the genre of animal fantasy. One class continued to request the song with every classroom guidance lesson whether the story included a donkey or not!

BOOKS FOR FOLLOW-UP LITERATURE STUDIES

Starred titles have full entries elsewhere in the book.

Gerstein, Mordicai. (1983). *Arnold of the Ducks.* Harper and Row.
> A little boy, Arnold, is mistaken by a pelican for a fish, then left with a family of ducks who adopt him. His curiosity leads him back home to his human family.

* Gerstein, Mordicai. (1987). *The Mountains of Tibet.* Harper and Row.
> There is a similarity between Sylvester's separation from his family, and the woodcutter in *The Mountains of Tibet*, who has a choice about another life. Reading the two books in sequence can lead to a more in-depth discussion of choices with older children.

Steig, William. (1976). *The Amazing Bone.* Simon and Schuster.
> On her way home Pearl finds a bone with magical powers.

Yorinks, Arthur. (1986). *Hey, Al.* Illustrated by Richard Egielski. Farrar Straus & Giroux.
> A mysterious adventure enables Eddie and his dog to appreciate their home and themselves.

John Steptoe, *Mufaro's Beautiful Daughters: An African Tale*

• •

Publisher and Date: Lothrop, Lee and Shepard, 1987
Illustrator: John Steptoe
Audience Level: Grades three and up
Main Theme: Responses to Goodness and Meanness
Other Possible Themes: Punishment, Kindness, Giving, Virtue Rewarded
Values to Target: Self-awareness, Good as a Response to Meanness

• •

ABOUT THE AUTHOR

In his acceptance speech for the Boston Globe-Horn Book Award for illustration (1988), John Steptoe spoke of his experience as an artist and writer during the two and one-half years he spent on this book. He went to southeast Africa in search of a variant of the Cinderella story. He was also in search of the dignity and beauty of his own heritage. The ruins he visited in Zimbabwe suggested to him that the builders of the city were a society working together for good. He pictured them behaving as people do today. "People love, laugh, and quarrel; some are kind, and some are selfish and spoiled." He found the African Cinderella theme to be similar to that in many other cultures. This led him to surmise that industrious, kind, and considerate behavior has "always been an ideal to be encouraged" (p. 27). He also spoke of making a connection with his own family. Seeing in his mind's eye that his ancestors were very much like his own family, he stated, "Then I knew who my characters were and that they had dignity and grace." He used members of his family as models for some of the characters—his mother as the queen mother, his nephew as the little boy in the forest, and his daughter, Bweela, as the model for both sisters. At 16 Bweela could model both the self-centeredness of Manyara and the generous nature of Nyasha.

Steptoe saw this book as a triumph. "I began to realize that I was actually capable of creating images that I've wanted to see all my life" (p. 28). Students will enjoy looking at his earliest works, such as *Stevie* and *Birthday,* where he was primarily a colorist, and compare these to later works in black-and-white, such as *Daddy is a Monster.* Steptoe said that his work on *Mufaro's Beautiful Daughters* helped him "to learn more about loving myself" (Steptoe, John. "Acceptance Speech for Boston Globe-Hornbook Award." *The Hornbook Magazine 14*(1): 25-28). John Steptoe died in 1989.

ABOUT THE STORY

The size and the glowing colors of this Caldecott honor book make it ideal for groups. Mufaro had two beautiful daughters, Manyara and Nyasha. The girls are tested in identical ways to reveal which of them is worthy to become the king's wife. Even though Nyasha proves to be kind and Manyara vain and mean, Mufaro proclaims that he is the happiest father in all the land, for he is blessed with two beautiful and worthy daughters. Folktale motifs such as the archetypal king, queen, journey, and tests make comparison to folktales from other cultures interesting.

Folktales are about moral behavior. Characters have no dimension. Good folks win out. Evil or meanness is punished. Wit, kindness, wisdom, and courage are rewarded. Thomas Lickona (1991) has commented that folktales survive because we "love the good." Children enjoy the predictability of the story structure, the catharsis of disliking the bad character, and the rewarding of the good. This story challenges children to think in a different way. Steptoe presents an unhappy Manyara rather than an evil character and a father and sister who love her nevertheless. There is no punishment for her, only her appropriate place in the palace.

The frontispiece has information about the art work and the meanings of the names in the Shona language. The reader will want to pause and allow the children to enjoy the visual clues to the plot outcome, such as the "uppermost branches (of the trees) seemed to bow down to Nyasha."

DIALOGUE

Talk about What You Notice in the Story

• •

In this fifth grade classroom students begin by noticing literary devices. Alan picks up a foreshadowing clue from the illustrations, an important literary skill. The teacher reflects the joy Chris is experiencing in understanding the clues provided by the author. He is obviously an experienced literary connoisseur.

• •

TEACHER:	LET'S TALK ABOUT WHAT IS REAL AND WHAT IS NOT.
C. J.:	Well, snakes don't talk.
Corey:	And they don't turn into princes.
Alan:	I noticed the ears on the little boy in the picture. That was the first time I knew that something magic was happening.
TEACHER:	SO YOUR CUE ABOUT THE MAGIC CAME FROM AN ILLUSTRATION. CAN YOU SAY MORE ABOUT THOSE WEIRD EARS?
Chris:	It's important because when you see them, it's like you have a hint that you can let yourself go on off into wonderland.
TEACHER:	WONDERLAND.... OH, I *LIKE* THAT WORD!
Chris:	It's like you don't believe it, but you don't care that it's not true.
Casey:	Yeah, it's fun. You can get into it.

• •

The teacher uses the opportunity to briefly mention suspension of disbelief as a literary device since it had already been so aptly described by Chris as "wonderland."

• •

TEACHER:	WHAT ABOUT THE WOMAN IN THE TREES? AND THE LITTLE BOY?
Iyam:	Probably not real, but the story wouldn't be good without them. There are other stories with fairy godmothers and other stuff in them.

Talk about How the Story Makes You Feel

• •

The teacher allows time for comparisons to real and imaginary aspects of Cinderella and a Chinese folktale the group has read recently. Chris makes a wise generalization indicating his ability to be a critical thinker.

• •

TEACHER:	LOOK AT THE FACES. IT'S EASY TO TELL WHO IS MEAN AND WHO IS GOOD.
Jessie:	I can't stand Manyara. *[laughing]* And it's fun not to like her.
Haley:	She's really mean.
Alan:	She hurts other people and she's not sorry.
TEACHER:	IS MEAN DIFFERENT FROM EVIL?
Chris:	I think evil is worse and more widespread.

Talk about What the Story Reminds You of in Your Life

• •

The teacher gives prompts that allow the children to relate their beliefs to the principles upon which the text is based. Corrie agrees with Steptoe that parents like their children even on their mean days. The comments show how folktales lead to discussion of principles of behavior more than to labeling people good or bad.

• •

Summer:	Really those sisters remind me of my brother and me.
TEACHER:	WHAT IF I TOLD YOU THAT STEPTOE USED HIS DAUGHTER AS THE MODEL FOR BOTH NYASHA AND MANYARA?
Alan:	Let's see it again.
Cassie:	Well, if he had a normal daughter she might be grouchy some days and not on some days.
Alan:	Maybe both on the very same day!
Denise:	My dad always notices when I have my pouting face.
Erin:	I liked that it turned out with Manyara as the servant, since she had bragged so at the beginning.
TEACHER:	ARE SERVANTS NOT AS GOOD AS QUEENS?
C.J.:	No, of course not. They have to do all the work.
Iyam:	I don't know about that. There could be a bad queen and a good servant.
Mati:	I think queens can do some work too.
TEACHER:	DOES GOODNESS HAVE TO DO ONLY WITH DOING WORK?

Cassie:	That's not all there is to it. Nyasha gave food to the little boy. And she wasn't mean back to her sister.
Jeremy:	And she didn't try to get even at the end by laughing or saying, "I told you so!"
TEACHER:	MANYARA SAYS THAT HER SISTER'S KINDNESS IS A SILLY WEAKNESS.
Chad:	Being kind is hard. So you can't call it weak.
Jennifer:	Manyara will make a grouchy servant. I don't think she's going to change her personality.
TEACHER:	WOULD SHE MAKE A GOOD QUEEN?
Chorus:	No!
Iyam:	Nyasha will make the best queen.
TEACHER:	WHAT IS BEING GOOD?
Group Consensus:	It's how you treat other people. If you hurt them you're mean inside.
TEACHER:	ONE THING I NOTICED WAS THAT MUFARO THINKS BOTH HIS DAUGHTERS ARE BEAUTIFUL.
Corrie:	Well, your real parents are like that, I think. They like you any way you are on your mean days and your good days.

TEACHER FOCUS

Compare and Contrast: Steptoe has changed the traditional folktale from good versus evil to one that shows evil stemming from unhappiness. Why do people behave as they do? The answer is provided in-depth in realistic fiction. In folktales we generally assume that it is our choice whether we are good or evil. This story raises another factor. Do people behave differently when unhappy?

Visual Literacy: These Caldecott honor pictures are exquisite in presenting a fairy tale setting with African motifs. The portraiture-like characters maintain the same characteristics: the beauty of Africans with the feeling of make-believe.

COUNSELOR FOCUS

Meanness: Steptoe presents a new way to look at meanness. Nyasha responds to the meanness of Manyara by being kind. That premise offers a new approach to conflicts among children.

Kindness: The trials set before the sisters require a kind response in order for one of them to become a queen. The metaphorical meaning can be explored in relation to antagonisms in children's lives.

Sexism: The purpose of the trials set before the sisters is to win the prince. Indeed, the prince himself is in on the judging of behavior. A question for discussion is whether the story could be told equally well if the princess put a prince to the test.

MAKING CONNECTIONS

Literature Study: *Mufaro's Beautiful Daughters* is similar to Robert D. San Souci's *The Talking Eggs* (see earlier entry) in several ways: good and bad sisters, the motif of tests, good versus meanness as theme. One teacher of behaviorally handicapped students constantly relies on metaphor to elicit thinking about behavior in the classroom. Folktales are ideal because they capture the imagination and offer the good/bad dilemmas that make for rich discussion. The teacher spent two weeks on *The Talking Eggs*, using character maps, character studies, plot summaries, discussion, bulletin boards, dramatization, video production, comparison with *Cinderella*, dialogues with talking eggs, and art work. She followed this study with *Mufaro's Beautiful Daughters*. The children were very successful with comparative character studies of Manyara and Nyasha with Rose and Blanche. Group discussions on this story centered on "Who is mean in my life?" Children maintained a continual dialogue about the story during everyday classroom interactions.

Comparisons to Other Fairy Tales: One group examined different approaches to good and evil, using a character map of Cinderella, the stepsisters, the stepmother, the fairy godmother, and the prince, along with the characters from this story. Knowing only Disney versions of the story, the students were shocked that the older versions of Cinderella were more violent, with punishment for the wicked stepsisters. (Birds came and plucked out their eyeballs!) The children noted the difference in the punishment theme in *Mufaro's Beautiful Daughters*.

Art: John Steptoe died soon after the publication of *Mufaro's Beautiful Daughters*, which was the only Caldecott honor book for 1989. His development as an artist is an interesting study of the relationship of artist and ideas. There are many modern versions of folktales being published. Students may want to continue with explorations of the old and the new.

BOOKS FOR FOLLOW-UP LITERATURE STUDIES

Other Cinderella Stories

Climo, Shirley. (1989). *The Egyptian Cinderella.* Crowell.
> Set in the sixth century B.C., Cinderella is a slave girl who is chosen by the Pharaoh to be queen.

Huck, Charlotte. (1989). *Princess Furball.* Illustrated by Arnold Lobel. Greenwillow.
> A spirited princess relies on her own ingenuity rather than waiting for a fairy godmother.

Louie, Ai-ling. (1982). *Yehshen: A Cinderella Story from China*. Philomel.
This version dates back 1000 years before the European Cinderella.

Another Folktale by John Steptoe

Steptoe, John. (1984). *The Story of Jumping Mouse: A Native American Legend*.
Lothrop, Lee and Shepard.
Jumping Mouse has gifts of magic which lead him to a far-off land where, thanks
to his unselfish spirit, no mouse goes hungry.

REFERENCES

Lickona, Thomas. (1991). *Educating for Character*. Bantam.
Steptoe, John. (1988) "Acceptance Speech for Boston Globe-Hornbook Award" *The Hornbook Magazine*. *14*(1): 25-28.

Chris Van Allsburg, *The Wretched Stone*

• •
Publisher and Date: Houghton Mifflin, 1991
Audience Level: Grades four and up
Illustrator: Chris Van Allsburg
Main Themes: Addiction, Obsession, Self-control
Other Possible Themes: Creativity, Conformity, Television,
    Mechanization, Education, Greed
Values to Target: Self-Knowledge
• •

ABOUT THE AUTHOR

Although he loved painting and drawing as a child, Chris Van Allsburg's interest in art had to compete with the numerous other activities enjoyed by young boys, such as playing baseball and building models. He tells a story about waking up sick one morning on a day when his class had art. He pretended not to be sick so he wouldn't have to miss school. But when his art teacher noticed his pale face and took him into the coat room to see if he was all right, he said, "Yes," and promptly threw up into Billy Marcus's boots. Van Allsburg enrolled in art school on a lark, but soon rediscovered his childhood interest in making things with his hands. He graduated from the University of Michigan as a sculptor and regarded drawing as a hobby. Van Allsburg wrote his first book somewhat casually and was surprised by its success. That first book, *The Garden of Abdul Gazazi*, was a Caldecott runner-up. He has won two Caldecott Medals since then. He writes his stories first, then makes many different sketches for each idea he wants to illustrate. His drawings are rich and provocative. Children will note his ability to use tones of dark and light in such a way that the forms appear three dimensional. He wants his stories to leave something to ponder at the end; "The book itself", he says, "is merely chapter one" (p. 169) (*SATA* v. 53, pp. 160-72).

ABOUT THE STORY

Using the device of a captain's log, Van Allsburg creates through story and illustration the last voyage of the Rita Anne. Conditions are ideal as the ship sets sail. The lively crew enjoys singing, dancing, and telling stories. But the text and illustrations take on an ominous tone after the crew unearths a luminous stone on an uncharted island. They load their treasure into the forward hold. The "wretched stone" soon begins to display an uncanny power. The men are so attracted to its light that they sit around it in silence, transfixed. Days later the captain is horrified to find that the once vivacious crew members have turned into grinning monkeys. The suspense and humor lend to enjoyment and thought-provoking inquiry. Upon first reading we were enchanted by the art work, but wondered if the message was *too* obvious: "TV is bad for us." Discussions with children, however, convinced us that there are many "wretched stones" in their lives. The book has merit not only for its suspense and artistry but for stimulating thought about responsibility and our priorities in life.

DIALOGUE

Talk about What You Notice in the Story

• •

Alan, like many fifth graders, is already a student of Van Allsburg's work. The teacher doesn't ask questions, but contributes to the conversation. Alan continues to make conceptual responses.

• •

Alan: Usually you expect in a Chris Van Allsburg book that it will go off into a fantasy.

TEACHER:	YOU BEGIN TO SEE CLUES OF SOMETHING MYSTERIOUS OR UNREAL.
Alan:	Things seemed pretty normal at first. The crew was dancing and singing and telling stories. Then they came to the uncharted island.
Casey:	The trees didn't bear fruit.
Jessica:	Look at the lighting in the picture of the island!
Aaron:	Then we *really* know it is unreal when we see all those grinning monkeys staring at the stone.
Chris:	Cool! One has an earring.
Alan:	Their brains are gone!
Jessica:	They are idiots.
Aaron:	The stone did it!
James:	Then the stone goes dark. It gets struck by lightning. That was a good thing!
TEACHER:	THE STONE WENT DARK BUT EVERYTHING DIDN'T RETURN TO NORMAL RIGHT AWAY. NOTICE THE FACES.
Chris:	They're still apes, but their faces are getting more alert.
Alan:	It's like they are coming to their senses.
Casey:	The captain is reading to them.

Talk about How the Story Makes You Feel

• •

The teacher provides sensory experiences to enhance the meaning of the text. Alan's remarks show that he is moving through the text to find meaning.

• •

Alan:	Actually I was amused at the end. Every good book has got to have a little joke.
TEACHER:	YOU'LL NEVER GUESS THAT WE MAY HAVE A SPECIAL SNACK TODAY!
Chorus:	Bananas!
	[Much laughter]
TEACHER:	THE HUMOR AT THE END WORKS WELL, WHAT OTHER FEELINGS DO YOU HAVE?
Chris:	Interested. Wanting to know what he means.
Jessica:	I'm still not sure what this is all about.
TEACHER:	NEITHER AM I. WE CAN TALK ABOUT IT.

Talk about What the Story Reminds You of in Your Life

Notice that the dictionary and thesaurus become the subject of study as well as the source of a definition. Casey connects the title with the theme of the story. The discussion moves from the concrete elements of story and familiarity with the word addiction offered by Jessica to the conceptual and a discussion of Nintendo and greed. "Wretched stone" is used by the teacher as a metaphor and the students make superb applications to their own lives.

TEACHER:	MAYBE WE COULD START TO THINK BY EXAMINING THE CHARACTERISTICS OF THE WRETCHED STONE.
Alan:	It had power over them. It was like a wizard.
Chris:	They kept staring at it. It kept them from doing their work.
James:	It was like they lost their real personalities.
Alan:	The stone did it!
TEACHER:	THE TITLE IS *THE WRETCHED STONE*. COULD IT HAVE BEEN CALLED SOMETHING ELSE?
Casey:	What does wretched mean anyway?
Chad:	I'll look it up. *[returning]* This is cool. The antonyms for wretched are animated, lively, content. That describes the crew *before* the stone!
Casey:	Oh, I get it. They were just the opposite when they were under the power of the stone. So it was wretched.
Jessica:	I think the stone was addictive.
Chorus:	"Yeah." "Like drugs." "Drugs make you keep doing drugs."
TEACHER:	I'M REMEMBERING THAT WE SAID THE STONE HAD POWER OVER THEM, CAUSED THEM TO LOSE THEIR REAL PERSONALITIES AND KEPT THEM FROM DOING THEIR WORK. YOU ARE SAYING THESE ARE THE CHARACTERISTICS OF DRUG ADDICTION.
Alan:	Right. Drugs make people like monkeys.
TEACHER:	SO THE STORY CAN BE A METAPHOR FOR OUR TIME AND OUR LIFE. THE METAPHOR MAY BE ABOUT MORE THAN DRUG ADDICTION. ARE THERE OTHER ADDICTIONS? WHAT ELSE IN OUR WORLD HAS THIS KIND OF POWER OVER US?
James:	I know! Nintendo!
Chad:	TV!
Jessica:	Yeah. You keep going back to it.
Casey:	You have it around all the time.
James:	Everybody's a couch potato sometimes.

Alan: It can keep you from doing your homework. Especially Nintendo.

Jessica: Have you noticed that people who are playing Nintendo can't talk to anybody while they are doing it?

TEACHER: DO YOU THINK WE SHOULD THROW OUR TV'S AND NINTENDO GAMES OVERBOARD LIKE THE STONE?

Alan: No. It's really good to have TV most of the time.

Jessica: We don't have to watch it so much. Nobody tells us we have to watch everything.

Chris: We can go outside more.

Alan: We don't *have* to be couch potatoes.

Chris: Right. We don't have to turn into monkeys.
[Laughter]

Jessica: We can read.

James: You know I don't really like MTV. I'd rather just hear a song. After I see the MTV I can't get those pictures out of my head.

Jessica: I'd rather think of how it should be on my own.

James: I know. It's more fun if you imagine the song to be what you have in your head.

Alan: Hey, I just thought of something else that the wretched stone might be. It might be greed.

TEACHER: CAN YOU SAY SOME MORE ABOUT THAT?

Alan: What I mean is that people seem to want so much stuff like cars and all, and it gets to be that they are controlled by wanting it, and they don't have much of a life.

TEACHER: ALAN HAS JUST REMINDED *ME* OF ANOTHER STORY AND SOME MORE DISCUSSION IDEAS. WOULDN'T YOU KNOW, OUR TIME IS UP AND WE ARE NOW JUST BEGINNING TO MAKE HEADWAY ON THIS METAPHOR. LET'S LEAVE WITH A RE-READING OF THE JUNE 29 ENTRY. "I AM HAPPY TO REPORT THAT THE MEN HAVE RETURNED TO NORMAL. IT SEEMS THAT THOSE WHO KNEW HOW TO READ RECOVERED MORE QUICKLY." WHAT DOES THIS MAKE YOU WANT TO DO ABOUT WRETCHED STONES?"

Chris: I think we can remember that it's up to us to be in charge.

Alan: We just have to know when something like the stone is taking over.

Jessica: I think this book is easy to remember because we have these illustrations of the grinning moneys in our heads to remind us.

TEACHER: *[PRESENTING BANANAS]* AND DON'T DEVELOP AN UNUSUAL APPETITE FOR BANANAS! HERE'S ONE FOR EACH OF YOU TO EAT!

TEACHER FOCUS

Allegory: The wretched stone, as the children realized, could be applied to anything in our lives to which we become addicted and can't easily justify. These fifth grade students had no trouble using synthesis skills and identifying what those addictions were for them.

Critical Viewing Skills: The remarks of these children about television would probably be repeated anywhere in the country. The book may provide an authentic purpose for studying television and its power to make children addictive.

COUNSELOR FOCUS

Addiction: The "just say no" campaign to prevent drug addiction is based on the belief that children will respond obediently to promises of reward or punishment. The study of this text provides an opportunity to have a more profound effect on children. They internalize the metaphor and apply it to themselves at whatever stage of cognitive development in which they may be functioning.

MAKING CONNECTIONS

Health: Children may research kinds of treatment plans for addiction. School nurses have access to "Smoking Cessation" and other treatment plans and may be guest speakers.

Television/Math: Children may survey the number of hours they spend watching television, and calculate the average number of hours per week for the class.

Creative Writing: Teachers may describe what they remember or know about life without television. This may inspire children to fantasize about what life would be like if all televisions were to be suddenly destroyed. Would there be "withdrawal"?

BOOKS FOR FOLLOW-UP LITERATURE STUDIES

Kennedy, Richard. (1987). "The Lost Kingdom of Karnica" from *Richard Kennedy: Collected Stories*. Harper and Row.

> In the previous conversation it was Alan's insightful discovery of the more subjective application of the metaphor that made a connection with the teacher, who recalled this intriguing story about a stone by Richard Kennedy. In this original tale Farmer Erd discovers an enormous glowing stone in his garden. "Life got worse, and quickly, after the stone was found." Kennedy's longer work, *The Blue Stone,* is included in this treasury of provocative tales.

Susan Varley, *Badger's Parting Gifts*

- -

Publisher and Date: Lothrop, Lee and Shepard, 1984
Illustrator: Susan Varley
Audience Level: Grades one and up
Main Theme: Death
Other Possible Themes: Memory, Friendship, Gifts, Loss
Values to Target: Kindness, Caring, Value of Others

- -

ABOUT THE AUTHOR

Susan Varley lives in her hometown of Blackpool, England. Since childhood she has enjoyed drawing more than any other activity. She discovered children's book illustration while in art college. She read Kenneth Grahame's *Wind in the Willows* at age 20 and acknowledges its influence. *Badger's Parting Gifts* was her first picture book and was completed while she was still in college. She credits her art school tutor with the book's concept (*SATA* v. 63, pp. 175-78).

ABOUT THE STORY

Old Badger's body wasn't working well anymore and he knew he must soon die. He wasn't afraid, but he was concerned about how his friends would feel when he was gone. He wrote a note to his friends about his dream of a "Long Tunnel," hoping they wouldn't be too sad when he was gone. When Badger died his friends did feel sadness. As they gathered to talk about the days when Badger was with them, each told of a gift Badger had given, a "parting gift which should become all the more special as it was passed on to others."

In our death-denying culture, this is an important book for adults as well as children. The story is unique in that it presents the topic of death from the point of view of the one dying. As Badger describes his vision of the "Long Tunnel," he feels liberated and joyful. The sadness of his friends upon losing him is not dismissed or discounted. It is depicted in the metaphor of winter's cold and spring's renewal. Badger's friends grieve. As they gather to remember their unique gifts from Badger, their sadness melts with the snow.

DIALOGUE

Talk about What You Notice in the Story

• •

These fourth graders sound almost eager to be able to talk about a taboo subject. They wonder if the story even mentions the word death, and Erin realizes that people hope to protect children by not using the word.

• •

Haley:	Did Badger really die?
Jeremy:	I don't think the word dead is in the book.
Erin:	It said, "down the tunnel."
Gerald:	The word "died" is hard to say.
Scott:	I think "dead" is in there. *[after teacher lends him the text]* After Fox read the note it says here, "Fox broke the news that Badger was dead."
Daniel:	But his picture was in the book after he died.
Erin:	Yes. But those were memories.
Teacher:	*[FINDING THE ILLUSTRATIONS OF MOLE AND THE PAPER DOLLS, AND FROG AND THE ICE SKATING EVENT]* AS ERIN SAID, THESE ARE FLASHBACKS TO AN EARLIER TIME. I NOTICED FROM YOUR COMMENTS THAT YOU NOTICE THAT PEOPLE TEND TO AVOID THE WORD "DEAD."
Jeremy:	I've always wondered why people just won't ever say "He died."
Scott:	They say "He passed away."
Denise:	Or "kicked the bucket."
Lashonda:	Or "went to sleep."
Teacher:	I WONDER WHY PEOPLE DO THIS.
Erin:	I think they don't want kids to get scared.

Talk about How the Story Makes You Feel

• •

The children move through the story feeling the sorrow and the poetry of it. Scott's response is aesthetic and Lashonda is empathetic with the friends left behind. The teacher points out the parallel theme of changing seasons.

• •

Erin:	Some kids are really scared of dying, or that their mama will die.

Denise: I used to get scared when my daddy left for work in the mornings. I thought he might be in a wreck and not come back. Some mornings I would cry. But I wouldn't tell anybody why I was crying.

Jeremy: I have never yet had anybody that is closely related to me die.

TEACHER: DENISE AND ERIN HAVE JUST SAID HOW THEY REMEMBER BEING AFRAID SOMEONE WILL DIE. AND JEREMY SAID NOT *YET* HAS ANYONE DIED WHO IS REALLY CLOSE TO HIM. I NOTICED THAT DEATH IS NOT SO FRIGHTENING TO BADGER WHO IS ABOUT TO DIE.

Scott: It almost seemed to me like he wanted to die.

Denise: I would still be scared to die even if I were old. I heard about a man who almost drowned but who was revived by the EMS. He talked about seeing clouds and a long tunnel. He said it on TV.

Erin: If I got too sick to know anything, I might decide I'd be better off dead.

Denise: Well, it depends on how sick you are.

Scott: I bet I know the reason Badger wasn't scared. I think he was old and tired and he wanted to get stronger. He could run again in his dream of the long tunnel.

Jeremy: I guess in a way dying could be happy and sad. If you die you don't have to worry any more about robberies and killing and stuff.

Denise: I know it's still sad for those left behind.

La Shonda: Mole and Frog and his friends didn't feel like doing much of anything.

TEACHER: I NOTICED HOW THE SEASON CHANGED. "THE SNOW COVERED THE COUNTRYSIDE, BUT IT DIDN'T COVER THE SADNESS."

Scott: Then the sadness melted as they remembered Badger.

Denise: Badger was good. You'd just as soon forget a bad person.

Talk about What the Story Reminds You of in Your Life

• •

The beauty of the story is in the concept of Badger leaving gifts behind. The responses reflect the caring tone of the story and create a greater appreciation for the temporary nature of life.

• •

TEACHER: LET'S NOTICE THE TITLE OF THE BOOK AGAIN. WHAT DOES THIS STORY MAKE YOU THINK ABOUT IN YOUR LIFE?

Gerald:	Parting gifts remind me of my uncle. He died. He always let me do things with him on the farm, like driving the tractor. He taught me like in the story.
Scott:	I never knew my grandfather. He died in 1980 right before I was born. All I ever saw were his pictures. A road is named after him.
Jeremy:	Well, you still have the road. That's good.
Scott:	Sure. I ride my bike on it every day.
TEACHER:	SO IN A WAY THAT WAS A PARTING GIFT. SOMEONE ELSE THOUGHT OF NAMING THE ROAD. ONE OF YOU SAID EARLIER THAT THE GIFTS COULD LAST FOREVER. IS THAT TRUE FOR YOU IN YOUR LIFE?
Daniel:	My grandfather taught me how to fish, and I can teach somebody else now.
Denise:	My grandmother is still alive. She has time to play games with me.
TEACHER:	THAT'S A GIFT YOU CAN PASS ON.
Denise:	I do. To my little brother.
Summer:	I know how to cut paper dolls like Mole. I could pass on that gift now!

TEACHER FOCUS

Life Cycle: Badger leaves his friends the gifts that represent his life. The story of Badger gives children an affective dimension to the study of the life cycle. The story will remain in the minds (hearts) of children and can serve as a engaging point of reference throughout scientific study.

Language: Death is a taboo subject in our culture, but not all cultures. Taboos, however, are evident in all cultures. For upper grades the subject of taboos could be studied by finding cultural taboos in a folklore index. Also, euphemisms are a way of avoiding a taboo subject and can provide a fascinating language study.

COUNSELOR FOCUS

Death: This story is unusual because it is told from the point of view of the character who is dying and connects with readers' fear of death. Badger faces death unafraid and serene. Children are unduly protected from discussions of death, which increases their fear. Intentional use of this story at any time is appropriate; we don't have to wait for a death to bring up the subject.

MAKING CONNECTIONS

Cooperative Learning: From the conversation above emerged the idea that children already had gifts to share—something they could teach another to do. Other groups may want to explore such possibilities.

BOOKS FOR FOLLOW-UP LITERATURE STUDIES

In unique ways the following titles address the issue of death or the theme of gifts that last through generations:

Babbitt, Natalie. (1975). *Tuck Everlasting.* Farrar Straus & Giroux.
> In this fantasy, Tuck and his family explore the possibility of dying or living forever with Winnie Foster, a young girl who has run away from home. This is a full-length book with prose that is exquisite for reading aloud.

Flournoy, Valerie. (1985). *The Patchwork Quilt.* Illustrated by Jerry Pinkney. Dial Books for Young Readers.
> A little girl helps her grandmother and mother make a quilt that tells the story of her family's life.

Martin, Bill and Archambault, John. (1987). *Knots on a Counting Rope.* Illustrated by Ted Rand. Henry Holt.
> An Indian grandfather shares family stories with his blind grandson to give him courage to handle their parting.

Miles, Miska. (1971). *Annie and the Old One.* Illustrated by Peter Parnall. Little, Brown.
> A Navajo girl unravels her grandmother's weaving because she believes the completion will mean her death.

Polacco, Patricia. (1988). *The Keeping Quilt.* Simon and Schuster.
> An autobiographical story of a little girl in whose family the quilt is passed down and used for four generations.

Judith Viorst,
The Tenth Good Thing about Barney

• •

Publisher and Date: MacMillan, 1971
Illustrator: Erik Blegvad
Audience Level: Kindergarten and up
Main Theme: Grief

Other Possible Themes: Changes, Loss, Friendship, Love of
Family
Values to Target: Joy and Sadness

• •

ABOUT THE AUTHOR

Judith Viorst and her husband, Milton, who is also a writer, are the parents of three children, Anthony, Nicholas, and Alexander. Children who know her books may recognize that the Viorst family has inspired several titles. When Anthony was picking on his younger brother, she decided to write *I'll Fix Anthony* to cheer up Nick. When Alexander said he was having "a terrible day," the result was *The Terrible, Horrible, No Good, Very Bad Day.* Nick's fear of Monsters inspired *Mama Says There Aren't Any Zombies.* Viorst began writing when she was seven. She has been a regular columnist for *Redbook Magazine* and has published numerous articles in other periodicals (*SATA* v. 7, pp. 200-01).

ABOUT THE STORY

Barney, the cat, dies and the little boy doesn't feel like eating or watching TV. His parents understand and do not downplay his need to be sad. His mom says they will have a funeral and advises him to think of ten good things about Barney. He has no trouble thinking of nine. His friend Annie from next door comes over with flowers. After the funeral, the boy helps his father plant seeds in the garden. From this experience comes the realization of the tenth good thing about Barney.

Children can readily discover in the story the value of ritual, and the need for loving support of parents and friends like Annie to help us deal with sadness. The boy's argument with Annie about heaven and the ground is welcomed by children who think concretely. The story depicts parents who help when a child is faced with such hard questions.

DIALOGUE

Talk about What You Notice in the Story

• •

The teacher does not pre-suppose that all the questions and wondering statements of these second grade children need a definitive answer.

• •

TEACHER:	YOU CAN STOP ME DURING THE READING IF YOU WANT TO SAY ANYTHING.
Keetha:	They're having a funeral.
Angelina:	Annie is at the funeral too.
	[The teacher pauses to allow children to count on their fingers the nine good things about Barney.]
Beth:	My grandma told me when we were driving to Wal-Mart that it's not the real "you" when you're buried.
Keetha:	It's your spirit.
Andy:	Yeah, your soul.
TEACHER:	IT IS HARD TO UNDERSTAND, ISN'T IT?
Justin:	*[thoughtfully]* Yeah. I always wonder how can you be in heaven and in the ground at the same time?
TEACHER:	BETH'S GRANDMA HAS TOLD HER WHAT SHE BELIEVES ABOUT HEAVEN.
Beth:	We were riding by the cemetery and I saw the graveyard and I asked her. It was when my other grandma was in the hospital.
TEACHER:	MAYBE YOU WERE AFRAID SHE MIGHT NOT GET WELL.
Beth:	Yes. *[now with more energy]* But she did get well.
TEACHER:	YOU WERE REALLY WORRIED THOUGH?
	[Nod of agreement]

Talk about How the Story Makes You Feel

• •

The children have so many stories to tell, and many about crying. It makes us wonder if we allow enough time for this on a regular basis. One teacher has suggested that when she sees this reaction in her class she stops and simply says, "Now take two minutes and tell your neighbor what you want to say. Ready? Begin."

• •

Jason:	I know just how he feels because my cat got hit by a car.
Chorus:	"My dog died..." "Please can I tell something?..." "My little kitten died..."
TEACHER:	ONE AT A TIME PLEASE.
Chase:	One night when I was sleeping we heard a gunshot. The next morning my dad and I found our dog. We buried him in the garden, too, just like in the story.
TEACHER:	SO OTHERS HAVE LOST A PET...
Chorus:	"Me..." "I have..." "I've lost two."
TEACHER:	JASON SAID DURING THE STORY THAT HE KNOWS HOW IT FEELS. HOW WOULD YOU DESCRIBE THE FEELING?

Jeremy:	Sad.
Chase:	A feeling of crying.
Shari:	If you feel sad, then you start to cry. Like when you feel like you're all by yourself with nobody there. You'd be sad and you'd cry.
Chase:	I cried when my cat died, and his name was Dennis. And I was sad when my other cat ran away.

Talk about What the Story Reminds You of in Your Life.

• •

This conversation reflects feeling and thinking. Beth knows that for sadness to leave takes more than a day and Keetha isn't sure it ever goes away. Jason displays thinking skills as he compares what dogs and cats usually do and what happens after burial.

• •

TEACHER:	THE TITLE IS IMPORTANT IN THIS STORY.
Keetha:	The tenth thing is helping the flowers grow.
Andy:	Annie said heaven is in the ground. I think it's in the sky.
TEACHER:	SO PEOPLE HAVE DIFFERENCES IN THE WAY THEY THINK ABOUT HEAVEN.
Beth:	I figure out stuff with my Grandma.
TEACHER:	MAYBE FUNERALS HELP PEOPLE REMEMBER GOOD THINGS.
Jason:	Hmm. I don't know.
Keetha:	I think the funeral helped them because they'll remember Barney. And they can come back to the place to see him every day and remember he was special.
Jeremy:	My grandpa died and we had a funeral. I got to see my grandpa one last time. It was sad.
Shari:	Churches give us funerals.
TEACHER:	THE FUNERAL IN THE STORY IS NOT IN A CHURCH.
Keetha:	It can still be a funeral.
Jeremy:	They were all there, like on the cover picture. His mom, his dad, and his friend.
Beth:	They sang a song. We sing in church.
Justin:	The boy and his father planted seeds where Barney was buried.
Beth:	The seeds will change into flowers.
TEACHER:	WHAT ELSE CHANGES?
Chorus:	The ground.
TEACHER:	BARNEY WAS DEAD. LIFE WILL BE DIFFERENT FOR THE BOY.
Shari:	I know. He'll be sad and lonely.

Jeremy:	I think he will get to feel better after a while.
TEACHER:	HIS FATHER SAID HE MIGHT FEEL BETTER THE VERY NEXT DAY.
Beth:	I think it takes more than a day.
Keetha:	I don't think it goes away.
Shari:	You may feel it in your stomach for a long time.
TEACHER:	YOU ALL KNOW ABOUT SADNESS. I NOTICED THE WORDS, "THAT'S A PRETTY NICE JOB FOR A CAT."
Jason:	*[laughing, changing the mood of the conversation]* Yeah. I usually think of cats and dogs digging and tearing up the ground, not helping things to grow.
Larry:	Well, my dog Max is in the ground. I guess it's a pretty nice job for a dog too.

TEACHER FOCUS

Ritual: Instead of depriving children of participation in ritual, use of this book helps children understand the importance of it. Children are very familiar with home and classroom rituals, and going through established motions affirms the reality of death. The loss of a pet is not uncommon and children may not have the necessary ritual to shed their grief. This book is no doubt responsible for thousands of home and classroom ceremonies.

Life Cycle: We often limit the life cycle lesson to one of facts. This story could add an affective dimension to engage the children and stimulate thought.

COUNSELOR FOCUS

Loss: A child's first experience with loss is most often with a pet. This story provides an elementary experience upon which counselors can build as children will inevitably face other kinds of losses.

MAKING CONNECTIONS

Don't miss the opportunity to allow children to become conscious of the rituals you create together in the classroom. Some teachers have found that the establishment of rituals frees them from having to always be in a directive role. The children know what to do. Their consciousness of funeral rituals eases the sorrow associated with loss and grief.

BOOKS FOR FOLLOW-UP LITERATURE STUDIES

Starred titles have full entries elsewhere in this book.

* Shreve, Susan. (1979). "The Death of Giles" from *Family Secrets*. Alfred A. Knopf.
Sammy finds Giles, his dog, dead. At first he doesn't even tell the family because
he hopes it might not be true.
* Varley, Susan. (1984). *Badger's Parting Gifts*. Lothrop, Lee and Shephard.
Badger's friends, like the little boy in this story, work through their grief by
remembering good times with their friend.
Wilhelm, Hans. (1985). *I'll Always Love You*. Crown.
A little boy tells his dog every day how much he loves him. When the dog dies,
this is some comfort. The simple text is good for the very youngest of children.

Vera Williams,
A Chair for My Mother

• •

Publisher and Date: Greenwillow, 1982
Illustrator: Vera Williams
Audience Level: Grades two and up
Main Theme: Working Together
Other Possible Themes: Sacrifice, Generosity, Unselfishness,
    Single Parents
Values to Target: Care, Cooperation, Work

• •

ABOUT THE AUTHOR

Vera Williams was born in California but grew up in New York City.
Her family was poor and moved frequently. Williams and her sister lived
for a time in foster homes and an orphanage. Her parents encouraged her
to participate in creative activities like art, dramatics, and dance. A teacher
at school recommended Vera for art classes, which she attended for nine
years. She is a graduate of Black Mountain College in North Carolina.

In 1953 her husband and friends established the Gate Hill cooperative community at Stony Point, New York. Their three children were
raised there. In 1970 she moved to Canada and returned to New York in
1981. She was 51 years old when her first book was published. Her books
feature people of color, women-centered families, and working class

people. The bright colors and bold lines in her drawings convey a wonderment and optimism she hopes all children can experience (*SATA* v. 53, pp. 189-93).

ABOUT THE STORY

Rosa's family fills a jar with coins for special purchases. Because of a fire in their house, the family lacks essentials. So this time the money is used to buy a beautiful easy chair for the family, but especially for mother, who is tired when she comes home from work, and for grandmother, who also needs to rest. Picking out the chair and bringing it home is cause for celebration.

This working class grandmother, mother, and daughter give the kind of care and support to each other that sustains families through hard times. Such fictional role models of family stability, industriousness, kindness, and courage serve our children well.

DIALOGUE

Talk about What You Notice in the Story

• •

Third grade students begin commenting on the story from the beginning. Heather's response makes the word "nice" sound poetic, enough to make James feel positive about the book too. His other responses indicate that he wasn't very happy that day. The counselor noticed and invited him back later for a talk about how he was feeling.

• •

TEACHER:	I THINK VERA WILLIAMS IS A WONDERFUL WRITER AND ILLUSTRATOR. YOU MAY STOP ME DURING THE READING AS YOU NOTICE HOW THE PICTURES HELP TO TELL THE STORY.
Josh:	I've been noticing all the time how the borders go with the story. Look at the one with the blue sky and clouds.
Patrick:	And in the one with the fire, she has droopy flowers and the page looks like smoke.
Josh:	Right. And the one with the fire trucks. It's just so cool how they favor the story.
Leigh Ann:	I notice that there's always a small picture on the other side too. It goes with the page.
Heather:	That's so neat!

TEACHER:	YOU ALL ARE REALLY OBSERVANT TODAY. YOU NOTICED SOME THINGS I DIDN'T NOTICE. ANYTHING ELSE?
Heather:	Mainly this story is just nice. It was nice about Josephine paying Rosa the money, and it was nice of Rosa to put it in the jar for her mother, and it was nice the neighbors helped them to clean up and start all over.
James:	*[a new student, first day at school]* Yeah, it was good. It was really nice.
Josh:	See, James, I told you it would be a lot of fun coming up here for guidance.
James:	Yeah. I like it here. I thought it was good when the little girl was filling the catsup bottles and got paid.
Jessica:	That *was* nice of that lady to pay her.
Josh:	Look, you can see the cake back there in the restaurant.
TEACHER:	VERA WILLIAMS' DRAWINGS ARE REALLY A TREAT! SO YOU NOTICED HOW EVEN ROSA THE LITTLE GIRL GOT TO PUT MONEY IN THE JAR.
Kayla:	She helped her mama in everything that she did.
Heather:	She wasn't always mean and angry. She could have said, "This is my money. Take me to the store, Mama."
James:	That's like me!
Ricky:	That's being mean.
Josh:	No, that's not being mean. It's being greedy.
James:	What's greedy mean?
Jessica:	It means somebody wants everything and they won't share. My cousin's greedy. He saves up his money and then all the time asks for more. That's greedy.
Josh:	That is such a big jar of money.
Patrick:	It's a lot.
James:	It just looks like it because it's all change.
Patrick:	There's something I don't understand about this story.
TEACHER:	YES...
Patrick:	I can't figure out how the house burned down, and the money didn't burn up with it.
TEACHER:	THAT'S A GOOD QUESTION.
Josh:	It was like back in time. They didn't have the money jar until after the fire. See, she starts out with telling about the restaurant and the money jar, then she goes back in time. That's when the fire was. It was before!
Patrick:	*[a light going on]* Oh, it makes sense now.
TEACHER:	THANKS FOR THE QUESTION, PATRICK. AND THANKS FOR WHAT YOU NOTICED, JOSH.

Talk about How the Story Makes You Feel

The children appreciate the goodness of the characters. Jessica commented that there were no mean people in the story. Heather wants to read the story to her mother.

Heather: Well, it's sad.

Kayla: Not all of it.

Heather: But it had a very sad thing in it. I mean the part about the fire. You'd feel sad if your house caught on fire.

Ricky: Yeah, if your Nintendo and stuff burned. Oh Man!

James: If that happened to me, I'd throw a rock at God.

Ricky: God doesn't cause that. You shouldn't be mad at God. He brought you to life.

Josh: Yeah, I don't think God causes stuff like fires on purpose or anything.

Heather: Me, neither. I read it in the Bible all the time.

Ricky: Can you read the Bible?

Heather: Well, mostly my grandma reads it to me.

Teacher: SO YOU ARE SAYING THESE ARE NOT PEOPLE WHO DESERVE PUNISHMENT OR HARD TIMES.

Jessica: Yeah, they weren't ever mean people. People didn't ever act mean in this story.

Josh: It was very nice what they did for each other. They brought food and beds and red checked curtains.

Heather: There are sad and happy feelings in the story. I really like it. I'm going to see if it is in the library. I want to take it home and read it to my mother.

Talk about What the Story Reminds You of in Your Life

In another classroom group, the teacher asked the children before discussion to write for five minutes on "what the story is about." As children share written responses, chances for some conversation in the large group is created and the teacher knows that each child has done some thinking on her or his own. The following written responses come from third graders. These responses allow teachers to assess the level of thinking of each of the students. Some are concrete, others conceptual. Some teachers use stories like this one during the first weeks of school in order to get acquainted with the students and understand how to assist their development. Paula's concrete response can be compared to Jackie's more abstract response.

• •

Paula: I think this story is about the house getting on fire and they want a chair, and the girl helps her mother at the Blue Tile Diner.

Jill: I think this story is about a chair that is special because they needed a chair because theirs were burned up. They really worked hard for the chair.

Jackie: I think this story is about love, care, feelings, and resting.

Tonya: I think the story is really about a money jar. It took one year to fill it. It was very large.

Larry: I think this story is about love and waiting for what you want. It is also about saving.

TEACHER FOCUS

Community: Rosa's family is close-knit, but it is clear in the story that they are a part of a larger community. The family derives strength from each other and the community.

Women: This book shows three generations of women enjoying each other's company, helping each other, and, in spite of difficult times, making it.

COUNSELOR FOCUS

Hardship: The existence of hardship is a given in the book not just the fire, but the tired feet and shortage of money. If there is a message in this story, it is that people overcome hardship by helping each other.

Decentering: Children experience this story and think about their own selfishness and selflessness. Everyone is "nice" and to Heather, in the above dialogue, that means being kind and caring about the needs of others.

MAKING CONNECTIONS

Art: Since the borders in this book are so inspiring, allow the children to make a border around the sentences in their "five minute writing."

BOOKS FOR FOLLOW-UP LITERATURE STUDIES

The first two Vera Williams books listed below are companion pieces to *A Chair for My Mother*. The second two titles also celebrate family relationships.

Williams, Vera. (1984). *Music, Music for Everyone*. Greenwillow Books.
>In this third book in this series, the jar is empty because Rosa's grandmother is sick and her care costs money. The big chair is empty because grandmother must stay upstairs. But Rosa has her accordion, and after school, along with her friends, she makes music for Grandma. Their playing makes Grandma feel like a girl again, like dancing at a party. This gives Rosa a great idea. She and her friends become a "real band." And even Grandma is able to come to the party!

———. (1983). *Something Special for Me*. Greenwillow Books.
>This time it is Rosy's turn to spend the money in the jar. It is so hard to decide. She almost buys a dress; then she thinks about skates. But when she hears music from an accordion, she realizes that it is like the one grandmother used to play!

———. (1988). *Stringbean's Trip to the Shining Sea*. Greenwillow Books.
>Stringbean and his brother travel across country to the Pacific and, along the way, send postcards that are reproduced here as a travelogue. Some of these are illustrated by Williams's daughter Jennifer.

———. (1981). *Three Days on a River in a Red Canoe*. Greenwillow Books.
>Brother Sam, cat Sixtoes, Aunt Rosie, and Mom take an eventful trip in the red canoe.

Audrey Wood,
Elbert's Bad Word

• •

Publisher and Date: Harcourt, 1988
Illustrator: Don Wood
Audience Level: Kindergarten and up
Theme: Bad Words
Other Possible Themes: Affectation, Anger, Hurt
Values to Target: Rational Thinking about Language

• •

ABOUT THE AUTHOR AND ILLUSTRATOR

Audrey and Don Wood are married and work together to create books. She is the story writer, and they collaborate on the art. She grew up in Florida where she remembers accompanying her father, an artist, to paint the large murals used by Ringling Brothers Circus. She always loved color, and knew from the time she was a child that she wanted to write children's books. She started by stashing ideas in a cigar box on her desk in elementary school. *Elbert's Bad Word* started as a doodle on the pad by the telephone. Audrey noticed it and remembered how their son Bruce Robert "caught" a bad word when he was in kindergarten. The Woods live in California. Their studio is home to a mouse, a pigeon, a parrot, and a tortoise. They take in wounded birds and rehabilitate them (*SATA* v. 50 p 118-231).

ABOUT THE STORY

At an elegant garden party young Elbert overhears a "bad" word (one he has never heard before). It takes the shape of an ugly bristly creature as it floats by. Elbert stuffs it into his back pocket, never suspecting how soon it will fly into his mouth. It appears the moment that Sir Hilary's croquet mallet lands on Elbert's great toe. The word flies out of his mouth and the plot thickens. The gardener wizard tells him, "Sometimes we need strong words to say how we feel." After some interesting turns of events, Sir Hilary's croquet mallet crashes once again on Elbert's great toe. This time the bad word loses its power.

Every element of this story contributes to an understanding of the politics of language. The sirs and madames at an elegant garden party symbolize polite society where language must be as appropriate as the dress, music, and deviled eggs. The bad word chooses Elbert rather than the other way around. His innocence is believable and accurate. The wizard gardener offers advice that can benefit all of us. Elbert prefers to please rather than alienate the crowd, leaving the bad word to slip quietly away.

DIALOGUE

Talk about What You Notice in the Story

• •

The sixth grade children recognize that some words are labeled bad by society. The "beep" on television is understood to censor bad words. Daniel shows analytical thinking skill in making this connection. Dyrell and Marie also know a bad word when they hear one. They and Angela even understand that bad words are designed to get a particular kind of response, and they do.

• •

TEACHER:	I NOTICE BY YOUR EXPRESSIONS THAT YOU WERE INTRIGUED AND THAT THE ILLUSTRATIONS ARE REALLY IMPORTANT TO THIS STORY. *[Laughter]*
Marie:	All the people are at this fine party. They're like movie star people.
Kevin:	I guess that shows you can find a bad word anywhere.
B.J.:	Maybe even *more* in high society.
Angela:	We *never* did know what the word was.
Daniel:	I know! It's "beep." *[More laughter]*
TEACHER:	SO YOU THINK IT'S POSSIBLE TO CATCH A BAD WORD AT AN ELEGANT GARDEN PARTY. *[Chorus of agreement]*
B.J.:	I learned my very first bad word from Yosemite Sam on TV. My mother was shocked!
Dyrell:	I learned one from two spy dudes on TV.
Marie:	I learned one in kindergarten! *[A chorus of "first bad word" experiences]*
TEACHER:	LIKE ELBERT, IF YOU NEVER HEARD THE WORD BEFORE, HOW WOULD YOU EVER KNOW IT IS A BAD WORD?
Daniel:	Oh, you can tell by the dirty laugh.
Dyrell:	Or the way people be screaming it out!
Angela:	What about mean expressions on their faces?

Talk about How the Story Makes You Feel

• •

The children understand that bad feelings are associated with bad words. Kevin and Jennifer are being analytical, and explain the nuances and contexts involved in using bad words.

• •

Marie:	The story is mainly funny. But being called a bad name at school is not funny.
Kevin:	It feels terrible.
TEACHER:	SO BAD WORDS HURT PEOPLE.
Jennifer:	Those are really the worst kind of bad words.
Kevin:	The ones you say when you stub your toe don't really hurt other people as much. Those are just for being mad at something. Maybe not even a person.
Marie:	But the ones with God in them are bad. Did you know there's some bad words in the Bible?

*[The group shared information to clarify some real mean-
ings of words in the Bible and elsewhere.]*

Talk about What the Story Reminds You of in Your Life

• •

Angela and B.J. apply the age-old question: Is there noise if no ears
hear it? Kevin and Dyrell are developing an elementary understanding of the sexist nature of some language. Kevin is using application
skills to test how a bad word comes into being. The teacher's use of
role playing illustrates that bad words are used to hurt people.

• •

Dyrell:	I get so mad sometimes that I mutter bad words under my breath. I wonder if that's as bad as saying them aloud.
Angela:	Maybe if you said it out in the woods or somewhere it wouldn't be as bad.
B. J.:	The trees would hear! *[Laughter]*
David:	I still think the ones that hurt people are the worst.
Kevin:	Some of the ones we hear for name calling don't make any sense. Bitch means a female dog, and I like dogs.
Dyrell:	And people all the time go around talking about your mother. That doesn't make any sense if they're mad at you. Somebody's mama might even be dead.
Marie:	Well, maybe people don't think about that.
Dyrell:	*[with feeling]* It's just a shame. That's what!
Marie:	What I meant was they don't think what it means.
Dyrell:	*[with intensity]* Well, they should think about it!
Angela:	I always used to wonder why people make up bad words in the first place, because then you just have to go around and make rules to keep people from saying them.
Kevin:	*[reflectively]* I don't think there's really any such thing as a bad word. *[Some disagreement]*
Kevin:	What I mean is you could take any old word, like Jehosephat, and you could make it into a bad word.
Jennifer:	How would you do that?
Kevin:	You'd use it with some kind of a mean expression on your face and use it for name calling.
Teacher:	You think you could hurt somebody? *[Chorus of agreement]*

Daniel:	I wonder if you'd get in trouble for that. You could say, "I just said Jehosephat, that's all."
Marie:	Well, schools have to have rules.
Jennifer:	I think it's right to have rules against saying bad words on the bus, because most of them are name-calling words.
TEACHER:	LET'S TALK ABOUT WHAT YOU CAN DO IF YOU ARE CALLED A BAD NAME.
Marie:	Ignore it.
TEACHER:	GOOD IDEA. SOMETIMES THAT'S HARD BECAUSE YOU ARE VERY HURT. *[A short role play of "ignoring" with teacher as the one ignoring and Marie as name caller]*
Angela:	You have to take care of yourself some way. Calling someone a name back might make it worse, especially if you're on the bus. You get in trouble.
TEACHER:	WHEN YOU ARE GROWN, WHAT WILL YOU SAY TO YOUR CHILDREN ABOUT BAD WORDS?
Daniel:	I wouldn't be wanting my little kids to say them.
TEACHER:	AFTER SUCH A GOOD DISCUSSION, I WOULD THINK THEY'D BE OKAY IF THEY LEARNED WORDS FROM YOU!

TEACHER FOCUS

Language: The concept of a bad word is more complicated than we sometimes care to consider. Different cultures have different bad words. Bad words change depending on the changes in the meaning of words over time. What the Woods present to us in this book is an exaggerated setting that explains that "bad" is usually defined in contextual terms. Don't use that word in polite society. They also make it clear that we need strong words to express feelings and we must be aware that we can get into trouble with words.

Critical Thinking: The sixth graders in the above class used several levels of thinking skills to make meaning out of the concept of bad words. They understood that words are good or bad because of their impact on others, and that words only have meaning in the context of use.

COUNSELOR FOCUS

Accurate Expression of Feelings: Usually bad words only express the feelings and not the reasons behind the feelings. Bad words are often misleading because the children don't know why it's a bad word nor the connotation. Children need not be scolded for using bad words, instead they need to be helped to find the appropriate words to explain why they feel as they do. One third grade group brainstormed such expressions as "Oh, fruit loop!" and "Oh, tofu!" to denote dismay and discouragement.

MAKING CONNECTIONS

Wizard Word Dictionaries: Discussion may seem to be enough with this book. Perhaps the group will want to make up some "Wizard Words" for continuing use. A project could be to make a dictionary of good words to use for strong feelings. Children may illustrate with scribble drawings and give instructions on when to use.

Art: Since the illustration of the "bad word" in the book is so successful, children may enjoy drawing pictures of the wizard words. Who can illustrate Hop Toads and Gadzooks? Suffering cats?

Child psychotherapist Violet Oaklander (1969) has an excellent chapter on "Drawing and Fantasy" in her book *Windows to Our Children*. Included are simple suggestions for using scribble drawings with children. One application she describes is for the expression of anger. Although her examples are from a clinical setting, her suggestions are adaptable to any group or to individual use.

BOOKS FOR FOLLOW-UP LITERATURE STUDIES

Cole, Brock. (1986). *The Giant's Toe*. Farrar, Straus & Giroux.
    This humorous parody of *Jack and the Beanstalk* can set the stage for further discussions of anger.
Hurwitz, Johanna. (1987). *Russell Sprouts*. Illustrated by Lillian Hoban. Morrow Junior Books. "Bad Words," pp. 9-18
    Russell's question, "How can a word be bad,?" gives impetus to discussion of unacceptable language through realistic fiction.

Appendix A
Story Connections in Our Family

by Jane Tarman

Reading is a very important part of our family life. Every evening we gather with all four children—Laura, 11; Janie, 9; Bill, 6; and John, 3—for family story time. The age range of our children adds a great dimension to our enjoyment of reading aloud. We sit close. The boys and girls alternate evenings sitting on the outside or next to Mom. We do read picture books, but we have a chapter book in progress at all times. Even our three year old looks forward to the next chapter with great anticipation.

My love of reading and being read to was fostered in my childhood as one of a family of six children. Some of my earliest memories are of listening to *Babar* and *Little House in the Big Woods* at my mother's knee. As I grew older, books and reading became a very important part of my life.

As a young mother I wanted to instill that love of reading in our family, so I started reading to Laura, my first child, at a very early age. As more children came along, each was included in our nightly ritual. The older ones would turn the pages as I nursed a baby and read at the same time.

Our first foray into chapter books came with the Little House series by Laura Ingalls Wilder. I loved these books as a child and couldn't wait to share them with my own children. Laura was six and Janie was four when we read them all. The nightly refrain was, "Please read another chapter, Mother, just one more!" Both our daughters have since reread every book. Some of our favorites have been *The Princess and the Goblin*, the Ramona series, and *The Borrowers*. When the boys came along we began reading *Treasure Island, The Legend of King Arthur,* and *Tom Sawyer,* our present book. I loved re-reading and sharing the books that I remembered from my childhood as well as discovering new favorites. Even though Laura and Janie are avid readers on their own, they love our read-aloud times as much as their younger brothers do.

From this experience we all sense a physical and emotional closeness that is difficult to duplicate in any of our other family experiences. We pause and talk about the story whenever a child has something to say. We share thoughts and ideas. John adds squeals of delight, Bill points out exactly what he notices; and the girls patiently encourage their brothers' responses. The girls' insights stimulate many long talks, some serious and some not. Often we simply collapse into giggles! We feel connected to each other, thanks to these special times together. The story time ritual is one we plan to keep in our family, and would recommend to all families.

Appendix B
Selected Bibliographies of Children's Books

Bernstein, Joanne E. (1983). *Books to Help Children Cope with Separation and Loss*. 2nd edition. R. R. Bowker.

Children's Catalog. (1909 to date). H. W. Wilson.

Dreyer, Sharon. (1985 to date). *The Bookfinder: A Guide to Children's Literature about the Needs and Problems of Youth Aged 2 and Up*. American Guidance Service.

The Elementary School Library Collection. (1986). Brodart.

Elleman, Barbara. (1984). *Children's Books of International Interest*. American Library Association.

Hearne, Betsy. (1982). *Choosing Books for Children*. Delacorte.

Lima, Carolyn W. (1986). *A to Zoo: Subject Access to Children's Picture Books*. R. R. Bowker.

Lipson, Eden Ross. (1991). *Parents' Guide to the Best Books for Children*. Times Books.

Lynn, Ruth Nadelman. (1983). *Fantasy for Children: An Annotated Checklist and Reference Guide*. R. R. Bowker.

Mahoney, Ellen. (1985). *Ready, Set, Read: Best Books to Prepare Preschoolers*. Scarecrow Press.

Oppenheim, Joanne F. et al. (1986). *Choosing Books for Kids*. Ballantine Books.

Roman, Susan. (1985). *Sequences: An Annotated Guide to Children's Fiction in Series*. American Library Association.

Smith, Charles A. (1989). *From Wonder to Wisdom: Using Stories to Help Children Grow*. New American Library.

Sutherland, Zena, ed. (1982). *The Best in Children's Books*. University of Chicago.

Tway, Ellen, ed. (1981). *Reading Ladders for Human Relations*. National Council of Teachers of English.

Bibliography

Aardema, Verna. (1975). *Why Mosquitoes Buzz in People's Ears.* Illustrated by Leo and Diane Dillon. Dial Books for Young Readers.

Alexander, Sue. (1983). *Nadia, the Willful.* Pantheon.

Anno, Mitsumasa. (1989). *Anno's Aesop: A Book of Fables.* Orchard Books.

Babbitt, Natalie. (1970). *The Something.* Farrar, Straus & Giroux.

———. (1975). *Tuck Everlasting.* Farrar, Straus & Giroux.

Bang, Molly. (1988). *Delphine.* Morrow Junior Books.

Bauer, Marion Dane. (1986). *On My Honor.* Clarion Books.

Bierhorst, John. (1987). *Doctor Coyote: a Native American Aesop's Fables.* Macmillan.

Bjork, Christina, and Lena Anderson. (1988). *Linea's Windowsill Garden.* Farrar, Straus & Giroux.

Blos, Joan V. (1987). *Old Henry.* Illustrated by Stephen Gammell. Morrow.

Blume, Judy. (1971). *Freckle Juice.* Illustrated by Sonia O. Lisker. Four Winds Press.

———. (1984). *The Pain and the Great One.* Illustrated by Irene Trivas. Bradbury Press.

Boyd, Candy Dawson. (1984). *Circle of Gold.* Scholastic.

Brown, Marcia. (1961). *Once A Mouse.* Scribner.

Bulla, Clyde R. (1975). *One Poppy Seed.* Hale.

———. (1989). *The Christmas Coat.* Illustrated by Sylvia Wickstrom. Alfred A. Knopf.

Burningham, John. (1971). *Mr. Gumpy's Outing.* H. Holt and Company.

———. (1983). *Mr. Gumpy's Motor Car.* Crowell Junior Books.

———. (1987). *John Patrick Norman McHennessy.* Crown Publisher.

Byars, Betsy. (1975). *The Lace Snail.* Viking Press.

Caines, Jeannette. (1982). *Just Us Women.* Illustrated by Pat Cummins. Harper and Row.

Carle, Eric. (1987). *A House for Hermit Crab.* Picture Book Studio.

———. (1990). *The Very Quiet Cricket.* Philomel.

Carlstrom, Nancy White. (1987). *The Moon Came Too.* Illustrated by Stella Ormai. MacMillan.

Cleary, Beverly. (1968). *Ramona the Pest.* Morrow.

———. (1975). *Ramona the Brave.* Morrow.

———. (1977). *Ramona and Her Father.* Morrow.

———. (1979). *Ramona and Her Mother.* Morrow.

———. (1981). *Ramona Quimby, Age 8.* Morrow.

Clifton, Lucille. (1983). *Everett Anderson's Nine Month Long.* Illustrated by Ann Grifalconi. Holt, Rinehart and Winston.

Climo, Shirley. (1989). *The Egyptian Cinderella.* Crowell.

Cohen, Barbara. (1983). *Molly's Pilgrim*. Illustrated by Michael Derany. Lothrop, Lee and Shepard.

Cole, Brock. (1986). *The Giant's Toe*. Farrar, Straus & Giroux.

Coleridge, Ann. (1987). *The Friends of Emily Culpepper*. Putnam.

Cooney, Barbara. (1985). *Miss Rumphius*. Viking Press.

———. (1990). *Hattie and the Wild Waves*. Viking Press.

Craven, Carolyn. (1987). *What the Mailman Brought*. Putnam.

dePaola, Tomie. (1975). *Strega Nona*. Prentice Hall.

———. (1980). *Now One Foot, Now the Other*. Putnam.

———. (1989). *The Art Lesson*. Putnam.

Estes, Eleanor. (1944). *The Hundred Dresses*. Illustrated by Louis Slobodkin. Harcourt Brace.

Fitzhugh, Louise. (1964). *Harriet the Spy*. Dell.

Flournoy, Valerie. (1985). *The Patchwork Quilt*. Illustrated by Jerry Pinkney. Dial Books.

Fox, Paula. (1984). *The One-Eyed Cat*. Bradbury Press.

Fox, Mem. (1985). *Wilfrid Gordon McDonald Partridge*. Illustrated by Julie Vivas. Kane/Miller.

Gerstein, Mordicai. (1983). *Arnold of the Ducks*. Harper and Row.

———. (1984). *The Room*. Harper and Row.

———. (1986). *Seal Mother*. Dial Books for Young Readers.

———. (1987). *The Mountains of Tibet*. Harper and Row.

Giff, Patricia. (1980). *Today Was a Terrible Day*. Illustrted by Susanna Natti. Viking Press.

———. (1984). *The Beast in Ms. Rooney's Room*. Dell.

———. (1986). *Watch Out, Ronald Morgan*. Illustrated by Susanna Natti. Penguin, Inc.

———. (1988). *Happy Birthday, Ronald Morgan*. Illustrated by Susanna Natti. Penguin, Inc.

Graham, Bob. (1987). *Charlotte and Henry*. Viking Penguin, Inc.

Greenfield, Eloise. (1974). *She Come Bringing Me That Little Baby Girl*. Illustrated by John Steptoe. Lippincott.

———. (1980). *Grandmama's Joy*. Illustrated by Carole Byard. Collins.

———. (1988). *Grandpa's Face*. Illustrated by Floyd Cooper. Philomel.

———. (1988). *Nathaniel Talking*. Illustrated by Jan Spivey Gilchrist. Black Butterfly Children's Books.

Griffith, Helen. (1986). *Georgia Music*. Illustrated by James Stevenson. Greenwillow Books.

———. (1987). *Grandaddy's Place*. Illustrated by James Stevenson. Greenwillow Books.

Hamilton, Virginia. (1967). *Zeely*. Macmillan.

Hederwick, Mairi. (1986). *Katie Morag and the Tiresome Ted*. Little, Brown.

Heide, Florence Parry. (1971). *The Shrinking of Treehorn*. Illustrated by Edward Gorey. Holiday House.

Henkes, Kevin. (1988). *Chester's Way*. Greeenwillow Books.

Hooks, William. (1990). *The Ballad of Belle Dorcas*. Illustrated by Brian Pickney. Alfred A. Knopf.

Houston, Gloria. (1992). *My Great Aunt Arizona*. Illustrated by Susan Condie Lamb. Harper and Row.

Howard, Elizabeth. (1991). *Aunt Flossie's Hats (and Crab Cakes Later)*. Illustrated by James Ransome, Clarion.

Huck, Charlotte. (1989). *Princess Furball*. Illustrated by Arnold Lobel. Greenwillow Books.

Hurwitz, Johanna. (1978). *The Law of Gravity*. Morrow Books.

———. (1987). *Class Clown*. Morrow Junior Books.

———. (1987). *Russell Sprouts*. Illustrated by Lillian Hoban. Morrow Junior Books.

———. (1989). *Russell and Elisa*. Illustrated by Lillian Hoban. Morrow Junior Books.

Hutchins, Pat. (1971). *Changes, Changes*. Bodley Head.

Keats, Ezra Jack. (1964). *Whistle for Willie*. Viking Press.

———. (1967). *Peter's Chair*. Harper and Row.

———. (1981). *Regards to the Man in the Moon*. Four Winds.

Kennedy, Richard. (1987). *Richard Kennedy: Collected Stories*. Harper and Row.

Knight, Margy Burns. (1992). *Talking Walls*. Illustrated by Sibley O'Brien. Tilbury House.

Komaiko, Leah. (1987). *Annie Bananie*. Harper and Row.

Korschunow, Irina. (1986). *Adam Draws Himself a Dragon*. Harper and Row.

Lasky, Kathryn. (1987). *Sea Swan*. MacMillan.

Leaf, Munro. (1936). *The Story of Ferdinand*. Illustrated by Robert Lawson. Viking Press.

Levoy, Myron. (1977). *Alan and Naomi*. Harper and Row.

Lionni, Leo. (1963). *Swimmy*. Alfred A. Knopf.

———. (1967). *Frederick*. Pantheon.

———. (1985). *Frederick's Fables: A Leo Lionni Treasury of Favorite Stories*. Pantheon.

Lobel, Anita. (1990). *Allison's Zinnia*. Greenwillow Books.

Lobel, Arnold. (1980). *Fables*. Harper and Row.

Louie, Ai-ling. (1982). *Yehshen: A Cinderella Story from China*. Philomel.

Lowry, Lois. (1977). *A Summer to Die*. Houghton, Mifflin.

MacLachlan, Patricia. (1980). *Arthur, for the Very First Time*. Harper and Row.

———. (1986). *Sarah Plain and Tall*. Caedmon.

Magorian, Michelle. (1981). *Good Night, Mr. Tom*. Harper and Row.

Martin, Bill Jr., and John Archambault. (1987). *Knots on A Counting Rope*. Illustrated by Ted Rand. Henry Holt.

Mathis, Sharon Bell. (1975). *The Hundred Penny Box*. Illustrated by Leo and Diane Dillon. Viking Press.

Mayer, Mercer. (1968). *There's a Nightmare in My Closet*. Dial Books for Young Readers.

Maxner, Joyce. (1989). *Nicholas Cricket*. Harper and Row.

McDonald, Megan. (1990). *The Potato Man*. Illustrated by Ted Lewin. Orchard Books.

Miles, Miska. (1971). *Annie and the Old One*. Illustrated by Peter Parnall. Little, Brown.

Myers, Walter Dean. (1988). *Me, Mop and the Moondance Kid*. Illustrated by Rodney Pate. Delacorte.

Ness, Evaline. (1966). *Sam, Bangs and Moonshine*. Henry Holt.

Paxton, Tom. (1990). *Belling the Cat and Other Aesop's Fables*. Morrow Junior Books.

Polacco, Patricia. (1988). *The Keeping Quilt*. Simon and Schuster.

Prelutsky, Jack. (1976). *Nightmares: Poems to Trouble Your Sleep*. Illustrated by Arnold Lobel. Greenwillow Books.

Rylant, Cynthia. (1972). *When I Was Young in the Mountains*. Illustrated by Diane Goode. E. P. Dutton.

———. (1983). *Miss Maggie*. Illustrated by Thomas Di Grazia. E. P. Dutton.

———. (1985). *The Relatives Came*. Illustrated by Stephen Gammell. Bradbury Press.

Sachs, Marilyn. (1981). *Hello, Wrong Number*. Illusstrated by Pamela Johnson. Dutton.

San Souci, Robert D. (1987). *The Talking Eggs: A Folktale from the American South*. Dell.

Schotter, Roni. (1990). *Captain Snap and the Children of Vinegar Lane*. Illustrated by Marcia Sewall. Orchard Books.

Schwartz, Amy. (1987). *Oma and Bobo*. Bradbury.

Sendak, Maurice. (1963). *Where the Wild Things Are*. Harper and Row.

Shreve, Susan. (1979). *Family Secrets.* Alfred A. Knopf.

Silverstein, Shel. (1964). *The Giving Tree.* Harper and Row.

Singer, Isaac Bashevis. (1980). *The Power of Light: Eight Stories for Hanukkah.* Illustrated by Irene Lieblich. Farrar, Straus & Giroux.

———. (1984). *Stories for Children.* Farrar, Straus & Giroux.

Slepian, Jan. (1980). *The Alfred Summer.* Macmillan.

Small, David. (1985). *Imogene's Antlers.* Farrar, Straus & Giroux.

———. (1987). *Paper John.* Farrar, Straus & Giroux.

Smith, Janice Lee (1988). *The Show and Tell War.* Illustrated by Dick Gackenbach. Harper and Row.

Spinelli, Jerry. (1984). *Who Put That Hair in My Toothbrush?* Little, Brown.

———. (1990). *The Bathwater Gang.* Little, Brown.

———. (1990). *Maniac Magee.* Little, Brown.

Steig, William. (1969). *Spinky Sulks.* Simon and Schuster.

———. (1969). *Sylvester and the Magic Pebble.* Prentice-Hall.

———. (1976). *The Amazing Bone.* Simon and Schuster.

Steptoe, John. (1984). *The Story of Jumping Mouse: A Native American Legend.* Lothrop, Lee and Shepard.

———. (1987). *Mufaro's Beautiful Daughters: An African Tale.* Lothrop, Lee and Shepard.

Stolz, Mary. (1988). *Storm in the Night.* Illustrated by Pat Cummings. Harper and Row.

Thompson, Peggy. (1988). *The King Has Horse's Ears.* Illustrated by David Small. Simon & Schuster.

Tolstoy, Leo. (1986). *Shoemaker Martin.* Adapted by Brigitte Hanhart. Translated by Michael Hale. Illustrated by Bernadett Watts. North-South Books.

Van Allsburg, Chris. (1988). *Two Bad Ants.* Houghton Mifflin.

———. (1991). *The Wretched Stone.* Houghton Mifflin.

Varley, Susan. (1984). *Badger's Parting Gifts.* Lothrop, Lee and Shephard.

Viorst, Judith. (1971). *The Tenth Good Thing about Barney.* Illustrated by Erik Blegvad. MacMillan.

———. (1972). *Alexander and the Terrible, Horrible, No Good Very Bad Day.* Atheneum.

———. (1974). *Rosie and Michael.* Illustrated by Lorna Tomei. Aladdin Books.

Waber, Bernard. (1988). *Ira Says Goodbye.* Houghton Mifflin.

Whitman, Sally. (1978). *A Special Trade.* Illustrated by Karen Gundersheimer. Harper.

Wilhelm, Hans. (1985). *I'll Always Love You.* Crown.

Williams, Vera. (1981). *Three Days on a River in a Red Canoe.* Greenwillow Books.

———. (1982). *A Chair for My Mother.* Greenwillow Books.

———. (1983). *Something Special for Me.* Greenwillow Books.

———. (1984). *Music, Music for Everyone.* Greenwillow Books.

———. (1988). *Stringbean's Trip to the Shining Sea.* Greenwillow Books.

Wood, Audrey. (1988). *Elbert's Bad Word.* Illustrated by Don Wood. Harcourt Brace Jovanovich.

Yorinks, Arthur. (1986). *Hey, Al.* Illustrated by Richard Egielski. Farrar, Straus & Giroux.

———. (1990). *Ugh.* Illustrated by Richard Egielski. Farrar, Straus & Giroux.

Zolotow, Charlotte. (1974). *My Grandson Lew.* Illustrated by William Pene du Bois. Greenwillow.

———. (1984). *I Know a Lady.* Illustrated by James Stevenson. Greenwillow.

Subject Index to Book Entries

This is an index of themes and subjects addressed by the books discussed in the entries. For basic subject access to Chapters 1 and 2 and the book entries, see the General Index.

Addiction
Van Allsburg. *The Wretched Stone,* 189
Aesthetics
Cooney. *Miss Rumphius,* 49
Craven. *What the Mailman Brought,* 58
Lionni. *Frederick,* 101
African Americans
Authors
Clifton. *Everett Anderson's Nine Month Long,* 44
Steptoe. *Mufaro's Beautiful Daughters,* 183
Characters
Clifton. *Everett Anderson's Nine Month Long,* 44
Keats. *Whistle for Willie,* 91
Affectation
Lobel. *Fables,* 108
Small. *Imogene's Antlers,* 165
Wood. *Elbert's Bad Word,* 209
Aging
Cooney. *Miss Rumphius,* 49
Fox. *Wilfrid Gordon McDonald Partridge,* 68
Griffith. *Grandaddy's Place,* 85
Rylant. *Miss Maggie,* 120

Allegory
Gerstein. *The Mountains of Tibet,* 73
Van Allsburg. *The Wretched Stone,* 189
Altruism
Cooney. *Miss Rumphius,* 49
Fox. *Wilfrid Gordon McDonald Partridge,* 68
Rylant. *Miss Maggie,* 120
Williams. *A Chair for My Mother,* 204
Anger
Blume. *The Pain and the Great One,* 20
Clifton. *Everett Anderson's Nine Month Long,* 44
Sendak. *Where the Wild Things Are,* 140
Steig. *Spinky Sulks,* 169
Wood. *Elbert's Bad Word,* 209
Appalachia
Rylant. *Miss Maggie,* 120
Rylant. *The Relatives Came,* 126
Application. *See also* Critical Thinking.
Wood. *Elbert's Bad Word,* 209
Archetypes
San Souci. *The Talking Eggs,* 134

Archetypes *(continued)*
Steig. *Sylvester and the Magic Pebble*, 176
Steptoe. *Mufaro's Beautiful Daughters*, 183

Art
Carle. *A House for Hermit Crab*, 30
Craven. *What the Mailman Brought*, 58
Gerstein. *The Mountains of Tibet*, 73
Lionni. *Frederick*, 101

Attention, Need for
See Behavior.

Bad Words
Wood. *Elbert's Bad Word*, 209

Beauty. *See also* Art.
Cooney. *Miss Rumphius*, 49
Lionni. *Frederick*, 101

Behavior
Attention, Need For
Blume. *The Pain and the Great One*, 20
Clifton. *Everett Anderson's Nine Month Long*, 44
Cleary. *Ramona Quimby, Age 8*, 37
Steig. *Spinky Sulks*, 169
Foolish and Wise
Lobel. *Fables*, 108
Reasons for
Blume. *The Pain and the Great One*, 20
Clifton. *Everett Anderson's Nine Month Long*, 44
Craven. *What the Mailman Brought*, 58
Estes. *The Hundred Dresses*, 62
Giff. *Today Was a Terrible Day*, 78
Griffith. *Grandaddy's Place*, 85
Komaiko. *Annie Bananie*, 96
Ness. *Sam, Bangs and Moonshine*, 114
Rylant. *Miss Maggie*, 120
San Souci. *The Talking Eggs*, 134
Sendak. *Where the Wild Things Are*, 140
Shreve. *Family Secrets*, 146
Small. *Imogene's Antlers*, 165
Steig. *Spinky Sulks*, 169
Steptoe. *Mufaro's Beautiful Daughters*, 183

Van Allsburg. *The Wretched Stone*, 189
Wood. *Elbert's Bad Word*, 209

Bicycles
Bang. *Delphine*, 16

Boredom
See Feelings.

Change. *See also* Life Cycle.
Clifton. *Everett Anderson's Nine Month Long*, 44
Komaiko. *Annie Bananie*, 96

Characterization
Burningham. *Mr. Gumpy's Outing*, 25
Cleary. *Ramona Quimby, Age 8*, 37
Giff. *Today Was a Terrible Day*, 78
Lionni. *Frederick*, 101
Ness. *Sam, Bangs and Moonshine*, 114
Rylant. *Miss Maggie*, 120
Shreve. *Family Secrets*, 146
Small. *Imogene's Antlers*, 165
Steig. *Spinky Sulks*, 169
Steig. *Sylvester and the Magic Pebble*, 176
Varley. *Badger's Parting Gifts*, 195

Cheating
Shreve. *Family Secrets*, 146

Choices. *See also* Moral Reasoning.
Cooney. *Miss Rumphius*, 49
Gerstein. *The Mountains of Tibet*, 73
Lobel. *Fables*, 108
Steptoe. *Mufaro's Beautiful Daughters*, 183

Cities
See Geography.

Community
Burningham. *Mr. Gumpy's Outing*, 25
Carle. *A House for Hermit Crab*, 30
Rylant. *Miss Maggie*, 120
Williams. *A Chair for My Mother*, 204

Compare and Contrast
Burningham. *Mr. Gumpy's Outing*, 25
Gerstein. *The Mountains of Tibet*, 73
Lionni. *Frederick*, 101
Rylant. *Miss Maggie*, 120
Rylant. *The Relatives Came*, 126

Silverstein. *The Giving Tree*, 153
Steptoe. *Mufaro's Beautiful Daughters*, 183
Van Allsburg. *The Wretched Stone*, 189

Compassion
Fox. *Wilfrid Gordon McDonald Partridge*, 68
Rylant. *Miss Maggie*, 120

Competence
Bang. *Delphine*, 16
Carle. *A House for Hermit Crab*, 30
Fox. *Wilfrid Gordon McDonald Partridge*, 68
Giff. *Today Was a Terrible Day*, 78
Keats. *Whistle for Willie*, 91
Lionni. *Frederick*, 101

Comprehension
Carle. *A House for Hermit Crab*, 30
Fox. *Wilfrid Gordon McDonald Partridge*, 68
Lobel. *Fables*, 108
Small. *Imogene's Antlers*, 165

Conformity. *See also* Fads. Individuality.
Cleary. *Ramona Quimby, Age 8*, 37
Van Allsburg. *The Wretched Stone*, 189

Connection
Fox. *Wilfrid Gordon McDonald Partridge*, 68
Griffith. *Grandaddy's Place*, 85
Komaiko. *Annie Bananie*, 96
Rylant. *The Relatives Came*, 126

Cooperation
Burningham. *Mr. Gumpy's Outing*, 25
Carle. *A House For Hermit Crab*, 30
Clifton. *Everett Anderson's Nine Month Long*, 44
Cooney. *Miss Rumphius*, 49
Fox. *Wilfrid Gordon McDonald Partridge*, 68
Griffith. *Grandaddy's Place*, 85
Komaiko. *Annie Bananie*, 96
Lionni. *Frederick*, 101
Rylant. *The Relatives Came*, 126
Singer. *The Power of Light*, 159
Steig. *Spinky Sulks,* 169
Steig. *Sylvester and the Magic Pebble*, 176
Van Allsburg. *The Wretched Stone*, 189

Varley. *Badger's Parting Gifts*, 195
Williams. *A Chair for My Mother*, 204

Coping
With Illness
Craven. *What the Mailman Brought*, 58
With Fear and Worry
Bang. *Delphine*, 16

Courage
Bang. *Delphine*, 16
Carle. *A House for Hermit Crab*, 30
Rylant. *Miss Maggie*, 120
Singer. *The Power of Light*, 159

Creativity
Craven. *What the Mailman Brought*, 58
Fox. *Wilfrid Gordon McDonald Partridge*, 68
Lionni. *Frederick*, 101
Van Allsburg. *The Wretched Stone*, 189
Varley. *Badger's Parting Gifts*, 195
Wood. *Elbert's Bad Word*, 209

Critical Thinking
Cleary. *Ramona Quimby, Age 8*, 37
Gerstein. *The Mountains of Tibet*, 73
Lionni. *Frederick*, 101
Lobel. *Fables*, 108
Ness. *Sam, Bangs and Moonshine*, 114
Rylant. *Miss Maggie*, 120
Singer. *The Power of Light*, 159
Small. *Imogene's Antlers*, 165
Steig. *Spinky Sulks*, 169
Van Allsburg. *The Wretched Stone*, 189
Varley. *Badger's Parting Gifts*, 195

Cruelty
Estes. *The Hundred Dresses*, 62
Ness. *Sam, Bangs and Moonshine*, 114
San Souci. *The Talking Eggs*, 134

Death
Ness. *Sam, Bangs and Moonshine*, 114
Varley. *Badger's Parting Gifts*, 195
Viorst. *The Tenth Good Thing about Barney*, 199

Differences, Acceptance of
Carle. *A House for Hermit Crab*, 30
Lionni. *Frederick*, 101

Differences, Acceptance of *(continued)*
    Rylant. *Miss Maggie*, 120
    Small. *Imogene's Antlers*, 165
    Steptoe. *Mufaro's Beautiful Daughters*, 183
Diligence
    Fox, *Wilfrid Gordon McDonald Partridge*, 68
    Keats. *Whistle for Willie*, 91
    Williams. *A Chair for My Mother*, 204
Discrimination
    See Prejudice.
Diversity. *See also* Differences.
    Gerstein. *The Mountains of Tibet*, 73

Ecology
    Carle. *A House for Hermit Crab*, 30
    Cooney. *Miss Rumphius*, 49
    Lionni. *Frederick*, 101
    Silverstein. *The Giving Tree*, 153
Embarrassment
    Cleary. *Ramona Quimby, Age 8*, 37
Empathy
    Blume. *The Pain and the Great One*, 20
    Clifton. *Everett Anderson's Nine Month Long*, 44
    Fox. *Wilfrid Gordon McDonald Partridge*, 68
    Giff. *Today Was A Terrible Day*, 78
    Viorst. *The Tenth Good Thing about Barney*, 199
    Williams. *A Chair for My Mother*, 204
Environment
    See Ecology.
Euphemisms. *See also* Language.
    Varley. *Badger's Parting Gifts*, 195

Fables
    Lionni. *Frederick*, 101
    Lobel. *Fables*, 108
Fads
    Cleary. *Ramona Quimby, Age 8*, 37
Failure
    Giff. *Today Was a Terrible Day*, 78
Fairness
    Lionni. *Frederick*, 101
    Silverstein. *The Giving Tree*, 153

Family
  Advice
    Cooney. *Miss Rumphius*, 49
    Griffith. *Grandaddy's Place*, 85
  Generations
    Cooney. *Miss Rumphius*, 49
    Fox. *Wilfrid Gordon McDonald Partridge*, 68
    Griffith. *Grandaddy's Place*, 85
    Ness. *Sam, Bangs and Moonshine*, 114
    Rylant. *Miss Maggie*, 120
    Rylant. *The Relatives Came*, 126
    Varley. *Badger's Parting Gifts*, 195
    Williams. *A Chair for My Mother*, 204
  Joy
    Rylant. *The Relatives Came*, 126
    Williams. *A Chair for My Mother*, 204
  Love
    Sendak. *Where the Wild Things Are*, 140
    Steig. *Sylvester and the Magic Pebble*, 176
  Relatives
    Bang. *Delphine*, 16
    Cooney. *Miss Rumphius*, 49
    Griffith. *Grandaddy's Place*, 85
    Rylant. *The Relatives Came*, 126
    Williams. *A Chair for My Mother*, 204
  Siblings
    Blume. *The Pain and the Great One*, 20
    Cleary. *Ramona Quimby. Age 8*, 37
    Clifton. *Everett Anderson's Nine Month Long*, 44
  Single Parents. See also Parents. Stepfather. Grandparents.
    Ness. *Sam, Bangs and Moonshine*, 114
    Steptoe. *Mufaro's Beautiful Daughters*, 183
    Williams. *A Chair for My Mother*, 204
Fantasy
    Craven. *What the Mailman Brought*, 58
    Gerstein. *The Mountains of Tibet*, 73

Lionni. *Frederick*, 101
Sendak. *Where the Wild Things Are*, 140
Silverstein. *The Giving Tree*, 153
Small. *Imogene's Antlers*, 165
Steig. *Sylvester and the Magic Pebble*, 176
Van Allsburg. *The Wretched Stone*, 189
Varley. *Badger's Parting Gifts*, 195
Wood. *Elbert's Bad Word*, 209

Fantasizing
Bang. *Delphine*, 16
Craven. *What the Mailman Brought*, 58
Ness. *Sam, Bangs and Moonshine*, 114
Small. *Imogene's Antlers*, 165

Farm Life
Griffith. *Grandaddy's Place*, 85

Fear. *See also* Feelings.
Bang. *Delphine*, 16
Carle. *A House for Hermit Crab*, 30
Griffith. *Grandaddy's Place*, 85
Rylant. *Miss Maggie*, 120
Sendak. *Where the Wild Things Are*, 140
Singer. *The Power of Light*, 159

Feelings. *See also* Death. Embarrassment. Grief. Loneliness. Power.
Accurate Expression of
    Clifton. *Everett Anderson's Nine Month Long*, 44
    Estes. *The Hundred Dresses*, 62
    Lionni. *Frederick*, 101
    Sendak. *Where the Wild Things Are*, 140
    Viorst. *The Tenth Good Thing about Barney*, 199
    Williams. *A Chair for My Mother*, 204
Anticipation
    Carle. *A House for Hermit Crab*, 30
    Cooney. *Miss Rumphius*, 49
Boredom
    Craven. *What the Mailman Brought*, 58
Fear
    Bang. *Delphine*, 16
    Carle. *A House for Hermit Crab*, 30

Griffith. *Grandaddy's Place*, 85
Sendak. *Where the Wild Things Are*, 140
Rylant. *Miss Maggie*, 120
Singer. *The Power of Light*, 159
Guilt
    Shreve. *Family Secrets*, 146
Joy
    Burningham. *Mr. Gumpy's Outing*, 25
    Rylant. *Miss Maggie*, 120
    Rylant. *The Relatives Came*, 126
    Steig. *Sylvester and the Magic Pebble*, 176
Left Out
    Clifton. *Everett Anderson's Nine Month Long*, 44
    Estes. *The Hundred Dresses*, 62
    Steig. *Spinky Sulks*, 169
Love. *See also* Family Love.
    Fox. *Wilfrid Gordon McDonald Partridge*, 68
    Steig. *Spinky Sulks*, 169
    Steig. *Sylvester and the Magic Pebble*, 176
    Williams. *A Chair for My Mother*, 204
Negative
    Bang. *Delphine*, 16
    Blume. *The Pain and the Great One*, 20
    Cleary. *Ramona Quimby, Age 8*, 37
    Clifton. *Everett Anderson's Nine Month Long*, 44
    Craven. *What the Mailman Brought*, 58
    Estes. *The Hundred Dresses*, 62
    Giff. *Today Was a Terrible Day*, 78
    Griffith. *Grandaddy's Place*, 85
    Keats. *Whistle for Willie*, 91
    Komaiko. *Annie Bananie*, 96
    Ness. *Sam, Bangs and Moonshine*, 114
    Rylant. *Miss Maggie*, 120
    Sendak. *Where the Wild Things Are*, 140
    Shreve. *Family Secrets*, 146
    Silverstein. *The Giving Tree*, 153
    Small. *Imogene's Antlers*, 165
    Steig. *Spinky Sulks*, 169

Feelings *(continued)*
 Viorst. *The Tenth Good Thing
  about Barney,* 199
 Wood. *Elbert's Bad Word,* 209
 Reasons for
  Blume. *The Pain and the Great
   One,* 20
 Rejection
  Giff. *Today Was a Terrible Day,*
   78
  Komaiko. *Annie Bananie,* 96
 Sadness
  Komaiko. *Annie Bananie,* 96
  Ness. *Sam, Bangs and Moon-
   shine,* 114
  Silverstein. *The Giving Tree,* 153
  Varley. *Badger's Parting Gifts,*
   195
  Viorst. *The Tenth Good Thing
   about Barney,* 199
 Sharing
  Blume. *The Pain and the Great
   One,* 20
  Komaiko. *Annie Bananie,* 96
  Silverstein. *The Giving Tree,* 153
 Worry
  Bang. *Delphine,* 16
  Clifton. *Everett Anderson's Nine
   Month Long,* 44
Folk Tales
 San Souci. *The Talking Eggs,* 134
 Steptoe. *Mufaro's Beautiful Daugh-
  ters,* 183
Following Directions
 Burningham. *Mr. Gumpy's Outing,*
  25
 San Souci. *The Talking Eggs,* 134
 Steptoe. *Mufaro's Beautiful Daugh-
  ters,* 183
 Wood. *Elbert's Bad Word,* 209
Forgiveness
 Estes. *The Hundred Dresses,* 62
 Sendak. *Where the Wild Things Are,*
  140
 Shreve. *Family Secrets,* 146
 Silverstein. *The Giving Tree,* 153
 Steptoe. *Mufaro's Beautiful Daugh-
  ters,* 183
Friends
 Burningham. *Mr. Gumpy's Outing,*
  25
 Carle. *A House for Hermit Crab,* 30

 Estes. *The Hundred Dresses,* 62
 Fox. *Wilfrid Gordon McDonald
  Partridge,* 68
 Komaiko. *Annie Bananie,* 96
 Rylant. *Miss Maggie,* 120
 Varley. *Badger's Parting Gifts,* 195
Gender
 See Sex Roles.
Geography
 Cooney. *Miss Rumphius,* 49
 Gerstein. *The Mountains of Tibet,*
  73
 Griffith. *Grandaddy's Place,* 85
 Keats. *Whistle for Willie,* 91
 Rylant. *The Relatives Came,* 126
 Singer. *The Power of Light,* 159
Gifts
 Bang. *Delphine,* 16
 Craven. *What the Mailman Brought,*
  58
 Fox. *Wilfrid Gordon McDonald
  Partridge,* 68
 Varley. *Badger's Parting Gifts,* 195
 Williams. *A Chair for My Mother,*
  204
Giving
 See Altruism.
Goal Setting
 Bang. *Delphine,* 16
 Cooney. *Miss Rumphius,* 49
 Fox. *Wilfrid Gordon McDonald
  Partridge,* 68
 Gerstein. *The Mountains of Tibet,*
  73
 Giff. *Today Was a Terrible Day,* 78
 Griffith. *Grandaddy's Place,* 85
 Keats. *Whistle for Willie,* 91
 Lionni. *Frederick,* 101
 Singer. *The Power of Light,* 159
 Steptoe. *Mufaro's Beautiful Daugh-
  ters,* 183
 Williams. *A Chair for My Mother,*
  204
Goodness
 San Souci. *The Talking Eggs,* 134
 Steptoe. *Mufaro's Beautiful Daugh-
  ters,* 183
Grandparents. *See also* Family.
 Bang. *Delphine,* 16
 Cooney. *Miss Rumphius,* 49
 Griffith. *Grandaddy's Place,* 85

Rylant. *Miss Maggie*, 120
Williams. *A Chair for My Mother*, 204

Grief. *See also* Death.
Komaiko. *Annie Bananie*, 96
Steig. *Sylvester and the Magic Pebble*, 176

Growing
Carle. *A House for Hermit Crab*, 30
Cleary. *Ramona Quimby, Age 8*, 37

Hardship
Estes. *The Hundred Dresses*, 62
Lionni. *Frederick*, 101
Singer. *The Power of Light*, 159
Williams. *A Chair for My Mother*, 204

Homesickness
Sendak. *Where the Wild Things Are*, 140
Steig. *Sylvester and the Magic Pebble*, 176

Honesty
Ness. *Sam, Bangs and Moonshine*, 114
Shreve. *Family Secrets*, 146
Silverstein. *The Giving Tree*, 153

Hope
Steig. *Sylvester and the Magic Pebble*, 176

Human Character
See Characterization. Individuality.

Humor
Lobel. *Fables*, 108
Komaiko. *Annie Bananie*, 96
Small. *Imogene's Antlers*, 165
Van Allsburg. *The Wretched Stone*, 189
Wood. *Elbert's Bad Word*, 209

Illness
Craven. *What the Mailman Brought*, 58
Fox. *Wilfrid Gordon McDonald Partridge*, 68

Imagination
Bang. *Delphine*, 16
Craven. *What the Mailman Brought*, 58
Keats. *Whistle for Willie*, 91
Komaiko. *Annie Bananie*, 96

Imperfection
Cleary. *Ramona Quimby. Age 8*, 37

Keats. *Whistle for Willie*, 91
Shreve. *Family Secrets*, 146
Silverstein. *The Giving Tree*, 153
Steig. *Spinky Sulks*, 169
Steptoe. *Mufaro's Beautiful Daughters*, 183
Van Allsburg. *The Wretched Stone*, 189

Individuality
Lionni. *Frederick*, 101
Lobel. *Fables*, 108
Small. *Imogene's Antlers*, 165
Van Allsburg. *The Wretched Stone*, 189

Jealousy
Blume. *The Pain and the Great One*, 20
Clifton. *Everett Anderson's Nine Month Long*, 44

Jews
Singer. *The Power of Light*, 159

Kindness
Fox. *Wilfrid Gordon McDonald Partridge*, 68
Giff. *Today Was a Terrible Day*, 78
Griffith. *Grandaddy's Place*, 85
Rylant. *Miss Maggie*, 120
San Souci. *The Talking Eggs*, 134
Steptoe. *Mufaro's Beautiful Daughters*, 183
Varley. *Badger's Parting Gifts*, 195

Language. *See also* Euphemisms. Punctuation.
Oral Language
Carle. *A House for Hermit Crab*, 30
Fox. *Wilfrid Gordon McDonald Partridge*, 68
Komaiko. *Annie Bananie*, 96
Taboos. See also Metaphor. Story Structure.
Van Allsburg. *The Wretched Stone*, 189
Varley. *Badger's Parting Gifts*, 195
Wood. *Elbert's Bad Word*, 209
Vocabulary
Fox. *Wilfrid Gordon McDonald Partridge*, 68
Rylant. *Miss Maggie*, 120

Language *(continued)*
  Rylant. *The Relatives Came,* 126
  Steig. *Spinky Sulks,* 169
  Steig. *Sylvester and the Magic
    Pebble,* 176
Learning
  Giff. *Today Was a Terrible Day,* 78
  Keats. *Whistle for Willie,* 91
  Van Allsburg. *The Wretched Stone,*
    189
Leisure
  Burningham. *Mr. Gumpy's Outing,*
    25
  Komaiko. *Annie Bananie,* 96
Librarians
  Cooney. *Miss Rumphius,* 49
Life Cycle
  Carle. *A House for Hermit Crab,* 30
  Cooney. *Miss Rumphius,* 49
  Gerstein. *The Mountains of Tibet,*
    73
  Lionni. *Frederick,* 101
  Varley. *Badger's Parting Gifts,* 195
  Viorst. *The Tenth Good Thing about
    Barney,* 199
Loneliness
  Craven. *What the Mailman Brought,*
    58
  Ness *Sam, Bangs and Moonshine,*
    114
Loss
  Komaiko. *Annie Bananie,* 96
  Ness. *Sam, Bangs and Moonshine,*
    114
  Varley. *Badger's Parting Gifts,* 195
  Viorst. *The Tenth Good Thing about
    Barney,* 199

Mail Carriers
  Bang. *Delphine,* 16
  Craven. *What the Mailman Brought,*
    58
Meanness
  See Cruelty.
Mechanization
  Van Allsburg. *The Wretched Stone,*
    189
Magic
  San Souci. *The Talking Eggs,* 134
  Steig. *Sylvester and the Magic
    Pebble,* 176
  Steptoe. *Mufaro's Beautiful Daugh-
    ters,* 183

Manners
  Burningham. *Mr. Gumpy's Outing,*
    25
Memories
  Fox. *Wilfrid Gordon McDonald
    Partridge,* 68
  Varley. *Badger's Parting Gifts,* 195
Metaphor
  Bang. *Delphine,* 16
  Gerstein. *The Mountains of Tibet,*
    73
  Lionni. *Frederick,* 101
  Ness. *Sam, Bangs and Moonshine,*
    114
  Sendak. *Where the Wild Things Are,*
    140
  Silverstein. *The Giving Tree,* 153
  Small. *Imogene's Antlers,* 165
  Van Allsburg. *The Wretched Stone,*
    189
Misbehavior
  See Rules.
Moral Reasoning
  Lionni. *Frederick,* 101
  Ness. *Sam, Bangs and Moonshine,*
    114
  Rylant. *Miss Maggie,* 120
  San Souci. *The Talking Eggs,* 134
  Shreve. *Family Secrets,* 146
  Singer. *The Power of Light,* 159
  Steptoe. *Mufaro's Beautiful Daugh-
    ters,* 183
  Van Allsburg. *The Wretched Stone,*
    189
  Wood. *Elbert's Bad Word,* 209
Mountain Life
  Rylant. *Miss Maggie,* 120
  Rylant. *The Relatives Came,* 126

Naming
  Blume. *The Pain and the Great One,*
    20
  Fox. *Wilfrid Gordon McDonald
    Partridge,* 68
  Griffith. *Grandaddy's Place,* 85
  Lionni. *Frederick,* 101
  Ness. *Sam, Bangs and Moonshine,*
    114
  Wood. *Elbert's Bad Word,* 209
Name Calling
  Cleary. *Ramona Quimby, Age 8,* 37
  Estes. *The Hundred Dresses,* 62
  Giff. *Today Was a Terrible Day,* 78

Nature
   See Ecology.
Neighborhood
   Fox. *Wilfrid Gordon McDonald Partridge*, 68
   Keats. *Whistle for Willie*, 91
   Williams. *A Chair for My Mother*, 204
Non-verbal Communication
   Komaiko. *Annie Bananie*, 96
   Ness. *Sam, Bangs and Moonshine*, 114
   Rylant. *Miss Maggie*, 120
   Van Allsburg. *The Wretched Stone*, 189
   Wood. *Elbert's Bad Word*, 209

Obedience
   Griffith. *Grandaddy's Place*, 85
   San Souci. *The Talking Eggs*, 134
   Wood. *Elbert's Bad Word*, 209
Obsession
   Van Allsburg. *The Wretched Stone*, 189

Parents. *See also* Family.
   Blume. *The Pain and the Great One*, 20
   Cleary. *Ramona Quimby, Age 8*, 37
   Clifton. *Everett Anderson's Nine Month Long*, 44
   Cooney. *Miss Rumphius*, 49
   Craven. *What the Mailman Brought*, 58
   Fox. *Wilfrid Gordon McDonald Partridge*, 68
   Giff. *Today Was a Terrible Day*, 78
   Griffith. *Grandaddy's Place*, 85
   Keats. *Whistle for Willie*, 91
   Ness. *Sam, Bangs and Moonshine*, 114
   San Souci. *The Talking Eggs*, 134
   Sendak. *Where the Wild Things Are*, 140
   Shreve. *Family Secrets*, 146
   Small. *Imogene's Antlers*, 165
   Steig. *Spinky Sulks*, 169
   Steig. *Sylvester and the Magic Pebble*, 176
   Steptoe. *Mufaro's Beautiful Daughters*, 183
   Viorst. *The Tenth Good Thing about Barney*, 199

   Williams. *A Chair for My Mother*, 204
   Wood. *Elbert's Bad Word*, 209
Patience
   Keats. *Whistle for Willie*, 91
   San Souci. *The Talking Eggs*, 134
   Sendak. *Where the Wild Things Are*, 140
   Steig. *Spinky Sulks*, 169
   Wood. *Elbert's Bad Word*, 209
Peer Pressure
   Cleary. *Ramona Quimby, Age 8*, 37
   Estes. *The Hundred Dresses*, 62
Perseverance
   Bang. *Delphine*, 16
   Fox. *Wilfrid Gordon McDonald Partridge*, 68
   Keats. *Whistle for Willie*, 91
   Williams. *A Chair for My Mother*, 204
Pets
   Keats. *Whistle for Willie*, 91
   Ness. *Sam, Bangs and Moonshine*, 114
   Viorst. *The Tenth Good Thing about Barney*, 199
Pleasure
   See Leisure.
Poetry
   Clifton. *Everett Anderson's Nine Month Long*, 44
   Komaiko. *Annie Bananie*, 96
   Lionni. *Frederick*, 101
Point of View
   Blume. *The Pain and the Great One*, 20
   Clifton. *Everett Anderson's Nine Month Long*, 44
   Gerstein. *The Mountains of Tibet*, 73
   Sendak. *Where the Wild Things Are*, 140
   Varley. *Badger's Parting Gifts*, 195
   Wood. *Elbert's Bad Word*, 209
Polish Characters
   Estes. *The Hundred Dresses*, 62
   Singer. *The Power of Light*, 159
Popularity
   Estes. *The Hundred Dresses*, 62
Possibilities
   See Choices.
Pouting
   Steig. *Spinky Sulks*, 169

Poverty
  Estes. *The Hundred Dresses*, 62
  Lionni. *Frederick*, 101
  Williams. *A Chair for My Mother*, 204
Power/Powerlessness
  Sendak. *Where the Wild Things Are*, 140
  Small. *Imogene's Antlers*, 165
Prediction (All stories lend themselves to prediction. These are the most obvious.)
  Burningham. *Mr. Gumpy's Outing*, 25
  Craven. *What the Mailman Brought*, 58
  Fox. *Wilfrid Gordon McDonald Partridge*, 68
  Gerstein. *The Mountains of Tibet*, 73
  Rylant. *The Relatives Came*, 126
  San Souci. *The Talking Eggs*, 134
  Sendak. *Where the Wild Things Are*, 140
  Small. *Imogene's Antlers*, 165
  Steig. *Spinky Sulks*, 169
  Steig. *Sylvester and the Magic Pebble*, 176
  Steptoe. *Mufaro's Beautiful Daughters*, 183
  Viorst. *The Tenth Good Thing about Barney*, 199
  Williams. *A Chair for My Mother*, 204
  Wood. *Elbert's Bad Word*, 209
Prejudice
  Estes. *The Hundred Dresses*, 62
  Rylant. *Miss Maggie*, 120
  Singer. *The Power of Light*, 159
Problem Solving. *See also* Critical Thinking. Prediction.
  Lobel. *Fables*, 108
  Steig. *Sylvester and the Magic Pebble*, 176
Punctuation. *See also:* Language.
  Giff. *Today Was a Terrible Day*, 78
Punishment
  San Souci. *The Talking Eggs*, 134
  Sendak. *Where the Wild Things Are*, 140
  Steptoe. *Mufaro's Beautiful Daughters*, 183
  Wood. *Elbert's Bad Word*, 209

Racism
  Singer. *The Power of Light*, 159
Rejection
  Estes. *The Hundred Dresses*, 62
  Small. *Imogene's Antlers*, 165
Responsibility
  Burningham. *Mr. Gumpy's Outing*, 25
  Shreve. *Family Secrets*, 146
Ritual
  Rylant. *The Relatives Came*, 126
  Singer. *The Power of Light*, 159
  Viorst. *The Tenth Good Thing about Barney*, 199
Rules
  Sendak. *Where the Wild Things Are*, 140
  Shreve. *Family Secrets*, 146

Sacrifice
  Singer. *The Power of Light*, 159
  Williams. *A Chair for My Mother*, 204
School
  See Teachers.
Science
  Carle. *A House for Hermit Crab*, 30
Secrets
  Estes. *The Hundred Dresses*, 62
  Shreve. *Family Secrets*, 146
Self-Acceptance. *See also* Imperfections.
  Blume. *The Pain and the Great One*, 20
  Carle. *A House for Hermit Crab*, 30
  Cleary. *Ramona Quimby, Age 8*, 37
  Estes. *The Hundred Dresses*, 62
  Giff. *Today Was a Terrible Day*, 78
  Komaiko. *Annie Bananie*, 96
  Lionni. *Frederick*, 101
  Lobel. *Fables*, 108
  Sendak. *Where the Wild Things Are*, 140
  Shreve. *Family Secrets*, 146
  Small. *Imogene's Antlers*, 165
  Steptoe. *Mufaro's Beautiful Daughters*, 183
  Varley. *Badger's Parting Gifts*, 195
Self-Awareness
  See Behavior. Power/Powerlessness.
Self-Control
  Burningham. *Mr. Gumpy's Outing*, 25

Van Allsburg. *The Wretched Stone,*
189
Self-Reliance
Bang. *Delphine,* 16
Craven. *What the Mailman Brought,*
58
Fox. *Wilfrid Gordon McDonald*
Partridge, 68
Lionni. *Frederick,* 101
Small. *Imogene's Antlers,* 165
Steig. *Spinky Sulks,*
Steig. *Sylvester and the Magic*
Pebble, 176
Selfishness
Silverstein. *The Giving Tree,* 153
Sensory Experience
Keats. *Whistle for Willie,* 91
Komaiko. *Annie Bananie,* 96
Separation
See Loss.
Setting
Cooney. *Miss Rumphius,* 49
Gerstein. *The Mountains of Tibet,*
73
Griffith. *Grandaddy's Place,* 85
Ness *Sam, Bangs and Moonshine,*
114
Rylant. *Miss Maggie,* 120
Rylant. *The Relatives Came,* 126
Small. *Imogene's Antlers,* 165
Steptoe. *Mufaro's Beautiful Daugh-*
ters, 183
Wood. *Elbert's Bad Word,* 209
Sex Roles
Silverstein. *The Giving Tree,* 153
Steptoe. *Mufaro's Beautiful Daugh-*
ters, 183
Williams. *A Chair for My Mother,*
204
Sharing
See Cooperation.
Shyness
Griffith. *Grandaddy's Place,* 85
Sibling Rivalry. *See also* Family.
Blume. *The Pain and the Great One,*
20
Stepfather. *See also* Family.
Clifton. *Everett Anderson's Nine*
Month Long, 44
Stereotypes
Blume. *The Pain and the Great One,*
20
Estes. *The Hundred Dresses,* 62

Fox. *Wilfrid Gordon McDonald*
Partridge, 68
Giff. *Today Was a Terrible Day,* 78
Rylant. *Miss Maggie,* 120
Silverstein. *The Giving Tree,* 153
Story Structure
Keats. *Whistle for Willie,* 91
Rylant. *The Relatives Came,* 126
Shreve. *Family Secrets,* 146
Small. *Imogene's Antlers,* 165
Steig. *Spinky Sulks,* 169
Suspension of Disbelief
See Fantasy.
Survival
Singer. *The Power of Light,* 159

Teachers
Cleary. *Ramona Quimby, Age 8,* 37
Giff. *Today Was a Terrible Day,* 78
Shreve. *Family Secrets,* 146
Small. *Imogene's Antlers,* 165
Television
Van Allsburg. *The Wretched Stone,*
189
Temptation
San Souci. *The Talking Eggs,* 134
Sendak. *Where the Wild Things Are,*
140
Steptoe. *Mufaro's Beautiful Daugh-*
ters, 183
Wood. *Elbert's Bad Word,* 209
Thinking Skills
See Critical Thinking.
Tradition
See Ritual.
Travel
Cooney. *Miss Rumphius,* 49
Griffith. *Grandaddy's Place,* 85
Rylant. *The Relatives Came,* 126
Truth
Ness. *Sam, Bangs and Moonshine,*
114

Uniqueness
Carle. *A House for Hermit Crab,* 30
Lionni. *Frederick,* 101
Small. *Imogene's Antlers,* 165

Viewing Skills
See Visual Literacy
Virtue Rewarded
San Souci. *The Talking Eggs,* 134
Sendak. *Where the Wild Things Are,*
140

Virtue Rewarded *(continued)*
Silverstein. *The Giving Tree*, 153
Steptoe. *Mufaro's Beautiful Daughters*, 183
Wood. *Elbert's Bad Word*, 209
Visual Literacy
Bang. *Delphine*, 16
Craven. *What the Mailman Brought*, 58
Fox. *Wilfrid Gordon McDonald Partridge*, 68
Gerstein. *The Mountains of Tibet*, 73
Komaiko. *Annie Bananie*, 96
Rylant. *The Relatives Came*, 126
Sendak. *Where the Wild Things Are*, 140
Silverstein. *The Giving Tree*, 153
Small. *Imogene's Antlers*, 165
Steig. *Spinky Sulks*, 169
Steig. *Sylvester and the Magic Pebble*, 176
Steptoe. *Mufaro's Beautiful Daughters*, 183
Van Allsburg. *The Wretched Stone*, 189
Williams. *A Chair for My Mother*, 204
Wood. *Elbert's Bad Word*, 209
Vocabulary
See Language.

War
Singer. *The Power of Light*, 159
Wishes
Estes. *The Hundred Dresses*, 62
Steig. *Sylvester and the Magic Pebble*, 176
Work
Burningham. *Mr. Gumpy's Outing*, 25
Cooney. *Miss Rumphius*, 49
Lionni. *Frederick*, 101
Silverstein. *The Giving Tree*, 153
Van Allsburg. *The Wretched Stone*, 189
Williams. *A Chair for My Mother*, 204
Working Together
See Cooperation.
Worry
Bang. *Delphine*, 16
Clifton. *Everett Anderson's Nine Month Long*, 44
Steig. *Spinky Sulks*, 169
Steig. *Sylvester and the Magic Pebble*, 176
Writing
See Language. Metaphor. Story Structure.

General Index

by Janet Perlman

Aardema, Verna, 140, 219
Adam Draws Himself a Dragon, 84, 221
Aesop's fables, 108-14
African-American authors
  Clifton, Lucille, 44
  Greenfield, Eloise, 49, 73, 90, 96
  Steptoe, John, 183-84
African-American characters
  Everett Anderson's Nine Month Long, 48
  The Hundred Penny Box, 49, 133
  Just Us Women, 133
  Mufaro's Beautiful Daughters, 183
  The Talking Eggs, 134-35
  Whistle for Willie, 91
Aiken, Joan, 7, 15
Alan and Naomi, 62, 221
Alex and the Cat, 85
Alexander, Sue, 120, 219
Alexander and the Terrible, Horrible, No Good Very Bad Day, 84, 200, 222
The Alfred Summer, 62, 222
All I Ever Wanted to Know I Learned in Kindergarten, 153
Allison's Zinnia, 57, 221
The Amazing Bone, 183, 222
Anderson, Lena, 57, 219
Annie and the Old One, 199, 221
Annie Bananie, 8, 37, 96-101, 221
Anno, Mitsumasa, 114, 219
Anno's Aesop: A Book of Fables, 114, 219
Archambault, John, 37, 199, 221

Arnold of the Ducks, 77, 183, 220
Art activities
  A Chair for My Mother, 208
  Delphine, 19
  Elbert's Bad Word, 214
  The Giving Tree, 158
  "The Hard Boiled Egg Fad," 43
  A House for Hermit Crab, 35-36
  The Hundred Dresses, 67
  Miss Maggie, 126
  The Mountains of Tibet, 77
  The Pain and the Great One, 24
  The Relatives Came, 133
  The Talking Eggs, 139
  What the Mailman Brought, 62
  Where the Wild Things are, 146
  Whistle for Willie, 95
  Wilfrid Gordon McDonald Partridge, 72
The Art Lesson, 107, 220
Arthur, for the Very First Time, 133, 221
Aunt Flossie's Hats (and Crab Cakes Later), 90, 220

Babbitt, Natalie
  The Something, 20, 219
  Tuck Everlasting, 199, 219
"The Baboon's Umbrella," 109-11
Badger's Parting Gifts, 195-99, 204, 222
Baker, Olaf, 127
The Ballad of Belle Dorcas, 140, 220
Bang, Molly, 16
  Delphine, 16-20, 219

The Bathwater Gang, 43, 222
Bauer, Marion D., 153, 219
The Beast in Ms. Rooney's Room, 84, 220
Belling the Cat and Other Aesop's Fables, 114, 221
Bibliotherapy, xii, 5, 6
    book choice, 7-10
    counselor focus, 4
    discussion prompts, 4-6
    environment, 11
    leader, 7-15
    listening, 13
    teacher focus, 4
    theoretical base, xii-xiii
Bierhorst, John, 114, 219
Birthday, 184
Bjork, Christina, 57, 219
Blegvad, Erik, 199
Blos, Joan, 126, 168, 219
"The Blue Stone," 194
Blume, Judy, 20-21
    Freckle Juice, 67, 219
    The Pain and The Great One, 20-25, 219
Bodart, Joni, 5, 6
Book discussion. See Bibliotherapy
The Book of Kids' Songs, 182
Borders, Sarah G., xi-xiv, 2
Borka, 25
"A Boy Named Sue," 154
Boyd, Candy, 49, 219
Brown, Marcia, 96, 219
Bulla, Clyde
    The Christmas Coat, 25, 219
    One Poppy Seed, 57, 219
Burningham, John, 25-26
    John Patrick Norman McHennessy, 20, 219
    Mr. Gumpy's Motor Car, 29, 219
    Mr. Gumpy's Outing, 12, 25-29, 219
Byars, Betsy, 158, 219

Caines, Jeannette, 133, 219
"The Camel Dances," 111-12
Captain Snap and the Children of Vinegar Lane, 126, 221
"Captain's log" activity, 190
Carle, Eric, 30-31
    A House for Hermit Crab, 12, 30-37, 219
    The Very Quiet Cricket, 95, 219

Carlstrom, Nancy W., 96, 219
Cassidy, Nancy, 182
Catharsis, 5
A Chair for My Mother, 13, 158, 204-09, 222
Changes, Changes, 37, 221
Chanticleer, 50
Chanukah, 159-64
Characterization, 9-10
Charlotte and Henry, 78, 220
"Cheating," 146-53
Chester's Way, 101, 220
The Christmas Coat, 25, 219
Cinderella stories, 188
Circle of Gold, 49, 219
Class Clown, 176, 220
Cleary, Beverly, 37-38
    "The Hard Boiled Egg Fad," 37-42
    "Ramona" series, 10, 38, 42, 44, 218
Clifton, Lucille, 44
    Amifika, 121
    Everett Anderson's Nine Month Long, 6, 13, 44-49, 219
Climo, Shirley, 188, 219
Close Harmony, 73
Cohen, Barbara, 67, 220
Cole, Brock, 214, 220
Coleridge, Ann, 9, 176, 220
Coles, Robert, xii, xiv
Collins, W. A., xiii, xiv
Cookin' with Queen Ida and the Zydeco Band, 139
Cooney, Barbara, 49-50
    Hattie and the Wild Waves, 56, 57, 220
    Miss Rumphius, 6, 9, 13, 49-57, 77, 220
Cornelius, 107
Cornell, Laura, 97
Counselor focus, 4
Craven, Carolyn, 58
    What the Mailman Brought, 58-62, 220
Cuffari, Richard, 146

Daddy is a Monster, 184
"The Death of Giles," 204
Delphine, 16-20, 219
DePaola, Tomie
    The Art Lesson, 107, 220
    Now One Foot, Now the Other, 73, 220

Strega Nona, 140, 220
DiGrazia, Thomas, 121
Discussion leader, 7-15
Discussion prompts, 4-6, 11-13
Do You Know What I'll Do?, 159
Do You Want to Be My Friend?, 30
*Doctor Coyote: A Native American
    Aesop's Fables*, 114, 219
"Don't Let the Light Go Out," 12, 164
Dramatic activities
    The Giving Tree, 158
    The Pain and the Great One, 25
Drawing. *See* Art activities

Eeds, Mary, xii, xiv
The Egyptian Cinderella, 188, 219
Elbert's Bad Word, 8, 20, 209-14, 222
Empathy game, 24
Estes, Eleanor, 63
    The Hundred Dresses, 62-67, 220
Ethics, 152
Everett Anderson's Nine Month Long,
    6, 13, 44-49, 219

Fables, 113-14
Fables, 5, 108-14, 221
Fairy tales, 188
*Family Secrets: Five Very Important
    Stories*, 10, 146, 204, 222
Feeling charades, 21
Fish is Fish, 107
Fitzhugh, Louise, 29, 220
Flournoy, Valerie, 199, 220
Fox, Mem, 7, 8, 10, 15, 68-69
    *Wilfrid Gordon McDonald Par-
        tridge*, 68-73, 158, 220
Fox, Paula, 153, 220
Freckle Juice, 67, 219
Frederick, 101-07, 221
*Frederick's Fables: A Leo Lionni
    Treasury of Favorite Stories*, 107,
    221
The Friends of Emily Culpepper, 9,
    176, 220

Games, 139
Gammell, Stephen, 126-28
The Garden of Abdul Gazizi, 190
"The Garden Song," 57
Genealogy, 133
George, Jean, 114
Georgia Music, 89, 90, 158, 220
Gerstein, Mordicai, 73-74
    Arnold of the Ducks, 77, 183, 220

The Mountains of Tibet, 10, 12, 73-
    77, 183, 220
The Room, 78, 220
Seal Mother, 78, 220
The Giant's Toe, 214, 220
Giff, Patricia Reilly, 78-79
    The Beast in Ms. Rooney's Room,
        84, 220
    Happy Birthday, Ronald Morgan,
        84, 220
    Today Was a Terrible Day, 78-84,
        220
    Watch Out, Ronald Morgan, 84, 220
Ginger Pye, 63
The Giving Tree, 102, 153-59, 222
Good Night, Mr. Tom, 30, 221
Government, activity on, 152
Graham, Bob, 78, 220
Grandaddy's Place, 37, 85-91, 158,
    220
"Grandma Slid Down the Mountain,"
    90
Grandmama's Joy, 73, 220
Grandpa's Face, 90, 220
Greenfield, Eloise
    Grandmama's Joy, 73, 220
    Grandpa's Face, 90, 220
    Nathaniel Talking, 96, 220
    *She Come Bringing Me That Little
        Baby Girl*, 49, 220
Grief work, 72, 120, 203
Grifalconi, Ann, 44-45
Griffith, Helen, 85, 91, 158
    Georgia Music, 89, 90, 158, 220
    Grandaddy's Place, 37, 85-91, 158,
        220

Hall, Brent, 50
Hamilton, Virginia, 62, 220
Hanukkah, 159-64
Happy Birthday, Ronald Morgan, 84,
    220
"The Hard Boiled Egg Fad," 37-42
Harriet the Spy, 29, 220
Hattie and the Wild Waves, 56, 57, 220
Hederwick, Mairi, 25, 220
Heide, Florence P., 62, 220
Hello, Wrong Number, 68, 221
"The Hen and the Apple Tree," 113
Henkes, Kevin, 101, 220
Hey, Al, 183, 222
Hooks, William, 140, 220
A House for Hermit Crab, 12, 30-37,
    219

Houston, Gloria, 78, 220
Howard, Elizabeth, 90, 220
Huck, Charlotte, 188, 220
The Hundred Dresses, 62-67, 220
The Hundred Penny Box, 49, 133, 221
Hurwitz, Johanna
    Class Clown, 176, 220
    The Law of Gravity, 153, 220
    Russell and Elisa, 43, 220
    Russell Sprouts, 214, 220
Hutchins, Pat, 37, 221

I Know a Lady, 73, 222
Identification, 5
I'll Always Love You, 204, 222
I'll Fix Anthony, 199
Illustrations, 2, 9, 132
Immigrant experience, 62-67
Imogene's Antlers, 165-68, 222
"Inch by Inch," 57
Insight, 3, 5
Ira Says Goodbye, 101, 222
It's Mine, 107

John Patrick Norman McHennessy, 20, 219
Julie of the Wolves, 114
"Just say no" antidrug campaign, 194
Just Us Women, 133, 219

Kaleidoscope activity, 77
Katie Morag and the Tiresome Ted, 25, 220
Keats, Ezra Jack, 91
    Peter's Chair, 96, 221
    Regards to the Man in the Moon, 120, 221
    Whistle for Willie, 91-96, 221
The Keeping Quilt, 199, 221
Kelly, Patricia, 4, 6
Kennedy, Richard, 194, 221
"Kindergarten Wall," 153
The King Has Horse's Ears, 43, 168, 222
Knight, Margy B., 164, 221
Knots on a Counting Rope, 37, 199, 221
Komaiko, Leah, 96
    Annie Bananie, 8, 37, 96-101, 221
Korschunow, Irina, 84, 221

The Lace Snail, 158, 219
Langer, Judith A., xiv, 6
Lasky, Kathryn, 57, 221

The Law of Gravity, 153, 220
Leaf, Munro, 107, 221
"Leaving on a Jet Plane," 36
Levoy, Myron, 62, 221
Lieblich, Irene, 159
Light in the Attic, 154
Linea's Windowsill Garden, 57, 219
Lionni, Leo, 101-02, 107, 146, 221
    Cornelius, 107
    Fish is Fish, 107
    Frederick, 101-07, 221
    It's Mine, 107
    Swimmy, 107, 146
Listening, 13
Little Blue and Little Yellow, 102
Lobel, Anita, 108, 221
    Allison's Zinnia, 57
Lobel, Arnold, 20, 108
    Fables, 5, 108-14, 221
"The Lost Kingdom of Karnica," 194
Louie, Ai-Ling, 189, 221
Lowry, Lois, 120, 221

MacLachlan, Patricia
    Arthur, for the Very First Time, 133, 221
    Sarah Plain and Tall, 101, 221
"Magic Penny," 126
Magorian, Michelle, 30, 221
"Mail Myself to You," 62
Mama Says There Aren't Any Zombies, 200
Mandala, art activity with, 77
Maniac Magee, 8, 176, 222
Manners
    Mr. Gumpy's Outing, 29
Martin, Bill, Jr., 37, 199, 221
Mathis, Sharon B., 49, 133, 221
Maxner, Joyce, 107, 221
Mayer, Mercer, 146, 221
McCutcheon, John, 153
McDonald, Megan, 140, 221
Me, Mop and the Moondance Kid, 43, 221
Metaphor, xiii, 6
Miles, Miska, 199, 221
Miss Maggie, 73, 120-26, 221
Miss Rumphius, 6, 9, 13, 49-57, 77, 220
Mr. Gumpy's Motor Car, 29, 219
Mr. Gumpy's Outing, 12, 25-29, 219
Molly's Pilgrim, 67, 220
The Moon Came Too, 96, 219

"Moral imagination," xii
The Mountains of Tibet, 10, 12, 73-77, 183, 220
Mufaro's Beautiful Daughters: An African Tale, 135, 140, 183-89, 222
Music activities
    "Cheating," 153
    Grandaddy's Place, 90
    A House for Hermit Crab, 36
    Miss Maggie, 126
    Miss Rumphius, 57
    My Great Aunt Arizona, 78
    The Power of Light, 164
    Sylvester and the Magic Pebble, 182
    The Talking Eggs, 139
    What the Mailman Brought, 62
    Where the Wild Things Are, 146
    Whistle for Willie, 95
Music, Music for Everyone, 107, 209, 222
My Grandson Lew, 120, 222
My Great Aunt Arizona, 78, 220
Myers, Walter Dean, 43, 221

Nadia, The Willful, 120, 219
Nathaniel Talking, 96, 220
Natti, Susanna, 78-79
Naylor Alice P., ix-x, xii, xiii
Ness, Evaline, 114-15, 120
    Sam, Bangs and Moonshine, 114-20, 221
Nicholas Cricket, 107, 221
Nightmares: Poems to Trouble Your Sleep, 20, 221
Now One Foot, Now the Other, 73, 220

Oaklander, Violet, 214
Old Henry, 126, 168, 219
Oma and Bobo, 90, 221
On My Honor, 153, 219
"On the Road Again," 36
Once a Mouse, 96, 219
The One Eyed Cat, 153, 220
The One in the Middle Is a Green Kangaroo, 21
One Poppy Seed, 57, 219
The Oxcart Man, 50

The Pain and the Great One, 20-25, 219
Paper John, 168, 222
The Patchwork Quilt, 199, 220

Paxton, Tom, 114, 221
Peege, 73
Peter, Paul, and Mary, 164
Peter's Chair, 96, 221
Peterson, Ralph, xii, xiv
Picture books, 9
Pinkney, Jerry, 134-35
Plot, 9
"Plus One," xiii
Poetry activities
    Everett Anderson's Nine Month Long, 49
    Whistle for Willie, 95
Polacco, Patricia, 199, 221
Possum Magic, 69
The Potato Man, 140, 221
The Power of Light: Eight Stories for Hanukkah, 12, 159-64, 222
Prelutsky, Jack
    Nightmares: Poems to Trouble Your Sleep, 20, 221
    "Whistling," 95
Princess Furball, 188, 220

Ramona Quimby, Age 8, 37, 38
"Ramona" series, 10, 38, 42, 44, 219
"Red River Valley," 36
Regards to the Man in the Moon, 120, 221
The Relatives Came, 8, 9, 126-33, 221
Richard Kennedy: Collected Stories, 194, 221
Role playing
    A House for Hermit Crab, 35, 36
    Miss Rumphius, 56
    Mr. Gumpy's Outing, 29
    Sylvester and the Magic Pebble, 182
    Today Was a Terrible Day, 83-84
The Room, 78, 220
Rosenblatt, Louise M., xiii, xiv
Rosie and Michael, 25, 222
Russell and Elisa, 43, 220
Russell Sprouts, 214, 220
Rylant, Cynthia, 121
    Miss Maggie, 73, 120-26, 221
    The Relatives Came, 8, 9, 126-33, 221
    When I Was Young in the Mountains, 121, 132, 133, 221

Sachs, Marilyn, 68, 221
Saint Nicholas, 57
Sam, Bangs and Moonshine, 114-20, 221

San Souci, Robert D., 134
    The Talking Eggs, 134-40, 188, 221
Sarah Plain and Tall, 101, 221
Schotter, Roni, 126, 221
Schrank, F. A., 5, 6
Schwartz, Amy, 90, 221
Sea Swan, 57, 221
Seal Mother, 78, 220
Sendak, Maurice, 141-42
    Where the Wild Things Are, 8, 20,
        140-46, 221
Service projects, 73
She Come Bringing Me That Little Baby
    Girl, 49, 220
"She'll Be Comin' Round the Moun-
    tain," 90
Shoemaker Martin, 140, 222
The Show and Tell War, 84, 222
Shreve, Susan, 10, 147, 222
    "Cheating," 146-53
    "The Death of Giles," 204
The Shrinking of Treehorn, 62, 220
Silverstein, Shel, 154
    The Giving Tree, 102, 153-59, 222
Singer, Isaac Bashevis, 159-60
    The Power of Light: Eight Stories for
        Hanukkah, 12, 159-64, 222
    Stories for Children, 164, 222
Slepian, Jan, 62, 222
Small, David, 43, 165
    Imogene's Antlers, 165-68, 222
    Paper John, 168, 222
Smith, Janice Lee, 84, 222
The Snowy Day, 91, 95
The Something, 20, 219
Something Special for Me, 209, 222
The Song and Dance Man, 127
A Special Trade, 73, 222
Spinelli, Jerry
    The Bathwater Gang, 43, 222
    Maniac Magee, 8, 176, 222
    Who Put Hair in My Toothbrush?,
        49, 222
Spinky Sulks, 9, 169-76, 222
Sprinthall, Norman A., xiii, xiv
Steig, William, 169
    The Amazing Bone, 183, 222
    Spinky Sulks, 9, 169-76, 222
    Sylvester and the Magic Pebble, 12,
        176-83, 222
Steptoe, John, 49, 183-84
    Mufaro's Beautiful Daughters, 135,
        140, 183-89, 222

The Story of Jumping Mouse, 189,
    222
Stevenson, James, 37, 85, 90
Stevie, 184
Stolz, Mary, 91, 222
Stories for Children, 164, 222
Storm in the Night, 91, 222
The Story of Ferdinand, 107, 221
The Story of Jumping Mouse, 189, 222
Storytelling
    Miss Rumphius, 57
    Wilfrid Gordon McDonald Par-
        tridge, 73
Strega Nona, 140, 220
Stringbean's Trip to the Shining Sea,
    209, 222
A Summer to Die, 120, 221
Swimmy, 107, 146, 221
Sylvester and the Magic Pebble, 12,
    176-83, 222

The Talking Eggs: A Folktale from the
    American South,134-40, 188, 221
Talking Walls, 164, 221
Tarman, Jane, 215
Teacher focus, 4
The Tenth Good Thing about Barney,
    5, 199-204, 222
There's a Nightmare in My Closet, 146.
    221
Thompson, Peggy, 43, 168, 222
Three Days on a River in a Red Canoe,
    209, 222
"Ting-a-Lay-O," 182
Today Was a Terrible Day, 78-84, 222
Tolstoy, Leo, 140, 222
Touchton, Jacque, vii, 14
Trivas, Irene, 20
Tuck Everlasting, 199, 219

Ugh, 78, 222
"Uncle Shelby," 154

Van Allsburg, Chris, 189-90, 222
    The Wretched Stone, 3, 13, 189-94,
        222
Vandergrift, Kay, 10, 15
Varley, Susan, 195
    Badger's Parting Gifts, 195-99, 204,
        222
The Very Quiet Cricket, 95, 219
Viorst, Judith, 200
    Alexander and the Terrible,
        Horrible, No Good Very Bad
        Day, 84, 222

Rosie and Michael, 25, 222
The Tenth Good Thing about
    Barney, 5, 199-204, 222
Vivas, Julie, 68-69
Vygotsky, Lev, xiii, xiv

Waber, Bernard, 101, 222
"Waltzing Matilda," 72
Watch Out, Ronald Morgan, 84, 220
Water from Another Time, 153
What the Mailman Brought, 58-62, 220
When I Was Young in the Mountains,
    121, 132, 133, 221
Where the Buffaloes Begin, 127
Where the Sidewalk Ends, 154
Where the Wild Things Are, 8, 20, 140-
    46, 221
Whistle for Willie, 91-96, 221
"Whistling," 95
Whitman, Sally, 73, 222
Who Put That Hair in My Toothbrush?,
    49, 222
Why Mosquitos Buzz in People's Ears,
    14, 140, 219
Wilfrid Gordon McDonald Partridge,
    68-73, 158, 220
Wilhelm, Hans, 204, 222
Williams, Vera, 204-05
    A Chair for My Mother, 13, 158,
        204-09, 222
    Music, Music for Everyone, 107,
        209, 222
    Something Special for Me, 209, 222
    Stringbean's Trip to the Shining Sea,
        209, 222

Three Days on a River in a Red
    Canoe, 209, 222
Windows to Our Children, 214, 222
Wolves, 114
Women, 208
Wood, Audrey, 209-10
    Elbert's Bad Word, 8, 20, 209-14,
        222
The Wretched Stone, 3, 13, 189-94,
    222
Writing activities
    Annie Bananie, 97-98
    Delphine, 19
    The Giving Tree, 157-58
    "The Hard Boiled Egg Fad," 43
    A House for Hermit Crab, 36
    The Pain and the Great One, 24-25
    Today Was a Terrible Day, 83-84
    The Wretched Stone, 194

Yarrow, Peter, 164
Yehshen: A Cinderella Story from
    China, 189, 221
Yorinks, Arthur
    Hey, Al, 183, 222
    Ugh, 78, 222
"You Sing a Song," 95

Zeely, 62, 220
Zlateh, the Goat, 160, 164
Zolotow, Charlotte
    Do You Know What I'll Do?, 159
    I Know a Lady, 73, 222
    My Grandson Lew, 120, 222

SARAH G. BORDERS, Ed.S., is an elementary school counselor at William R. Davie School, Mocksville, North Carolina. She is a member of the American Association for Counseling and the North Carolina Association of School Counselors (NCASC). She presents workshops and seminars on bibliotherapy to school counselors and therapists for associations such as the NCASC, and her specialty is using quality literature, expressive arts, and play media in counseling children. She is also an adjunct professor at Appalachian State University.

ALICE PHOEBE NAYLOR, Ph.D., is a professor of children's literature at Appalachian State University, Boone, North Carolina. She is a member of the Center for the Expansion of Language and Thinking, the American Library Association, the Children's Literature Association, and the National Council of Teachers of English. In 1990, Dr. Naylor received the Appalachian Alumni Award for Outstanding Teaching and the Innovation in Teaching faculty award from the Reich College of Education. Dr. Naylor also chaired the 1991 John Newbery Award Selection Committee.